Glocal Religions

Glocal Religions

Special Issue Editor

Victor Roudometof

MDPI • Basel • Beijing • Wuhan • Barcelona • Belgrade

MDPI

Special Issue Editor
Victor Roudometof
University of Cyprus
Cyprus

Editorial Office
MDPI
St. Alban-Anlage 66
Basel, Switzerland

This is a reprint of articles from the Special Issue published online in the open access journal *Religions* (ISSN 2077-1444) from 2015 to 2018 (available at: https://www.mdpi.com/journal/religions/special_issues/glocal_religions)

For citation purposes, cite each article independently as indicated on the article page online and as indicated below:

LastName, A.A.; LastName, B.B.; LastName, C.C. Article Title. *Journal Name* **Year**, *Article Number, Page Range.*

ISBN 978-3-03897-316-4 (Pbk)
ISBN 978-3-03897-317-1 (PDF)

Contents

About the Special Issue Editor

Victor Roudometof (PhD Sociology and Cultural Studies, University of Pittsburgh, 1996) is associate professor of Sociology with the University of Cyprus and Professor (adj.) with the University of Tampere, Finland. He has also held appointments with Princeton University, Washington and Lee University and Miami University, OH. His main research interests include global and transnational sociology, culture, religion, and nationalism. He is the author of over 100 articles, book chapters, encyclopedia entries, etc. He is the author of four monographs and editor or co-editor of six volumes and five special issues of refereed journals. His latest monograph is Glocalization: a critical introduction (London: Routledge, 2016). Currently, he is Faculty Fellow with Yale University's Center for Cultural Sociology and Director of the Historical and literary Archives of Kavala, Greece (www.ilak.org). He has served as external reviewer for evaluations conducted by major research centers as well as for international publishers & for governmental organizations. Currently, he is a member in the editorial boards of the European Journal of Social Theory, Nations and Nationalism, Επιθεώρηση Κοινωνικών Ερευνών (Greek Review for Social Research), Interreligious Studies & Intercultural Theology and Religions. For full academic profile and additional information, see www.roudometof.com.

religions

MDPI

Editorial

Glocal Religions: An Introduction

Victor Roudometof

Department of Social and Political Sciences, University of Cyprus, P.O. Box 20537, Kallipoleos 75, Nicosia CY-1678, Cyprus; roudomet@ucy.ac.cy

Received: 3 September 2018; Accepted: 28 September 2018; Published: 29 September 2018

Abstract: This introductory article offers an overview of the volume's major problematic. It examines the literature on religion and globalization and then moves on to an overview of the literature on religion and glocalization. Throughout the discussion, the article refers explicitly to the volume's chapters and outlines how their specific themes fit within the broader problematic of glocal religions.

Keywords: religion; glocalization; globalization; hybridity

1. Introduction

This volume originated from the 2015 panel on glocal religion, which I organized and chaired for the biannual meetings of the International Society for the Sociology of Religion. Following the panel, contributions were invited for a special issue of the journal Religions, and over the next two years a series of articles were published in the journal. Although several of this volume's chapters originated from the initial panel, the list of contributions was subsequently expanded. I should express my gratitude to the scholars whose work is featured in the following pages. My thanks also go to the publisher, whose support for this project has been critically important.

The goal of this volume is to bring the theme of glocal religions to the attention of a broader scholarly audience as well as to demonstrate the relevance of glocality for the cross-cultural study of religion. It is not accidental that this volume features work that covers different regions of the globe and comes from different disciplines and specializations. The theme of glocal religion is far from novel; the notion of global–local or glocal religion as a 'genre of expression, communication and legitimation' of collective and individual identities (Robertson 1991, p. 282; Robertson and Garrett 1991, p. xv) has been on the agenda for more than two decades. More explicit scholarly engagement with the problematic of glocalization and religion is far more recent and remains relatively limited—especially if contrasted with the widespread popularity of the theme of globalization and religion (for an overview, see Roudometof 2016a). In this introductory chapter, I address two important issues that should be useful in offering a general means of orientation to readers with regard to the material featured in this collection. Firstly, I offer a brief account of the historical trajectory of the ideas associated with the problematic of the relationship among religion, globalization and glocalization, and secondly, I briefly discuss the ongoing and interdisciplinary scholarly production on the glocalization–religion nexus. Hopefully, this volume provides further incentive for additional work on this topic. There is plenty of room for future growth along the lines suggested by the theme of glocal religion, and numerous cases of religious expression from different corners of the globe can come under scrutiny and examination using the problematic of glocal religion.

2. Religion and Globalization

The intertwining of religion and globalization is quite well known, and religion is one of the primary areas demonstrating the significance of globalization in cultural and social life (for an overview, see Altglas 2010). It should be noted that key ideas about the very notion of globalization as a distinct process emerged from within the study of religion, although this is still largely unacknowledged. According to post-World War II modernization theory, modernization meant the success of universalism, secularism and at least a certain level of cross-cultural convergence (which remained a contested issue throughout the heyday of these perspectives in the 1960s and 1970s). However, since the 1970s, social scientists were confronted with a series of phenomena that offered a practical refutation of the predictions of modernization theory; on top of the list is the 1979 Iranian revolution, followed by the subsequent rise of fundamentalism and various religious revivals in Islamic countries but also in the US itself. Modernization did not translate into secularization—and the empirical refutation of this connection meant the delegitimization of post-World War II modernization and secularization theories.

The alternative perspective came with the notion of globalization, formulated in the early 1980s by Roland Robertson in a series of publications that eventually became his volume titled Globalization: Social Theory and Global Culture (1992). Robertson (1992, p. 8) defines globalization as 'the compression of the world'. By 'compression', Robertson means the accelerated pace of contact among cultures, peoples and civilizations or the sense that the world is 'shrinking'. Robertson does not equate globalization with universalism—but proposes the interpenetration of universalism and particularism. His approach is an alternative that highlights the significance of the 'search for fundamentals' as part of globalization. Fundamentalism or religious revivals are not seen as 'anomalies' but are accounted for as responses to globalization. The key idea is the notion of relativization—that is, the notion that, once a group encounters a new reality or condition or comes into contact with hitherto alien cultures, worldviews or ideas, it readjusts or 'relates' its own condition to the new realities. To avoid misunderstandings, relativization does not mean relativism. In Maffesoli's (2016, p. 745) analysis, a similar term is proposed ('relationniste') to denote the idea that concepts, ideas or practices become meaningful through their being related to other concepts, ideas or practices. Meaning is a property located only within a specific cultural milieu or context and nested in webs of relationships; when such relationships are reconfigured, meaning is adjusted too.

The post-1989 fall of communism in Eastern Europe contributed to the further proliferation of scholarship. For a short list of prominent or influential publications see, among others, Berger and Huntington (2002), Stackhouse and Paris (2000), Hopkins et al. (2001), Beckford (2003), Juergensmeyer (2003), Beyer and Beaman (2007), Beyer (2006) and Levitt (2007). Different organizational schemes have been proposed by Robertson (1992), Therborn (2000) and Campbell (2007) to capture the historicity of globalization. Although these authors are not in agreement in terms of the temporal phases or stages of globalization, they all share a long-term perspective that extends globalization further into the past and, *de facto*, separates globalization from modernization. Within the study of religion, scholarship has taken additional steps to address the everlasting and inconclusive debate on the definition of religion through the articulation of theories and interpretations that explain not just the phenomenon labeled 'religion' in the West alone but, rather, the development of 'world religions', as such (for accounts, see Masuzawa 2005; Beyer 2006; Hedges 2012). From within these lenses, then, the emergence of world religions is intertwined with the extension of commercial linkages and networks over the Euro–Asian landmass and is related to the political–military projects of several empires (see Tehranian 2007). Of special importance for the incorporation of the problematic of globalization within the sociology of religion is the gradual extension of Appadurai's (1990) notion of –scapes into the area of religion. Although religion is not included within his original typology of –scapes, the notion of religious landscape or religioscape has been gradually introduced into social–scientific discourse (McAlister 2005) and used to study the differential signification and contested nature of religious sites that operate within competing religioscapes (Hayden and Walker 2013). It has also been further applied to religious traditions within Christianity (Roudometof 2014a) as a means of capturing the religious unity formed by such traditions.

The globalization of various religious traditions, faiths and other subgroups, or more accurately their spread across borders (Kennedy and Roudometof 2006), brings forth the problematic of global–local interaction. This problematic is of course well known to researchers. The various patterns of the global–local binary relationship are typically seen as forming either an adversarial or a nonadversarial relationship. One of the primary forms nonadversarial relationships take are the multitude of processes that are conventionally referred to as indigenization, hybridization or glocalization (Pieterse 2003; Burke 2009; Roudometof 2016b). These processes register the ability of religion to mold into the fabric of different communities in ways that connect it intimately with communal and local relations. Religion sheds its universal uniformity in favor of blending with locality. Several authors have focused more on individual cases that highlight the mutability of religion; suitable examples include Warburg's (2006) impressive study of the Baha'i, Beyer's (2009) discussion of the differential adaptations of customs and practices such as the Islamic hijab, and Dessi's (2014) discussion of religious change as glocalization and analyses of Al Qaeda's international terrorist organizational blueprint as 'glocal' (global–local) (Marret 2008). The broader point here is that practices depicted as 'traditional' (such as the Muslim veil) are frequently innovations that transform past practices into contemporary cultural forms to express a felt incongruity with what is perceived to be a threat to identities and traditions.

3. The Religion–Glocalization Nexus

Social scientists' increased engagement with glocalization reflects a reality that has become gradually apparent to most people around the globe in the aftermath of the 2008 Great Recession. Globalization has entered into a more cautious and regulated phase, whereby walls have been created to obstruct the free flow of trade, money and people as governments adopt a more selective approach concerning their trade partners, the capital that is welcomed within their borders and the individuals who are viewed as legitimate candidates for inclusion in their societies. In a classical statement that helped introduce the term into the social sciences, Robertson (1995) argued that

> the global is not in and of itself counterpoised to the local. Rather, what is often referred to as the local is essentially included within the global. In this respect, globalization, defined in its most general sense as the compression of the world as a whole, involves the linking of localities. But it also involves the 'invention' of locality, in the same general sense of the idea of the invention of tradition. (p. 35)

Accordingly, global–local or glocal religion thus emerges as a key domain of inquiry as groups and individuals use religious traditions symbolically as emblematic of membership in an ethnic or national group. Both institutional avenues and private means are employed in this symbolic appropriation, and these are usually interwoven into a web of other associations and relationships. Although communities continue to be formed around the notion of 'locality', this category is further divorced from its original connection with a specific geographical area and it can be transnationally and/or symbolically reconstituted (Kennedy and Roudometof 2006). These processes involve the construction of cultural hybrids that blend religious universalism with several forms of local (national or ethnic) particularisms. For example, consider the case of Santo Daime, a syncretic religion, founded in the Amazon region of Brazil, that combines elements of folk Catholicism with influences of spiritualism, African animism and indigenous South American shamanism (see Dawson 2012).

Although the study of glocalization has become an area of growth for the study of religion, interest in this topic is by no means limited to the social–scientific or sociological and anthropological study of religion. In fact, it has extended into diverse fields ranging from marketing glocal yoga (Askegaard and Eckhardt 2012) and the relationship between science and religion (Drees 2015) to the fields of theology and constitutional law (see, for example, Hirschl 2010). The significance of glocal for new conceptions of theological thought that need to confront contemporary challenges is an important consideration in these debates. In theology, glocalization has been evoked as a conceptual vehicle for interpreting Christianity's adaptation strategies in China (Ng 2007) and has been debated as an interpretative strategy for public theology (Storrar 2004; Pearson 2007). In theology, as Küster (2016) remarks, the shift from contextualization to glocalization is visible in the works of African and Asian theologians, whereby late modern blueprints of enculturation theology are superseded by contextual and intercultural theological reflection. Discussions of missionary work have further noted the significance of glocalization as a highly relevant missionary strategy for engaging with diverse cultural milieus (Atido 2017; Engelsviken et al. 2011; Fujino 2010).

The above clearly suggests that the religion–glocalization nexus is by no means restricted to fields within the social sciences. This is evident in this volume's pages, with contributions coming from seemingly surprising fields—such as archaeology. Even more, the necessity to study empirical phenomena that involve a broad range of transnational and hybrid religiosity forms a solid foundation for future engagements with the notion of glocalization. Within the social sciences, the glocalization–religion nexus involves the consideration of an entire range of responses as outcomes instead of a single master narrative of secularization and modernization (Beyer 2007) and is among the developing research frontiers (for an overview, see Roudometof 2014c). Contributions to this research area cover a wide range, from analyses of the German religious landscape (Nagel 2014) to Japanese religiosity (Fujino 2010) to Afro-folk religious practices in Puerto Rico (Romberg 2005) and analyses of Orthodox Christianity's historical record (Roudometof 2013, 2014a, 2014b). Spickard (2004) also has studied the transnational expansion of Sekai Kyusei-kyo—a new Japanese religion—by specifically examining issues of transnational religious coordination. Spickard argues that culture has shaped the religion's local reception, whereas local culture has further overturned initial organizational hierarchies and models. Of special importance is the study of social movements related to religions (Luz 2014) and minority–majority relations (Burity 2015; Topel 2017). Such research helps relate glocality to the making and remaking of identities around the globe.

Of particular significance for the empirical consideration of this problematic are the cases of Japan (Dessi 2013; Dessi 2017) and Brazil (Matsue 2014; Rocha 2016; Shoji and Usarski 2014). In *Japanese Religions and Globalization*, Dessi (2013) offers a highly instructive study of the variety of glocalized adaptations of Japanese religions that highlights both inclusive and exclusive tendencies within Japanese forms of religiosity. In his contribution to the present volume, Dessì further expands upon his long-standing research agenda concerning the use of glocalization as a heuristic means for understanding varied practices. In his article, he focuses on two case studies: the first one concerns the ongoing greening of Japanese Buddhism, whereas the second concerns the adoption of meditational techniques by priests and lay practitioners in Hawaiian Shin Buddhism. He argues that the glocalization of Japanese Buddhism is shaped by four factors: global consciousness, resonance with the local tradition, decontextualization and quest for power. Buddism of course has been a prominent example of glocalization—not solely in Brazil or Japan but also in France (for a discussion, see Obadia 2012). Alongside varieties of Hinduism and eclectic adaptations of initially esoteric or mystical practices that originated in the Indian subcontinent, it offers classic examples that substantiate the thesis of the "Easternization of the West" (Campbell 2007). More than simply showing that cultural influences do not invariably run from West to East but in the opposite direction as well, this research agenda is also intimately related to the problematic of glocalization, as in most instances the versions of religious practices imported into the West are not faithful replicas of the originals but instead undergo creative adaptations to their new Western surroundings, thereby glocalizing themselves in order to endure and thrive in their newfound cultural milieus.

As the above clearly shows, research on the glocalization–religion nexus involves a large number of cases coming from a tapestry of regions around the globe: Brazil, Japan, US, Puerto Rico, Palestine, Germany and China are some prominent examples. These cross-cultural and inter- or transdisciplinary lenses of such research are also echoed in several chapters within the present volume. In her article, Tatiana Tiaynem-Qadir adopts the notion of glocalization to the transnational and anthropological exploration of liturgy within the Orthodox Church of Finland. Her research is based largely on ethnographic fieldwork with participants from Finnish, Russian and Greek cultural and linguistic backgrounds. In their chapter about the specifics of funeral feasts in St. Lucia, Sabita Manian and Brad Bullock explore the migrant narratives and Indo–Caribbean religious practices through ethnographic research. The authors inquire into the ways diasporic identity is reconfigured in a local–global nexus as well as the degree to which this particular funeral feast has acquired glocal characteristics.

Use of the notion of glocal within the study of religion is not, of course, solely restricted to the contemporary era—for once it has been introduced into our conceptual vocabulary, glocalization can be further applied to the historical record. Focusing on the *longue durée* of the history of Eastern Christianity, Roudometof (2013, 2014a) defines four forms of glocalization: indigenization, vernacularization, nationalization and transnationalization. Vernacularization involved the rise of vernacular languages (such as Greek or Latin or Arabic in the case of Islam) endowed with the symbolic ability to offer privileged access to the sacred, whereas indigenization connected specific faiths to ethnic groups, whereby religion and culture were often fused into a single unit. Vernacularization was often promoted by empires, whereas indigenization was connected to the survival of particular ethnic groups. It is important to stress that this is *not* an exclusively contemporary phenomenon. The creation of distinct branches of Christianity—such as Orthodox and Catholic Christianity—bears the mark of this particularization of religious universalism. Nationalization connected the consolidation of specific nations with particular confessions and has been a popular strategy both in Western and Eastern Europe (Hastings 1997; Gorski 2000). Transnationalization has complemented religious nationalization by forcing groups to identify with specific religious traditions of real or imagined national homelands or to adopt a universalist vision of religion. In this volume, Marco Guglielmi's article offers a highly nuanced assessment of this work. Addressing a very different cultural and geographical region, in her chapter Barbara Watson Andaya explores the degree to which the Christian missionary activities of the past centuries in East Asia were subject to a 'repackaging' or 'glocalization' that would render Christianity (most often Roman Catholicism) amenable to the local cultural milieu. She argues that the glocalization of Christianity set up a series of 'power-laden tensions' that continue to be the subject of ongoing negotiations to this day. This research might be seen in close connection with the series of arguments developed by José Casanova (2018) about the differential historical pathways to religious pluralism and secularization. In this regard, Brand's chapter on the relationship between US-based evangelical ideals and the founding of the US is also a highly relevant contribution. Brand highlights the strong influences that have historically contributed to the view of the US as a promised land or a new Jerusalem. It might be relevant here to mention that the metaphor of the 'new Jerusalem' is not exclusive to the US, as it is also present in narratives that contributed to the founding of the 16th century Russian Empire under Ivan the Terrible (for details, see Roudometof 2014a, pp. 62–64). Another far less expected area of research is revealed in David C. D. van Alten's chapter, in which he uses glocalization to interpret the features of the Roman Antiquity. The author interprets archaeological source material from within the glocalization framework, which helps account for the traits observed in religious material culture. This intertwining between archaeology and glocalization is not as idiosyncratic as one might think, as the relationship between the two has been the subject of a scholarly exchange (see Barrett et al. 2018).

Lastly, no discussion of the glocalization–religion nexus is adequate without addressing the theoretical ties between the concepts of glocalization and transnationalism. Conventionally, transnationalism has been applied primarily in connection to the lived experiences of individuals that are simultaneously embedded in two or more nation-states. In contrast, globalization is often used to signify processes that are planetary, interregional and intercontinental. But the line between the two is not clear cut. Although scholars of transnationalism have attempted to distinguish transnationalism from 'strong' versions of globalization as a set of worldwide or interregional processes, it is nevertheless true that 'given the complexity of today's world, the boundaries among the transnational, global, and diasporic religious modalities are very porous' (Vasquez 2008, p. 164).

In this regard, the interdisciplinary field of Transnational Studies is a fellow traveler with the scholarship on the religion–glocalization nexus. Transnational Studies emerged in the 1990s in connection with the study of post-World War II new immigrants or trans-migrants who moved from Third World and developing countries into developed First World nations (for an overview, see Levitt and Khagram 2007). New immigrants no longer assimilated into the cultures of the host countries but, rather, openly maintained complex links to their homelands, thereby constructing, reproducing and preserving their transnational ties. Immigrant transnationalism recast the relationship between people and religion (Van Der Veer 2002; Levitt 2001; Levitt 2007; Csordas 2009). In this volume, the relationship between transnationalism and glocalization is explored in Manéli Farahmand's article, in which she examines the uses of neo-Mayanity in diverse cultural contexts (Switzerland, Guatemala and Mexico). She traces the various transformations of this cultural and religious identity and analyzes them through a historical–ethnographic approach that offers important clues about the largely invisible cultural influences of this trend in several countries around the globe.

4. Conclusions

In conclusion, it is important to view the glocalization–religion nexus not solely from within the inter- or transdisciplinary area of the study of religion but equally from within the transdisciplinary area of glocalization, sometimes also referred to as Glocal Studies (Roudometof 2015). Glocalization is a focal area of interest in a diverse tapestry of fields, areas of study, disciplines and/or specialties that include humanities and social sciences but also areas of research—such as information and communications technology and geoscience—that combine technological and social–scientific aspects (for an overview, see Roudometof 2016b). Cast in this light, religion comes under the rubric of the various forms of glocal belonging of which people avail themselves. The significance of glocal religions then rests in demonstrating that religiosity is not divorced from other forms of glocal hybridity.

Funding: This research received no external funding.

Conflicts of Interest: The authors declare no conflict of interest.

References

Appadurai, Arjun. 1990. Disjuncture and difference in the global cultural economy. In *Global Culture: Nationalism, Globalization and Modernity*. Edited by M. Featherstone. London: Sage, pp. 295–310.

Altglas, Vèronique, ed. 2010. *Religion and Globalization: Critical Concepts in Social Studies*. London: Routledge, vol. I–IV.

Askegaard, Søren, and Giana M. Eckhardt. 2012. Glocal yoga: Re-appropriation in the Indian consumptionscape. *Marketing Theory* 12: 45–60. [CrossRef]

Atido, George Pirwoth. 2017. Church revitalization in Congo: Missiological insights from one church's efforts at glocalization. *International Bulletin of Mission Research* 41: 326–34. [CrossRef]

Barrett, James H., Roland Robertson, Victor Roudometof, Noel B. Salazar, and Susan Sherratt. 2018. Discussion: Interdisciplinary perspectives on glocalization. *Archaeological Review from Cambridge* 33: 11–32.

Beckford, James A. 2003. *Social Theory and Religion*. Cambridge: Cambridge University Press.

Berger, Peter L., and Samuel P. Huntington, eds. 2002. *Many Globalizations: Cultural Diversity in the Contemporary World*. Oxford: Oxford University Press.

Beyer, Peter. 2006. *Religion in Global Society*. London: Routledge.

Beyer, Peter. 2007. Globalization and glocalization. In *The Sage Handbook of the Sociology of Religion*. Edited by J. A. Beckford and N. J. Demerath III. London: Sage, pp. 98–117.

Beyer, Peter. 2009. Glocalization of religions: Plural authenticities at the centres and at the margins. In *Sufis in Western Society: Global Networking and Locality*. Edited by Markus Dressler, Ron Geaves and Gritt Klinkhammer. London: Routledge, pp. 13–25.

Beyer, Peter, and Lori Beaman, eds. 2007. *Religion, Globalization and Culture*. Leiden: Brill.

Burity, Joanildo. 2015. Politics of religious minoritisation and glocalisation: Notes towards a study of religious networks of transnational. *Revista Latinoamericana de Estudios Sobre Cuerpos, Emociones y Sociedad* 18: 19–30.

Burke, Peter. 2009. *Cultural Hybridity*. London: Polity.

Campbell, Colin. 2007. *Easternization of the West: A Thematic Account of Cultural Change in the Modern Era*, 1st ed. London: Routledge.

Campbell, George Van Pelt. 2007. Religion and phases of globalization. In *Religion, Globalization and Culture*. Edited by Peter Beyer and Lori Beaman. Leiden: Brill, pp. 281–304.

Casanova, José. 2018. The Karel Dobbelaere lecture: Divergent global roads to secularization and religious pluralism. *Social Compass* 65: 187–98. [CrossRef]

Csordas, Thomas J. 2009. *Transnational Transcendence: Essays on Religion and Globalization*. Berkeley: University of California Press.

Dawson, Andrew. 2012. *Santo Daime: A New World Religion*. London: Bloomsbury.

Dessì, Ugo. 2013. *Japanese Religions and Globalization*. London: Routledge.

Dessì, Ugo. 2014. Religious change as glocalization: The case of Shin Buddhism in Honolulu. In *Buddhist Responses to Globalization*. Edited by L. Kalmanson and J. M. Shields. Lanham: Lexington Press, pp. 33–50.

Dessì, Ugo. 2017. *The Global Repositioning of Japanese Religions*. London: Routledge.

Drees, Willem B. 2015. Glocalization: Religion and science around the world. *Zygon: Journal of Religion and Science* 50: 151–54. [CrossRef]

Engelsviken, Tormod, Erling Lundeby, and Dagfinn Solheim, eds. 2011. *The Church Going Glocal: Mission and Globalisation*. Oxford: Regnum Books International.

Fujino, Gary. 2010. 'Glocal' Japanese self-identity: A missiological perspective on paradigmatic shifts in urban Tokyo. *International Journal of Frontier Missiology* 27: 171–82.

Gorski, Philip S. 2000. The mosaic moment: An early modernist critique of modernist theories of nationalism. *American Journal of Sociology* 105: 1428–68. [CrossRef]

Hastings, Adrian. 1997. *The Construction of Nationhood: Ethnicity, Religion and Nationalism*. Cambridge: Cambridge University Press.

Hayden, Robert M., and Timothy D. Walker. 2013. Intersecting religioscapes: A comparative to trajectories of change, scale, and competitive sharing of religious spaces. *Journal of the American Academy of Religion* 81: 399–426. [CrossRef]

Hedges, Paul. 2012. The old and new comparative theologies: Discourses on religion, the theology of religions, orientalism and the boundaries of traditions. *Religions* 3: 1120–37. [CrossRef]

Hirschl, Ran. 2010. Holy glocalization: Constitutions and sacred texts in the 'non-secular' world. *Harvard International Review* 32: 38–42.

Hopkins, Dwight N., Lois Ann Lorentzen, Eduardo Mendieta, and David Batstone, eds. 2001. *Religions/Globalizations: Theories and Cases*. Durham: Duke University Press.

Juergensmeyer, Mark, ed. 2003. *Global Religions: An Introduction*. Oxford: Oxford University Press.

Kennedy, Paul, and Victor Roudometof, eds. 2006. *Communities across Borders: New Immigrants and Transnational Cultures*. London: Routledge.

Küster, Volker. 2016. From Contextualization to glocalization: Intercultural theology and postcolonial critique. *Exchange* 45: 203–26. [CrossRef]

Levitt, Peggy. 2001. *The Transnational Villagers*. Berkeley: University of California Press.

Levitt, Peggy. 2007. *God Needs No Passport: How Immigrants Are Changing the American Religious Landscape*. New York: Free Press.

Levitt, Peggy, and Sanjeev Khagram, eds. 2007. *The Transnational Studies Reader: Intersections and Innovations*. London: Routledge.

Luz, Nimrod. 2014. The glocalization of al-Haram al-Sharif: Designing memory, mystifying place. In *Islamic Myths and Memories: Mediators of Globalization*. Edited by Itzchak Weismann, Mark Sedgwick and Ulrika Mårtensson. London: Routledge, pp. 99–120.

Maffesoli, Michel. 2016. From society to tribal communities. *The Sociological Review* 64: 739–47. [CrossRef]

Marret, Jean-Luc. 2008. Al-Qaeda in Islamic Maghreb: A 'glocal' organization. *Studies in Conflict & Terrorism* 31: 541–52.

Masuzawa, Tomoko. 2005. *The Invention of World Religions*. Chicago: Chicago University Press.

Matsue, Regina Yoshie. 2014. The glocalization process of Shin Buddhism in Brasilia. *Journal of Religion in Japan* 3: 226–46. [CrossRef]

McAlister, Elizabeth. 2005. Globalization and the religious production of space. *Journal for the Scientific Study of Religion* 44: 249–55. [CrossRef]

Nagel, Alexander-Kenneth. 2014. German religioscapes: Global and local perspectives. *Theological Review* 35: 13–29.

Ng, Peter Tze Ming. 2007. 'Glocalization' as a key to the interplay between Christianity and Asian cultures: The vision of Francis Wei in early twentieth century China. *International Journal of Public Theology* 1: 101–11. [CrossRef]

Obadia, Lionel. 2012. Localised deterritorialisation? The case of the glocalisation of Tibetan Buddhism in France and worldwide. *International Social Science Journal* 63: 185–95. [CrossRef]

Pearson, Clive. 2007. The quest for a glocal public theology. *International Journal of Public Theology* 1: 151–72. [CrossRef]

Pieterse, Jan Nederveen. 2003. *Globalization and Culture: Global Mélange*. Lanham: Rowman and Littlefield.

Robertson, Roland. 1991. Globalization, modernization, and postmodernization: The ambiguous position of religion. In *Religion and Global Order*. Edited by Roland Robertson and William R. Garrett. New York: Paragon House, pp. 281–91.

Robertson, Roland. 1992. *Globalization: Social Theory and Global Culture*. London: Sage.

Robertson, Roland. 1995. Glocalization: Time-space and homogeneity-heterogeneity. In *Global Modernities*. Edited by Mike Featherstone, Scott Lash and Roland Robertson. London: Sage, pp. 25–54.

Robertson, Roland, and William R. Garrett, eds. 1991. Religion and globalization. An introduction. In *Religion and Global Order*. New York: Paragon House, pp. ix–xxiii.

Rocha, Christina. 2016. The glocalization of John of God movement: Cultural translation as glocalization. In *Handbook of Contemporary Religions in Brazil*. Edited by Bettina Schmidt and Steven Engler. Leiden: Brill, pp. 346–60.

Romberg, Racquel. 2005. Glocal spirituality: Consumerism and heritage in a Puerto Rico Afro-Latin-folk religion. In *Contemporary Caribbean Cultures and Societies in a Global Context*. Edited by Franklin W. Knight and Teresita Martinez-Vergne. Chapel Hill: University of North Carolina Press, pp. 131–55.

Roudometof, Victor. 2013. The glocalisations of Eastern Orthodox Christianity. *European Journal of Social Theory* 16: 226–45. [CrossRef]

Roudometof, Victor. 2014a. *Globalization and Orthodox Christianity: The Transformations of a Religious Tradition*. London: Routledge.

Roudometof, Victor. 2014b. Orthodox Christianity and globalization. In *Eastern Christianities and Politics in the Twenty-First Century*. Edited by Lucian N. Leustean. London: Routledge, pp. 776–94.

Roudometof, Victor. 2014c. Religion and globalization. In *The Sage Handbook of Globalization*. Edited by Manfred Steger, Paul Battersby and Joseph Siracusa. London: Sage, pp. 151–65.

Roudometof, Victor. 2015. The glocal and global studies. *Globalizations* 12: 774–87. [CrossRef]

Roudometof, Victor. 2016a. Globalization. In *Handbook of Religion and Society*. Edited by David Yamane. New York: Springer, pp. 505–24.

Roudometof, Victor. 2016b. *Glocalization: A Critical Introduction*. London: Routledge.

Spickard, James V. 2004. Globalization and religious organizations: Rethinking the relationship between church, culture, and market. *International Journal of Politics, Culture and Society* 18: 47–63. [CrossRef]

Shoji, Rafael, and Frank Usarski. 2014. Japanese new religions in Brazil and the dynamics of globalization versus glocalization. *Journal of Religion in Japan* 3: 247–69. [CrossRef]

Stackhouse, Max L., and Peter J. Paris, eds. 2000. *God and Globalization: Religion and the Powers of the Common Life*. Harrisburg: Trinity International.

Storrar, William F. 2004. Where the local and the global meet: Duncan Forrester's glocal public theology and Scottish political context. In *Public Theology for the 21st Century*. Edited by William F. Storrar and Andrew R. Morton. London and New York: T&T Clark, pp. 405–30.

Tehranian, Majid. 2007. Globalization and religious resurgence: A historical perspective. *The Muslim World* 97: 385–94. [CrossRef]

Therborn, Göran. 2000. Globalizations: Dimensions, historical waves, regional effects, normative governance. *International Sociology* 15: 151–79. [CrossRef]

Topel, Marta F. 2017. Brazilian Jewish communities: Globalization and glocalization. In *Religion, Migration, and Mobility: The Brazilian Experience*. Edited by Cristina Maria de Castro and Andrew Dawson. London: Routledge, pp. 57–71.

Warburg, Margit. 2006. *Citizens of the World: A History and Sociology of the Baha'i from a Globalization Perspective*. Leiden: Brill.

Van Der Veer, Peter. 2002. Transnational religion: Hindu and Muslim movements. *Global Networks* 2: 95–109. [CrossRef]

Vasquez, Manuel A. 2008. Studying religion in motion: A networks approach. *Method and Theory in the Study of Religion* 20: 151–84. [CrossRef]

![religions](religions logo) **MDPI**

Article

Sensing Hinduism: Lucian-Indian Funeral "Feast" as Glocalized Ritual

Sabita Manian [1],*,† **and Brad Bullock** [2],†

[1] Department of Political Science, Liberal Arts Studies, Lynchburg College, 1501 Lakeside Drive, Lynchburg, VA 24501, USA

[2] Department of Sociology, Randolph College, 2500 Rivermont Avenue, Lynchburg, VA 24503, USA; bbullock@randolphcollege.edu

* Correspondence: manian@lynchburg.edu; Tel.: +1-434-544-8449

† These authors contributed equally to this work.

Academic Editors: Peter Iver Kaufman and Victor Roudometof

Received: 15 October 2015; Accepted: 24 December 2015; Published: 6 January 2016

Abstract: Migrant narratives of Indo-Caribbean religious practices in the *smaller* island states of the Caribbean are rare, and that Diaspora's funerary traditions are even less explored. This scholarly lacuna is addressed here by using data from ethnographic research conducted in St. Lucia to examine the funerary ritual of a Lucian-Indian "feast" through the multidisciplinary lens of *glocalization*. Specifically, we investigate the following: (a) ways that the diasporic identity of Lucian-Indians has been adapted and re-configured within a local-global nexus; (b) the extent to which there has been a local construction of a distinct socio-spatial identity among Lucian-Indians, one retaining "Hinduness" even as they assimilated into the larger St. Lucian society; and (c) whether *glocal* characteristics can be identified in the performance of a particular funeral feast. Following Roudometof, we posit that many aspects of a Lucian-Indian ethno-religious funerary ritual demonstrate *indigenized* and *transnational* glocalization.

Keywords: globalization; glocalization; glocal ethnography; Caribbean; St. Lucia; Indo-Caribbean; Hindu; funeral

---

1. Introduction

"Kala Pani" (black water) migrant narratives of Indo-Caribbeans are rare, and accounts of their religious practices in the *smaller* island states of the Caribbean are even rarer. Accordingly, relatively little about their funerary traditions is documented, especially in Caribbean countries like St. Lucia, where people of East Indian origin constitute a small minority. This paper focuses specifically on the sociocultural adaptations observed in a contemporary funerary ritual in St. Lucia, particularly as they relate to global Hinduism and an East Indian Diaspora that signify a form of transnational material culture. Using original ethnographic research, we reveal how Indo-Lucians have crafted a socio-religious space that represents an important and enduring fragment of their ethnic identity, one shaped by their indentureship in this small Caribbean island, starting in the mid-nineteenth century. This funeral ritual has evolved according to an interplay of global and local forces, and the resulting hybrid practices are best understood using the concept of *glocalization* [1,2].

---

[1] A version of this paper was presented at the SISR-ISSR (International Society for the Sociology of Religion) conference in Louvain la Neuve, Belgium in July 2015. We wish to thank Ms. Wendy Bailey, Mr. Guy Joseph (former Minister of Communications and Transportation in St. Lucia), and Ms. Erma Khodra for their invaluable assistance in identifying Lucians of Indian ethnicity and heritage and for facilitating this research; we also gratefully acknowledge funding support from both Lynchburg College and Randolph College.

Foremost in form, we seek to provide a *glocal ethnography* along the lines suggested by Salazar ([3], p. 180), described as "the complex connections, disconnections and reconnections between local and global phenomena and processes . . . achieved by firmly embedding and historically situating the in-depth study of a particular socio-cultural group, organization or setting within a larger and ultimately global context." To this end, we include information from extensive interviews of Lucian-Indians, as well as video documentation of a funeral feast to examine the following: (a) ways that the diasporic identity of Lucian-Indians has been adapted and re-configured within a local-global nexus; (b) the extent to which there has been a local construction of a distinct socio-spatial identity among Lucian-Indians, one retaining "Hinduness" even as they assimilated into the larger St. Lucian society; and (c) whether glocal characteristics can be identified in the performance of a particular funeral feast.

2. Indo-Caribbean Identity

General scholarship on Indo-Caribbean history, culture, and politics emphasizes the common narrative of indentureship of women and men from India who crossed the "kala pani" (or "black waters") to work on Caribbean plantations, regardless of their linguistic and social diversity. Many historical narratives discuss the arrival of Indian women and men who brought with them physical and cultural pieces of their homeland, along with their dreams of making an honest living and saving enough to re-start their lives upon returning to India. Instead, as we know from the recorded histories of 19th century Indian immigrants, a majority of them had to lead a life tantamount to slavery, with neither a meaningful chance to fulfill their dreams nor return to their homeland. Despite the common travails among Indian indentured laborers in many parts of the Caribbean, what remains distinctly different is the unique sociocultural context that led them to shape particular individual or group identities as opposed to those of others.

Such transnational identity-shaping does vary from one Caribbean society to another. Consequently, the post-migration trajectories of Indians in their new homeland—requiring mediation, negotiation, innovation, and cultural production and re-production—are qualitatively and quantitatively different in various parts of the Caribbean. For instance, Guyana and Trinidad are characterized by what Hilbourne Watson calls the "the racialization of global politics" as "a dialectical process of construction and deconstruction," whereby race and racialization have contributed to the "colonial construction of the region" that affected the internal and regional consciousness of the Caribbean ([4], pp. 449–50). In this context, Indo-Caribbean identity has been forged primarily in opposition to a creolized or an Afro-Caribbean one within a cultural arena of conflict. Unlike their counterparts in Guyana or Trinidad and Tobago, St. Lucia's Indo-Caribbean population is considerably more assimilated into this majority Afro-Caribbean island state and their relationship with the Afro-Caribbean majority has not been surrounded by ostensible and comparable acrimony, hostility or segregation. Partly as a consequence of this context, inter-marriage among the various groups has contributed to an erosion of any acute sense of their East Indian Hindu heritage and identity. Yet, the funeral feast we describe reveals a primary way that ethnic "Hindu" norms are retained even as they are interspersed or intertwined with their contemporary Christian practices (Catholic, Methodist, Evangelical, or Pentecostal).

Lucian-Indians are Indo-Caribbeans who are descendants of East Indian indentured servants who began to arrive in St. Lucia starting in the 1850s (and through the early 1900s) following the abolition of slavery (in Britain, in 1833, but not fully realized until 1843). Many had been duped into labor contracts for migrant work on plantations, and were forced to settle in the Caribbean when the contractual agreements were reneged by the planter class. As Harmsen [5,6] reports:

> Just over 1600 people arrived here [St. Lucia] between 1856 and 1865 and another 4427 Indians sailed to St. Lucia between 1878 and 1893. By 1891, there were some 2500 East Indians in St. Lucia (colloquially known as 'coolies'), in a total population of 42,220 souls. Two years later, the last batch of indentured workers arrived on a ship called the 'Volga',

totaling 156 people .... By the turn of the century, St. Lucia had a free East Indian population of 2560 persons.

This diasporic population survived suffering, dislocation and relocation partly from their ability to use "religion as a process of transculturation" ([7], p. 4), thereby adapting to their new homeland by forging collective neo-identities.

From here out, we will exclusively use the term *Lucian-Indian* rather than Indo-Lucian to define and describe Indo-Caribbeans in St. Lucia. This draws a distinction between those of Indian descent in St. Lucia and their counterparts in countries such as Guyana, Trinidad, Surinam, Jamaica, St. Vincent, or Guadeloupe. In these other societies, a larger percentage of the Indo-Caribbean population have successfully retained more of their "Indian-ness". By placing "Lucian" before "Indian" we attempt to capture both the importance of the Lucian identity, which appears stronger than the Indian one but simultaneously does not erase East-Indian heritage.

St. Lucia's current population is approximately 183,645 (according to a 2014 World Bank report), of which an estimated 3%–3.25% is identified as Indo-Caribbean—resulting in 5000–6000 Lucians of East-Indian descent. Nearly 12% of that population is of "mixed" ethnicity, representing miscegenation of other racial/ethnic groups (primarily Afro-Caribbean) with their East Indian counterparts. Whatever their exact number, St. Lucia's comparable Indo-Caribbean population is rather small in relation to Jamaica, Trinidad and Tobago, or even Guyana (see Table 1 below). Likewise, by comparison to St. Lucia, the number and proportion of Indo-Guyanese and Indo-Trinidadians are considerably larger. Historically and politically, the inter-ethnic relations of the East-Indian and African populations in these two countries have often been less than amicable.

Table 1. Population of select Caribbean states.

Country	Total Population
Belize	351,700
French Guiana*	229,000
Grenada	106,300
Guadeloupe*	452,776
Guyana	763,900
Jamaica	2,721,000
St. Lucia	183,645
St. Vincent & the Grenadines	109,400
Trinidad & Tobago	1,354,000

Notes: Source: Data compiled from the 2014 World Bank Population Statistics except for French Guiana and Guadeloupe (data from INSE, France).

Among Trinidad and Tobago's approximately 1.3 million people, about 40% are East Indian and 38% are of African heritage. In Guyana, with a population of about 764,000, roughly 45% are of East Indian descent while 30% claim African heritage). The size of a country seems to matter less than the size of the minority when addressing identity politics. In fact, we contend that, along with the length of time since the bulk of migrants arrived, the proportional size of the Indo-Caribbean population may be the most important variable to explain differences in the subsequent retention of an "Indian" identity. Yet, St. Lucia itself is not without its inter-ethnic dynamic. Simply because the Lucian-Indian population is small does not mean one can ignore their contributions to Lucian history, culture, and society.

In his comparative study of the Hindu diaspora in the Caribbean countries of Guyana, Surinam and Trinidad, Vertovec ([8], pp. 110–11) observed that there are strong, distinct "Indian patterns" of Hinduism because of "inadvertent permutation as well as conscious manipulations which have taken place over the course of three to five generations". We argue here that for Lucian-Indians, despite their smaller number and their assimilation within the ethnic majority, there has been "inadvertent permutation" and "conscious manipulation" of identity taking place. Despite their integration—one that includes aspects of "acculturation" (adopting the new homeland's culture) and "assimilation" (building strong inter-ethnic ties with the new homeland's majority)—there are certain cultural spaces where Lucian-Indians continue to rely on their Hindu antecedents. These cultural spaces usually surround rites of passage related to life and death, accompanied by foodways that inform and structure such rituals as the funeral "feast". While religious festivals and rituals relating to Hossay (Muharram) in Trinidad, diwali or Kali worship in Guyana, or even carnival and its symbolism have all been studied before, Indo-Caribbean funeral rites are less studied and, in the St. Lucian case, poorly understood.

3. Theoretical Framework and Methods

We employ an interpretation of glocalization favored by Roudometof ([9], p. 9), who contends that "glocalization is globalization refracted through the local." By Roudometof's account, previous conceptions of hybrid practices have been developed within a dialectic about the influence and result of global forces on local practices. On one hand, ongoing work launched by theorists such as Robertson [10,11] basically argues that globalization is not a separate, binary opposite to the local or a force that overwhelms or displaces local practices, but rather a force that is invariably merged to the local so that it can only manifest itself within myriad new, hybrid or glocal forms. This monistic view suggests that globalization can encourage either heterogeneity or homogeneity among local practices, and delivers not integration but fragmentation. We stress that it also implicitly celebrates the eternal presence of the micro. On the other hand, work fueled by theorists such as Ritzer [12,13] sees globalization as an external force in mutual opposition to the local, one that is driven by the profane character of international capitalism to exterminate the local. Ritzer's dualistic view predicts integration inside the structure of a largely homogenized global culture, where remaining glocal forms reflect the ideas and values of capitalist hegemony. We believe that Ritzer's view explicitly bemoans the ultimate victory of the macro.

Roudometof presents his view of glocalization as an alternate to previous views, one that proposes we consider the processes and results of globalization as neither ultimately subsumed by the local nor causing the local in effect to disappear. In what we view is an effective synthesis of a dialectic, glocalization becomes "an analytically autonomous concept" and resulting glocal forms are not required in essence to be either local or global. In Roudometof's words, "The local is not annihilated or absorbed or destroyed by globalization but, rather, operates symbiotically with globalization and shapes the telos or end state ... " ([9], p. 9). That end state, or glocality, produces fertile glocal hybrid forms that are experienced locally, yet reflect multiple levels of power relations and agency at both the macro and micro levels. For example, in Roudometof's conception, the spread of powerful global memes may be buffered or "refracted" by waves of cultural resistance at the local level. We find this view the most effective from which to analyze the global and glocal forms we observed in St. Lucia.

We wish to demonstrate how the contemporary localized bricolage of ostensibly "Hindu" practices surrounding a ritualistic "Indian feast"—part of funerary practice performed by Lucian-Indians who are today self-identified as Christians—intersects innovatively with the global dynamics of historical colonialism to produce glocal practices. Those global dynamics led mostly Hindu migrants to become indentured laborers, arriving from India starting in the late 1850s. This Lucian-Indian funerary space is one that is distinct: while it contains a few elements we may describe as transnational hybridity, it is primarily glocal, and goes beyond the simple dichotomy of extracting and identifying global "Hindu" strands or global "Christian" strands. Instead, we attempt to understand this ritual as a heterotopic phenomenon, one founded on a collective and constructed memory in the context of a dominant culture and two dominant global religions, and performed locally in a unique social space. The various adaptations of Lucian-Indians, e.g., in comparison to the feast rituals of historical India, preserve what is now considered as "Indian" for their collective future identity, and the local space is in itself "context generating" (see Appadurai, [14]).

We restate that glocalization here is defined as "the refraction of globalization through the local ... a blend of the local and the global" (Roudometof [9], p. 13).[2] Elsewhere, Roudometof has lamented that "the glocal is conspicuously absent" from research agendas that tend to view "Creolization or hybridization" as "competing terms used to designate the production of various forms of heterogeneity under conditions of intensified cultural contact" ([1], p. 8). Other primary sources guiding our analysis include Pieterse [16] and Kriady [17] on forms of hybridity, and Khondker [18] on distinguishing the global and local features of glocal phenomena.[3]

This research is based on original ethnographic work. Over three week periods in June 2011 and May 2015, we conducted semi-structured interviews with a total of 35 women and men of Indo-Caribbean descent living in St. Lucia. Interviewees were first identified through local contacts and then later by word-of-mouth, either from earlier participants or through self-identified volunteers following local radio and television coverage of the project. The interviews were designed, conducted, and recorded by the authors. Since responses were digitally recorded, all interviewees were required to grant written consent. Respondents were also given the option to allow a recorded interview without recording their images (only one of our interviewees chose this option). In instances where a respondent was not fluent in English, a local interpreter translated between Creole and English.

While the Indo-Caribbean population is scattered throughout St. Lucia, small pockets of Lucian-Indians are geographically concentrated in certain areas (see Figure 1). Other than commercial centers such as Rodney Bay, Gros Islet, and the Castries area, we conducted the majority of our interviews in towns and parishes with high concentrations of Lucian-Indians: Babboneau in Forestiere parish (northeast), Choiseul in Laborie parish (southwest), Desruisseaux in Micoud parish (southeast), and Vieux Fort (south).

Figure 1. Map of St. Lucia and its eleven parishes.

---

[2] This definition deviates from Peter Beyer's assertion of Robertson's view of globalization as glocalization, but corresponds with the former's identification of glocalization as "the global expressed in the local and the local as particularization of the global" ([15], p. 98).

[3] Literature on the Caribbean has thoroughly developed numerous ways to understand the common condition of hybridity, including the conceptual tools of Creolization, douglarization, negritude, coolitude and so on. A previous draft of this paper attempted to address fertile connections between these and concepts associated with glocalization, but we decided in favor of leaving this discourse to a larger paper that could do justice to that enterprise. Though we adopt a narrower focus for the purposes of this work, we recommend several studies that will be useful for an overview of major concepts: Denis [19], Bongie [20] and Khan [21] on Creolization; for douglarization, Khan [22]; and for coolitude, Carter and Torabully [23], Crosson [24], and Mohammed [25]. Literature on the history of negritude is extensive, but we would suggest starting with any of the numerous works of Frantz Fanon or his teacher, Aimé Césaire.

Our 35 respondents consisted of 13 women and 22 men of varied ages. With some success, we prioritized interviewing older Lucians, octogenarians and nonagenarians, to excavate from their memories precious oral histories about their foremothers and forefathers that only they could still recollect. The interviews averaged about 45–50 min each, though a few went on for over an hour.

The interview questions, structured to provide a personal "life-history" narrative, were later transcribed. Our focus is qualitative, so that perspectives about social, economic, political and cultural life expressed by our respondents lend themselves to possible, generalized conclusions concerning the extent of, and reasons for, their assimilation and, for many others, their *dougla* (hybrid) identity. We particularly emphasized cultural markers relating to food, birth/marriage/death rituals, and social values as elements that cement either a latent or manifest identity. Then, by using a broad corpus of identity and assimilation theories, we have attempted to make sense of how Lucian-Indians now articulate an identity in their particular political and sociocultural context—that is, as a very small minority in a small island state. Generally, we assert that: (1) Lucian-Indians' contributions to St. Lucia's heritage and contemporary society are not insignificant, therefore it is essential to fully understand and incorporate their influence when constructing a pan-Lucian historical narrative or collective identity; and (2) there exists a unique context containing particulars of identity-shaping for Lucian-Indians that can offer a comparative case for the wider Caribbean.[4]

For this paper, however, we should emphasize some points related to these assertions. First, we do include some comparisons to help us to draw distinctions about what is uniquely St. Lucian; we believe that comparative analysis is invaluable and inevitable. But making fuller use of comparisons to related funereal practices (e.g., in the Caribbean or India or even other diaspora groups) is beyond the scope and aims of this paper. Case studies are intended to stand on their own, even when useful comparisons may be drawn to similar practices. The point remains that very little ethnographic work is done on Indo-Caribbean people in places where they are a substantial minority, and thus such work is valuable in its own right. To our knowledge, no other fully-documented Lucian-Indian funeral feast readily exists. Next, this study is not meant to be exhaustive but instead is located within an ongoing project on Lucian-Indian identity, so we choose to focus on some common themes that emerge from the narratives and practices we have already documented.

4. The Funeral Feast

In June of 2011, we were invited by one of our interviewees to attend and document an "Indian funeral feast" in Belle Vue (Vieux Fort parish) given by family members for a recently deceased uncle. She explained that this ritual was once common among Lucian-Indians but were now rarely performed except for older members of their communities, something corroborated by others we interviewed. In the Lucian tradition, the feast is always hosted and performed by family members after the corpse has received a Christian burial, sometimes 8 to 9 months after the death of their loved one, as was the case in the rite we documented. It was explained that the monetary cost and the time for arranging the feast often led to the delay in its performance, as it required not only the construction of a "shrine" or make-shift "house", but also time to amass provisions for feeding anywhere from 50 to 100 guests—relatives, friends and neighbors of all classes and ethnicities who are routinely invited to such ceremonies.

According to some of our respondents who provided extensive narratives about the feast, it is traditionally managed and prepared by men-folk in the family or the immediate community, and no women are permitted to be involved in this effort. In earlier times, this effort included the following: first, a shrine or what was described to us as a "house" for the departed, was constructed deep in the woods with bamboo and leaves, away from where people lived. This feature is now changed so that

---

[4] We are sensitive to Allahar's warnings that a unique Caribbean-ness as an identity category may be seen as a device foisted on the Caribbean by colonial authorities, a legacy of a colonial mind-set [26].

the "house" is constructed in the yard next to the home where the deceased lived, though it remains outside that building (see Figure 2). But it was still men who prepared the ritual meal for the feast we observed, when cooking is otherwise almost exclusively done by women.

Figure 2. The Funeral Shrine and the Drawing or Motif tradition of *Kohbar*.

Typically, men wake up before dawn and are required to wash and "cleanse" themselves. They clothe themselves either in clean black or black-and-white garments before they start their work in the kitchen, as early as 3 a.m., cooking about 8–10 different food items. In the feast we documented, the following food items were prepared: *dalpuri, suhari* (puffed bread), *chawal/bhaat* (rice), eggplant *tarkari*, pumpkin *tarkari*, potato *tarkari*, fish curry, a meat (goat) curry, and *gulgula* (mini donut balls). The food was contained in large metal pots covered with clean banana leaves. The banana leaves are significant because that material is traditionally used in India for all such rituals—metal lids and plates are considered polluted from previous use, whereas the biodegradable banana leaf is purer and cannot be re-used. Both in India and in St. Lucia, banana leaves serve to prevent food from drying out or being contaminated by flies, and fresh leaves function as plates from which food is consumed (traditionally taken to the mouth by one's fingers).

The full ritual is meant to be witnessed by assembled family and neighbors. A significant moment arrives when a select group of seven family members, later to serve as a processional group, assemble in the room where the food is housed to set up a ritual meal for the spirit of the deceased, who is served first. Before this however, the seven must undergo a highly choreographed "purification" ritual of washing their hands and feet. Immediately after washing their hands, each must sprinkle some clean "holy water" behind their back to stave off evil spirits. They go through a ritual cleansing of their hands, and then on clean banana leaves reserved for this purpose, they take turns spooning portions of each dish for the dead loved one's spirit. This is also done in a ceremonial way: they form a circle, placing precisely three pieces or spoons of each food item in the banana leaf, and the food is served always with the right hand, cradled at the elbow or wrist by the left hand.

Once the food for the deceased is set aside, the next step is to collect on a tray (not a banana leaf) some consumable items dear to the deceased so that the select members may take them into the shrine in a solemn procession. In the case we documented, this included a packet of cigarettes and matches, a favorite soda beverage, water and coffee. But the tray also included incense, wax candles, and a traditional Indian lamp or *diya* (which our hosts called a "local candle") made from dough and shaped like a cup or crucible and filled with oil and a cotton wick. The seven select members of the funeral feast group included 3 men and 4 women. All were dressed in casual black clothing, including t-shirts, except for one man at the back of the procession. We discovered that he remained in regular clothing since he was a friend of the deceased but unrelated to the family. Each of the women's heads were covered by a black scarf, and all seven members wore matching funeral ribbons of purple and white to signify their status both as special members of the feast group and as mourners.

For the procession (done in silence), the food for the dead is carried out first by a daughter, followed by a grandson who was charged with lighting the candles and incense. Slowly reaching the shrine, the grandson entered the space first to produce light inside. Then the procession kneels and carefully sets each item into the shrine in turn, remaining for some time in a position of prayer, meditation or reflection. One male member, in this case the family friend, stands guard at the rear of the procession carrying two ceremonial items: a smoldering log or "torch" and a machete or "cutlass" as it is called by Lucians. The shrine portion of the ceremony concludes when the supplicants rise and make their way out of the shrine space into the family home for their ritual meal.

Before the waiting guests can begin the feast, the seven processioners first gather in the house and sit in a circle on the floor where they are each served a portion of the prepared food items, again on banana leaves. In the middle of this circle, a banana "plate" is ritually set for the deceased, who is included in the group by receiving a serving of rum. Once the select group begins their meal, eaten with their fingers, everyone else begins to feast, and the solemn atmosphere turns to merriment. The many guests were served their fill from long tables set outside and the party went on for many hours.

5. Analysis: Global and Glocal

If the particular history, culture, or religion of any one island in the Caribbean is, indeed, the composite result of a series of transnational processes over time, it is then critical to consider the global effects on the production of locality and the local construction of globality, or "glocality" [27].

The most important way that Indian heritage appears passed down in the St. Lucian context—recognizably and significantly—is through funeral rituals, commonly called "feasts", or "dinners" by Lucian-Indians. From our interviews and documentation of a funeral feast, some noteworthy features emerged. We find the Lucian-Indian funeral feast is laced with reconfigured Hindu symbolism. Our case study focuses squarely on Roudometof's call to identify the "glocal" in culture and religion, and we will draw upon his heuristic categories of glocal-cultural hybrids: *i.e.*, *vernacularization, indigenization, nationalization*, and *transnationalization* [28]. We expect to show that indigenization and transnationalization are clearly identifiable elements in the funeral feast we analyze, whereby the "glocal turn" is revealed as "continuous processes of hybridization and of incorporation of cultural items borrowed from elsewhere" ([28], p. 1020). We further attempt to unpack and decode the global and the glocal by dissecting various material and non-material elements that relate to the performance of the feast.

5.1. The Global

To be glocal, there must be an identifiable global stream to influence and blend with the local. Among the potential global streams, we consider these most important: (i) aspects of global culture (material and non-material); (ii) the Indian diaspora itself (that section of it that is constituted by descendants of indentured laborers in St. Lucia); (iii) its global imaginary (which involves negotiating the disjuncture between their historical place of origin and contemporary settlement, and which continues to be shaped and re-shaped by their sense of collective ethnic identity that connects the idea of "India" with memories of "Hindu" practices); (iv) the global religions of Hinduism and Christianity; and finally (v) pan-Caribbean relations and influence (which raises a theoretical point we address later). For example, identifiable items of global material culture include the aforementioned t-shirts worn by the males in the feast procession printed with the international brands Nike and Adidas, and other "feast" paraphernalia such as rum (exported around the world), the plastic tray, and candles, to name a few. Since these same items can be purchased almost anywhere, we would not offer them as glocal. Global non-material culture would include the fashion of t-shirts, consumerism, and other ideas behind global branding and consumption (such as Ritzer's well-known concept of *McDonaldization*).

5.2. The Glocal

Among the category of glocal elements, we offer: (i) the singularity of the feast ceremony as distinct from its Hindu origin; (ii) the shrine, or the "special place"—referred to by the locals as a "house" constructed for the sole purpose of the funeral feast; (iii) foodways related to the "dinner"; (iv) the home-made candle that supplements the ubiquitous wax candles and was conspicuously significant to the performance of the rite; and (v) the constitution and performance of the processional group of seven members, including their black clothing and head coverings (for women), as well as the funeral ribbons.

The feast ceremony is informed by Hinduism but has been thoroughly blended with the local. Hindu death and post-mortem rituals in India vary according to family, caste, sect, and region; however, most Hindus generally draw from two bodies of Hindu texts: the Vedas and the *Garuda Purana* – a funeral liturgy. In contemporary practice, most Indian and diasporic Hindus tend to follow the latter more than the former. Significant to our case, the Hindu last-rites (*antam samskara*) mandated in the rite of transition requires:

> On the 3rd, 5th, 7th or 9th day, relatives gather for a meal of the deceased's favorite foods. A portion is offered before his photo and later ceremonially left at an *abandoned place*, along with some lit camphor [29]. (Emphasis Added).

This liturgical tenet for the ritual meal, and its ceremonial offering at "an abandoned place", is but one part of a multi-phased and elaborate *sraddha* (post-mortem rites)—a ceremony that lasts ten to thirteen days as part of a purification process for the family, as well as a rite of passage for the spirit to become a *pitr* or ancestor.[5] The Lucian-Indians, however, have collapsed an elaborate, days-long process to a single-day, a singular ritual that is particular to Lucian-Indian praxis. The practitioners have no direct knowledge of Hindu customs but describe what they do as "Indian"—the emic view is therefore more ethnic than religious. From that, and the fact that many of the migrants were from lower castes arrived poor, and were forced to convert to Christianity, it makes sense that a collapsed ritual would evolve—one that skips most of the purification and instead emphasizes the communal celebration.

The Hindu liturgical rationale for the "abandoned place" remains a distinct part of the funeral feast in the Lucian context, but local dynamics produce a unique spiritual space that takes the physical form of a spirit-house. The shrine is constructed to look like a mini-shed with an altar, covered with palm leaves and festooned with colorful (plastic) garlands, where the special dinner for the hungry and thirsty spirit is placed (see Figure 2). As one interviewee observed:

> When grandfather died we had a dinner. . . . They had a *"special place"* where they would place it [dinner] . . . .[Recently] *it baffled me: they had decorated a little house* and everybody was dressed in black and white shirts . . . *as if it was a Church ceremony* . . . but all food at the feast was Indian. [Emphasis Added].

What this respondent and others confirmed is that the construction of a physical shrine is a variant local feature that was not previously practiced. Our respondents were unable to provide a rationale for this change to a physical construct of the "special place", nor for making public what used to be isolated and private. When prodded about this, their replies fell along the lines from another interviewee who said:

---

[5]   Indeed, the *Garuda Purana* [30–33] carefully lays out the complex outline for various rites distinct to each of the purification stages in three different chapters.

> ... we accept everything ... nobody asks questions .... The old Indians, they know how
> to do everything and they volunteer.

Our etic interpretation is that the increase in trans-Caribbean movement of people,
and subsequently of norms and ideas, has resulted in imitation of the Guyanese or Trinidadian *"kutiya"*
or religious shrine and thus has led to a Lucian inclusion of the same in their funeral feast [34,35]. Also,
there is no longer the perceived need to hide this "Indian" ritual from intolerant Christians, as in the
colonial past.

A parallel ritual, similar to Hindu counterparts in India, is drawing on the floor of the sacred space
with white rice flour. In Trinidad, this tradition of "drawings in coloured rice flour and multi-coloured
powders around the area of a house or temple consecrated as [a] prayer ground" ([36], p. 137) is known
as *kohbar*.[6] A closer look at the *kohbar* inside the shrine we observed reveals that the drawing is clearly
meant to resemble the Union Jack (refer again to Figure 2). This global artifice is complicated: on one
hand it celebrates their British and perhaps Christian identity, but on the other it bears the legacy of
empire, colonialism, and the brutal Kala Pani passage related to an indentureship that cut their link
with their original homeland. Yet, none of our interviewees at the funeral feast or elsewhere were able
to identify a name in the local lexicon for the geometric floor pattern, nor provide a particular reason
for the Union Jack motif.

As mentioned previously, the non-quotidian food and beverage items at the feast (such as *dalpuri*,
various forms of *tarkari*, mutton, fish, *gulgulla*, and rum) reveal local particularization of Indian foods
used in Hindu funeral rituals elsewhere. The Lucian-Indian feast foods are specially prepared to reflect
their collective memory of Hindu customs (as reflected by the *Garuda Purana*, Chapters III and IV),
but the "Indian" food items themselves are refracted through local lenses. For instance, the Lucian
dalpuri is closer to its Indo-Caribbean counterparts (arguably, there is variation even in intra-Caribbean
cuisine) than to the North Indian preparation [37,38]. In the Lucian (and pan-Caribbean) variant,
the *dalpuri* is generally made with white flour and split peas and is pan-tossed, unlike its Indian
counterpart that is typically made with whole wheat flour, Bengal gram or lentils, and is very much
deep-fried. In St. Lucia, accessibility to yellow split peas rather than Bengal gram or moong beans
accounts for some of this. But the variation is also a consequence of intra-American agro-trade in the
nineteenth century that led to using first wheat flour and then bleached flour that replaced whole
wheat flour throughout the Caribbean. Another divergence is that Indian Hindus serve rice balls
(*pindas*) and other items such as *ghee* (clarified butter) that are dissimilar from the food items served in
the St. Lucian feast [31,32].

What is a common thread, however, in both the sub-Continent's funeral foodways and the Lucian
one, is the significance of three servings of each item (described earlier). This may stand as a remnant
global practice, since it is done identically in India and St. Lucia. Likewise, it is significant that
banana leaves, rather than a plate or a lid, were used to cover the food—these leaves are not used on
an everyday basis either in Lucian or in Lucian-Indian households. This feature also seems global,
since those leaves are used for funeral feasts in India as part of a Hindu religious dictum against
encountering a non-pollutant, and because it is a pan-Caribbean practice. Among Indo-Trinidadians,
Aisha Khan describes the "pollution ideology" of *"juthaa"* (pronounced joot-ta)—a Hindi/Urdu word
for food "defiled by eating, drinking, or using otherwise"—and she elaborates on the extension of this
concept: *"Juthaa* in this sense does not refer to regurgitated food, that which already has been consumed;
it signifies the remaining food that has been symbolically tainted by association with another person
(really, another person's essence, concretized as bodily substance, e.g., saliva, sweat, *etc.*)" ([39], p. 246).
Whereas among Indo-Trinidadians this "pollution ideology" is extended to describe other aspects
of defilement, in St. Lucia, its conceptual meaning is neither recognized nor extended in this way.
We believe this is largely because of: (a) St. Lucia's very small East Indian minority that has not

---

6   It is called an *alpana* in Hindi or *kolam* in Tamil.

managed to salvage this cultural norm; and (b) its geopolitical insularity from Caribbean societies with larger majorities of East Indians, since the pollution norm is observed by Indo-Caribbeans not just in Trinidad and Tobago but also in Guyana, Suriname and Jamaica [40–46]. In those places, intra-Caribbean movement of Hindu ritual specialists is a norm, whereas in St. Lucia the better survival strategy would have favored integration over maintaining a manifestly Hindu identity.

Earlier we discussed the inclusion of a home-made candle made of flour dough, shaped into a lamp, containing oil and three wicks that was used in the funeral procession; it was ceremonially carried by the grandson, along with a bowl containing incense made out of potpourri. Our interviewees labeled it a "local candle" but it is a "*diya*" or "*dheep*" when used for worship among Hindu families in India. The coexistence of a traditional lamp and wax candles is again significant, since it mixes a traditional Hindu ritual feature with a non-Hindu one more common in Christian church rituals. The particular symbolism, meaning, and interpretation of the consumables and the "light" brought to the spirit of the deceased are not exactly comparable to their Indian antecedents nor are they comparable with the larger Caribbean trio (Guyana, Trinidad and Suriname). Despite this, Lucian-Indians assert as essential the inclusion of the *diya* because they know that it is "Indian". Once more, the emic lack of knowledge about the proper name or symbolism does not alter the fact that it is glocal, while it also emphasizes the cultural imaginary of "Indian" as ethnic more than religious.

Some Lucian-Indians perform the feast procession with men only while others have a mix of women and men, yet the constant is seven members. The procession we documented had four women and three men and was led by the daughter of the deceased. This gender structure is not what the *Garuda Purana* prescribes, but it has become common custom even among contemporary Indian-Hindu and diasporic Hindus in the absence of a son of the deceased who would otherwise lead the rites. We posit that two historical, global trends are at work in this shift of gender role and status. First, the Hindu funeral ritual that began in the nineteenth century in St. Lucia would have required constructing a "special place" in the woods, outside the purview of the established secular and religious authorities, which reinforced this ceremony as an all-male affair (*i.e.*, one meant to "protect" women from having to make their way through a dark, dangerous forest full of spirits and wild animals). The contemporary "Indian" funeral practice is less discreet in the context of more flexible and liberalized norms of ecumenical propriety, thereby allowing for an altogether different space, one that allows women to be active co-participants. Second, the globalized shift in women's roles, and their relative rise in status over colonial times is reflected in both the Indian and Lucian context. Beyond the direct global and ethnic tie of the ritual itself, there is perhaps an indirect influence from the global spread of industrialization that has caused the same phenomenon to evolve independently [44]. This aspect, then, does not appear glocal by our chosen framework.

Also noted earlier was the color and type of attire donned by the seven processioners. Two of the men wore black t-shirts emblazoned with the global brands Nike and Adidas, while the women were more formally attired in black Christian "church dress" and head scarves, a custom quite different from their Indian counterparts who wear exclusively white mourning garments. The Lucian-Indian procession, then, is clearly a glocal affair. The use of a purple and white bereavement ribbon pinned to their clothing is common among Catholics and is reflective of their Christian experience. The women's head-cover, a black scarf, mimics those of Hindu women who are required by tradition to cover their head, particularly during a prayer ritual, but the Lucian-Indians more closely mimic the Catholic influence of proper reverence during worship.

When the seven go through the "purification" ritual of washing their hands and feet, followed by sprinkling some water behind their back, this harkens to Hindu rituals that employ "holy water" to stave off evil spirits. In traditional Hindu custom, the "holy water" is the water of the River Ganga/Ganges known as "*ganga pani*", but in many parts of India tap water is used to symbolically represent "*ganga pani*". Among the Lucian-Indians we interviewed, the symbolism of the purification ritual was unknown. The procession is representative of the five Brahmin priests or in some instances nine, who are required to conduct the funeral rites of the deceased in Hindu families in India [31]. Significant here, in the case of the Lucian-Indians, is not just the retention of representatives of the Hindu priesthood, but the number seven (rather than five or nine). Seven is a prominent holy number in Christian traditions.

All of the characteristics emphasized above reflect the glocal and can be identified with two of Roudometof's glocalization classifications: indigenization and transnationalization. As shown above, "Indian" funeral practice has been *indigenized* through the fusion of religious and ethnic categories "in the absence of political authority" to create and re-create a symbiotic cultural product that assures a survival of Lucian-Indian history and a cohesive root identity. Hinduism has thus contributed to a public performance in a public-private space and can be sensed in the cultural reproduction of the funeral feast by Lucian-Indians. *Transnationalized* glocalization is evidenced in Lucian-Indians, since what we document reveals how they "reconstitute their ties to both host and home countries [as] they engage in a creative process of blending elements from both points of reference" ([28], p. 1028). In the context of a decentralized Hinduism and the absence of a clerical hierarchical authority, Lucian-Indians have successfully navigated their cultural and political space in their current homeland to creatively reconstitute their "Indian" customs relating to a final rite of passage from their land of origin. Their adaptations and reconfigurations demonstrate concomitant and non-sequential glocalization that are both *indigenized* and *transnational*.

One aspect from our analysis that invites more attention is the assertion that what is pan-Caribbean is sufficient to count as the "global in the local". This may require a revised or expanded understanding of globalization by our reading, but we defer to those with wider knowledge of globalization theory. For now, we can see no reason, given the framework employed here, to prevent such usage.

6. Conclusions

This paper was an ethnographic summary and analyses of how religious rituals involving Hindu funeral rites have been glocalized, retained, and adapted to the specific context of both acculturation and assimilation in St. Lucia. For Lucian-Indians, there is an absence of "many factors that help to keep alive (albeit in modified form) cultural patterns from the home country ... [such as] strong immigrant communities and institutions, dense ethnic networks and continued, transnational ties to the sending society" ([40], p. 963). In St. Lucia we did not find forms similar to those observed by Keith McNeal [41], such as overt "Shango-Baptist interface" or the "Hinduizing" of Orisha praxis.[7] What we see instead in St. Lucia is more subtle, and more akin to Rocklin's description in Trinidad of the subaltern's contesting of colonial institutions of religion by "crossing reified religious lines" through "norm-bending practices"[42], an adaptation and negotiation of memory to shape and reconfigure current and future identity.

We have argued that indigenized and transnational glocalization is concurrently evident in the Lucian-Indian funeral context. But in closing we dwell on the need to consider how much of what is glocal is informed by non-material construction—in this case a reification of what is an Indian imaginary. As Kaufman writes, "Innovation does not happen in free form but within the parameters of constrained disagreement. Divergent innovations must retain enough remnants of the original form to remain discernible to viewers familiar with that tradition" ([43], p. 338). It is not merely structure that shapes social actors/denizens and supplies a certain meaning. Instead, social actors/consumers create and add meaning to the cultural factors and thereby bring meaning to their lives.

In this Lucian-Indian case, we might celebrate the glocal. Early conversions to Christianity, whereby Catholic or Methodist church institutions substituted for Hindu institutions, have in turn led to an effacing of many Hindu religio-cultural norms and rituals. But modern Lucian-Indians are

---

[7] See his excellent historical ethnography of Hindu and African alter-cultural religious experiences in Trinidad and Tobago in the context of globalization.

not passive receivers of a dominant global or local culture: they have adapted and retained certain "Indian" cultural features in their social and spiritual lives, as in the memorial of a recently-dead family member who shares a still important (and altered) sense of Indian identity. In this sense, it makes little difference that such cultural constructions are poorly understood among Lucian-Indians themselves. Similar adaptations, such as those associated with gender and generation, should be further explored among comparable populations.

Author Contributions: Both authors contributed equally to the research, interviews, analysis and construction of this paper.

Conflicts of Interest: The authors declare no conflict of interest.

References

1. Victor Roudometof. "The Glocal and Global Studies." *Globalizations* 12 (2015): 774–87. [CrossRef]
2. Victor Roudometof. "The Glocalizations of Eastern Orthodox Christianity." *European Journal of Social Theory* 2 (2013): 226–45. [CrossRef]
3. Noel Salazar. "Studying Local-to-Global Tourism Dynamics through Glocal Ethnography." In *Fieldwork in Tourism: Methods, Issues and Reflections.* Edited by Michael Hall. London: Routledge, 2011, pp. 177–87.
4. Hilbourne Watson. "Theorizing the Racialization of Global Politics and the Caribbean Experience." *Alternatives* 26 (2001): 449–83. [CrossRef]
5. Jolien Harmsen. "The East Indian Legacy in St. Lucia." 2014. Available online: http://www.slucia.com/visions/2002/indian.html (accessed on 7 October 2015).
6. Jolien Harmsen, Guy Ellis, and Robert Duveaux. *A History of St. Lucia.* Castries: Lighthouse Road Publications, 2014.
7. Margarite Fernandez Olmos, and Lizabeth Paravisini-Gebert. *Creole Religions of the Caribbean: An Introduction from Vodou and Santeria to Obeah and Espiritismo,* 2nd ed. New York: New York University Press, 2011.
8. Steven Vertovec. *The Hindu Diaspora: Comparative Patterns.* London and New York: Routledge, 2001.
9. Victor Roudometof. "Theorizing Glocalization: Three Interpretations." *European Journal of Social Theory,* 2015, 1–18. [CrossRef]
10. Roland Robertson. *Globalization: Social Theory and Global Culture.* London: Sage, 1992.
11. Roland Robertson. "Glocalization: Time–space and Homogeneity–Heterogeneity." In *Global Modernities.* Edited by Mike Featherstone, Scott M. Lash, and Roland Robertson. London: Sage, 1995, pp. 25–54.
12. George Ritzer. "Rethinking Globalization: Glocalization/Grobalization and Something/Nothing." *Sociological Theory* 21 (2003): 193–209. [CrossRef]
13. George Ritzer. *The Globalization of Nothing.* Thousand Oaks: Pine Forge Press, 2006.
14. Arjun Appadurai. "The Production of Locality." In *Counterworks: Managing the Diversity of Knowledge.* Edited by R. Fardon. London: Routledge, 1995, pp. 204–25.
15. Peter Beyer. "Globalization and Glocalization." In *The Sage Handbook of the Sociology of Religion.* Edited by James Beckford, and N.J. Demerath III. London: Sage, 2007, pp. 98–117.
16. J. Nederveen Pieterse. *Globalization and Culture: Global Mélange.* Lanham: Rowman & Littlefield, 2004.
17. Marwan M. Kriady. *Hybridity, or the Cultural Logic of Globalization.* Philadelphia: Temple University Press, 2005.
18. Habibul Haque Khondker. "Globalisation to Glocalization: A Conceptual Exploration." *Intellectual Discourse* 13 (2005): 181–95.
19. Ann Denis. "Ethnicity and Race in the Sociology within the Commonwealth Caribbean." In *The ISA Handbook of Diverse Sociological Tradition.* Edited by Sujata Patel. London: Sage, 2010, pp. 292–99.
20. Chris Bongie. "The (Un)Exploded Volcano: Creolization and Intertextuality in the Novels of Daniel Maximin." *Callaloo* 17 (1994): 627–42. [CrossRef]
21. Aisha Khan. "Journey to the Center of the Earth: The Caribbean as Master Symbol." *Cultural Anthropology* 16 (2001): 271–302. [CrossRef]
22. Aisha Khan. "Sacred Subversions? Syncretic Creoles, the Indo-Caribbean and 'Culture's In-Between'." *Radical History Review* 89 (2004): 165–84. [CrossRef]

23. Marina Carter, and Khal Torabully. *Coolitude: An Anthology of the Indian Labour Diaspora*. London: Anthem Press, 2002.

24. J. Brent Crosson. "Own People: Race, 'Altered Solidarities', and the Limits of Culture in Trinidad." *Small Axe* 45 (2014): 18–34. [CrossRef]

25. Patricia Mohammed. "The Asian Other in the Caribbean." *Small Axe* 29 (2009): 57–71. [CrossRef]

26. Anton L. Allahar. "Unity and Diversity in Caribbean Ethnicity and Culture." *Canadian Ethnic Studies* 25 (1993): 70–85.

27. Raquel Lomberg. "Local Spirituality: Consumerism and Heritage in a Puerto Rican Afro-Latin Folk Religion." In *Contemporary Caribbean Cultures and Societies in a Global Context*. Edited by Teresita Martínez-Vergne, and Franklin Knight. Chapel Hill: University of North Carolina Press, 2005, pp. 131–56.

28. Victor Roudometof. "Forms of Religious Glocalization: Orthodox Christianity in the *Longue Durée*." *Religions* 5 (2014): 1017–36. [CrossRef]

29. Hinduism Today. "Death and Dying: Rites of Transition." *Hinduism Today* 29 (2007): 64–67.

30. Ernest Wood, and S. Venkata Subrahmanyam. *The Garuda Purana*. Charleston: Bibliolife, 2009.

31. Gian Guisep Filippi. *Mrtyu: Concept of Death in Indian Traditions*. New Delhi: D.K. Printworld, 1996.

32. Beena Ghimire Poudyal, and Binod Ghimire. *Hindu Death Rites (Antyeshti Samskar)*. Kathmandu: Lithographing Co. Ltd., 1998.

33. Sally Acharya. "Thirteen Days of Mourning & Release." *Hinduism Today* 36 (2014): 58–63.

34. Steve Ouditt. "Kutiya Geometries." *Small Axe* 20 (2006): 247–55. [CrossRef]

35. Ron Ramdin. *Arising from Bondage*. Bloomsbury: I.B. Tauris & Co. Ltd., 2000.

36. Patricia Mohammed. "Of Poteau Mitans, Bedis, Veve and Things." In *Island as Crossroads: Sustaining Cultural Diversity in Small Island Developing States*. Edited by Tim Curtis. Paris: UNESCO, 2011, pp. 129–40.

37. Peter Fung. *Dal Puri Diaspora*. Toronto: Canada Council of the Arts, 2012.

38. Peggy Mohan. "Indians under a Caribbean Sky." *India International Centre Quarterly* 28 (2001): 3–13.

39. Aisha Khan. "Jootha in Trinidad: Food, Pollution and Hierarchy in a Caribbean Diaspora Community." *American Ethnologist* 21 (1994): 245–69. [CrossRef]

40. Ruben G. Rumbaut. "Assimilation and Its Discontents: Between Rhetoric and Reality." *International Migration Review* 31 (1997): 923–60. [CrossRef] [PubMed]

41. Keith E. McNeal. *Trance and Modernity in the Southern Caribbean: African and Hindu Popular Religions in Trinidad and Tobago*. Gainesville: University Press of Florida, 2011.

42. Alexander Rocklin. "Obeah and the Politics of Religion's Making and Unmaking in Colonial Trinidad." *Journal of the American Academy of Religion* 83 (2015): 697–721. [CrossRef]

43. Jason Kaufman. "Endogenous Explanation in the Sociology of Culture." *Annual Review of Sociology* 30 (2004): 335–57. [CrossRef]

44. Lavina Melwani. "Women Augment the Priestly Ranks." *Hinduism Today* 29 (2007): 33–35.

45. Peter van der Veer, and Steven Vertovec. "Brahmanism Abroad: On Caribbean Hinduism as an Ethnic Religion." *Ethnology* 30 (1991): 149–66. [CrossRef]

46. Brinsley Samaroo, and Ann Marie Bissessar, eds. *The Construction of an Indo-Caribbean Diaspora*. St. Augustine: The University of the West Indies Press, 2004.

religions

MDPI

Article

Japanese Buddhism, Relativization, and Glocalization

Ugo Dessì

Institute for the Study of Religion, University of Leipzig, Schillerstr. 6, 04109 Leipzig, Germany;
ugo.dessi@uni-leipzig.de; Tel.: +49-341-97-37160

Academic Editor: Victor Roudometof
Received: 9 October 2016; Accepted: 9 January 2017; Published: 18 January 2017

Abstract: Within the field of study on Japanese religions, the issue of globalization tends to be associated with the missionary activities of some successful new religious movements, and there is a certain reluctance to approach analytically the dynamics of glocalization/hybridization and the power issues at stake. In this article, I address these and other related problems by taking my cue from the relativizing effects of globalization and a working definition of religion based on the concept of authority. To this aim, I focus on two case studies. The first concerns the ongoing greening of Japanese Buddhism. The second revolves around the adoption of meditational techniques by priests and lay practitioners in Hawaiian Shin Buddhism. My findings show that there are at least four factors underlying the glocalization of Japanese Buddhism, that is, global consciousness, resonance with the local tradition, decontextualization, and quest for power. Moreover, they indicate that it is possible to distinguish between two types of glocalization (glocalization and chauvinistic glocalization) and two configurations of glocalization (juxtaposition and integration).

Keywords: Japanese Buddhism; relativization; glocalization; globalization; ecology; meditation; religious authority; definition of religion

1. Introduction

Despite the increasing amount of research on religion and globalization worldwide published in the last two decades, the study of Japanese religions under globalizing conditions is to date still in an early stage. There is some irony in this, given the emphasis on "Japanese religion" found in Roland Robertson's early theorizations on globalization, and his association of glocalization with the Japanese term *dochakuka* [1,2].

Indeed, Robertson's work remains the major source of inspiration for the few Japanese scholars who have attempted to explore the interplay of religion and global dynamics. One can think, for example, of Kashimura Aiko's analysis of New Age religious culture, which relies on Robertson's reflections on the interplay between the local and the global [3], or Inoue Nobutaka's early observations of "neo-syncretism" among Japanese new religious movements [4]. In Japan, there have also been attempts to elaborate on Robertson's claim that Japanese culture is inclined toward syncretism by contrasting "glocalized" (i.e., "harmony-oriented") Japanese Buddhism to the allegedly anthropocentric Western worldview [5]. Yet, Japanese scholarship on this subject has rarely been able to build on this strand of globalization theory and develop original approaches, and the research output is fragmented and limited to a small number of journal articles and book chapters.

Outside of Japan, slightly more attention has been paid to Japanese religions under globalization. Besides some research published in article (e.g., [6–9]) or dissertation format [10], three full length monographs have been published so far: Cristina Rocha's study of Zen Buddhism in Brazil through Appaduraian categories [11], and my two books [12,13] based on several case studies in Japan and overseas. Moreover, a Special Issue of the *Journal of Religion in Japan* has recently focused on the interplay of several Japanese religious traditions with global dynamics from different perspectives ([14];

for an exhaustive review of scholarly sources on Japanese religions and globalization by both Japanese and non-Japanese scholars, cf. ([13], pp. 16–24).

However, within the field of study on Japanese religions, the issue of globalization still tends to be seen as something self-explanatory, or is at best associated with the missionary activities of some successful new religious movements. Even when a larger array of phenomena is taken into account, there is a certain reluctance to approach analytically the dynamics of glocalization and hybridization and the power issues at stake.

In the following sections, I will address these and other related problems by taking my cue from the relativizing effects of globalization and a working definition of religion based on the concept of authority. In this way, I aim to provide a contribution to a more nuanced understanding of Japanese Buddhism under globalization.

2. Religion, Relativization and Authority

Although there is hardly any general agreement on the definition of globalization, many scholars in the field of studies on globalization and culture would agree that globalization is related to the increasing interconnectedness and the compression of time and space brought about by the new communication technologies. The metaphor of global flows has been widely used to describe the new global condition, in which people, goods and ideas circulating worldwide elicit the creation of new identities and networks at the local level (e.g., [15,16]). As aptly noted by some critical scholars, this does not necessarily mean that we are living in an age of global emancipation, since the circulation of these flows is generally regulated by powerful agents in search for power and legitimation (cf. [17–19]).

In this connection, it has also been suggested that the aquatic metaphor of flows should be replaced by others related to networks, which would allow for a better approach to the mechanisms of inclusion and exclusion underlying globalization [20]. Indeed, the metaphor of a global cultural network would also seem to express more clearly the agency of local actors, which are not just "caught" in global flows, but rather provide at any given moment with their interactions meaning and practical content to the process of globalization.

As illustrated by George Van Pelt Campbell, the new global condition brings about higher chances for local traditions to be relativized and produce a wide range of responses [21]. Campbell, who implicitly identifies tradition with "religious tradition", distinguishes four main aspects of it: the hermeneutic aspect (tradition as an interpretive scheme), the normative aspect (tradition as a set of norms), the legitimation aspect (tradition as a source of authority), and the identity aspect (tradition as a source of identity-formation) ([21], pp. 2–3). Campbell argues that relativization especially affects the hermeneutic and identity aspects of tradition, and much less the remaining two (normative and legitimation) ([21], pp. 3–4).

Campbell's model is meaningful and instructive in that it exposes the key role played by relativization within global dynamics. However, I think that its full application to *religious* traditions is rather problematic for the following reasons. First, Campbell's emphasis on the hermeneutic (as "making sense of the world") and identity aspects comes too close to the Western-centric idea that the focus on the ultimate meaning of life or social solidarity represent the core of religion. Second, as far as the relativization of religious traditions is concerned, it does not seem appropriate to downplay the role of the normative aspect, not least because this dimension of religion is still very relevant for a multitude of spiritual seekers around the globe.

Therefore, this approach centered on relativization requires some adjustments if it is to be applied to religion and Japanese Buddhism. In my view, a viable solution to this problem can be found by giving more emphasis to the issues of authority and legitimation, which are downplayed in Campbell's model. It is true that, as far as the legitimation aspect is concerned, Campbell makes reference to Max Weber's distinction between rational-legal, charismatic, and traditional authority, upon which three corresponding types of legitimation are based. However, Weber's analysis can also be used to support a rather different approach. Specifically, I am referring here to Weber's definition of a "hierocratic organization" as something "which enforces its order through psychic coercion by distributing or denying religious benefits" ([22], p. 54). This idea has been further elaborated by Mark Chaves, who noted that psychic coercion is not a satisfactory basis for authority, and suggested that it should be substituted for a concept that indicates religion's means of legitimation, namely, a "supernatural" component ([23], p. 756).

Based on these premises, I consider religion as a social system that regulates the access to a variety of worldly/other-worldly goods through the authority of a superempirical agency. The term superempirical is given preference here over terms such as supernatural and superhuman, the problematical status of which has been illustrated by previous scholarship [24], and refers to what lies beyond the intersubjectively observable and testable phenomena (cf. [12], pp. 11–17; [13], pp. 29–36).

The contents of the global cultural network can impact different parts of the religious system: the superempirical source of authority (whether or not it is something "real" existing out there); the constellation of goods mediated by religion; the structure of legitimation (the way in which the nexus between the superempirical agency and these goods is envisioned, narrated and performed); the main guardians of this authority structure, the religious professionals; and the ordinary practitioners.

Against this framework, relativization can be characterized as the process through which the pressure exercised by the increasing presence of external ideas (or other social/religious systems) calls into question the autonomy of a given religious system and the stability of its different parts. This pressure may affect, for example, the constellation of goods mediated by religion and push for the inclusion of new items (or the exclusion of old ones), or weaken the authority of the superempirical source of authority. Religious systems do not necessarily remain unstable as a consequence of relativization. Rather, they are pressed to reframe themselves against the broader context by way of strategies of global repositioning. As I illustrated elsewhere, the creative adaptation of external ideas or glocalization is one of these processes of repositioning ([13], pp. 162–89), which constitutes the focus of this article.

To some extent, my argument parallels Victor Roudometof's general discussion on "waves of globalization" ([25], pp. 63–68). Roudometof has recently introduced the metaphor of refraction to suggest that "glocalization is globalization refracted through the local" ([25], p. 65). My research intends to shed light on the why and how of the repositioning of Japanese Buddhism within global society (Roudometof's refraction), with specific attention to its underlying factors. To this aim, I will focus on two case studies: (a) The first concerns the ongoing greening of several strands of Japanese Buddhism, that is, their progressive involvement with the issue of global environmentalism. It focuses on the institutional level, and relies on participant observation and primary sources such as books, pamphlets, and other documents published by Buddhist institutions. (b) The second case study revolves around the somewhat controversial adoption of meditational techniques by priests and lay practitioners of the Hawaii Kyodan, the largest branch of Hawaiian Shin Buddhism. It mainly focuses on the individual level and relies on in-depth interviews with around sixty of these Shin Buddhist meditators (which were conducted privately and mostly within temple facilities), and material published by the head temple and local temples of this Buddhist organization.

3. The Greening of Japanese Buddhism

In this article, Japanese Buddhism is used as a label for different forms of traditional Buddhism (e.g., Zen, Shin, Tendai) and new religious movements with a clear Buddhist background (Sōka Gakkai, Risshō Kōseikai) operating in contemporary Japan. Despite the different sectarian emphases found within this multifaceted world, from the perspective of the working definition of religion presented above, Japanese Buddhism can be considered as a relatively unified religious system. As far as religious authority is concerned, the various forms of Japanese Buddhism basically regulate the access by practitioners to a constellation of goods through reference to superempirical agencies such as the Buddhist Dharma and the buddhas/bodhisattvas. Moreover, combinations of buddhas and Shintō deities (*kami*), spirits and ancestors can also be used as sources of superempirical legitimation.

The goods mediated by Buddhism can be other-worldly, such as awakening (*satori, gedatsu*, etc.), but also worldly benefits of various kinds (*genze riyaku*). The nexus between these goods and the superempirical sources of authority is envisioned and performed through a structure of legitimation, which is mainly based on religious narratives (e.g., the Buddhist sutras) and practices (e.g., meditation, memorial rites). This structure is generally managed by religious professionals, but lay practitioners can achieve considerable autonomy from them.

Against this background, I will focus on the extent to which the ongoing global discourse on ecology has been able to relativize the religious system of Japanese Buddhism and elicit the development of new glocal forms.

Despite the common stereotype that Japanese spirituality is inherently close to nature, ecology became for the first time a popular topic in Japan around the 1970s. It soon caught the attention of the Japanese Buddhist world, and, since the late 1980s, some Buddhist priests belonging to various denominations have promoted environmentalist activism at the local level. In the 1990s, there were the first attempts to engage with this issue at the institutional level. Among these, Sōtō Zen Buddhism (Sōtōshū) initiated a Green Plan in 1995, and similar endeavors were undertaken within Tendai Buddhism (Tendaishū), Shin Buddhism (Jōdo Shinshū), Sōka Gakkai and Risshō Kōseikai [26,27].

The Sōtō Zen campaign was initiated with the aim of promoting surveys on acid rain and saving water and energy in temples and private households, and focuses on the ideas of interdependence (*engi*) and buddha-nature [28]. For example, within the Green Plan the principle of "harmonious coexistence with nature" is validated through founder Dōgen's (1200–1253) identification of mountains and streams with the Buddha and his frugal lifestyle ([12], p. 53).

In the late 1990s, also Tendai Buddhism started placing emphasis on environmental protection, and the ecologically-oriented practice of "living in harmony" figures nowadays as one of the main themes in the slogan of its revitalization movement, the Light Up Your Corner Movement (Ichigū o Terasu Undō). Tendai Buddhist institutions encourage their members not to waste natural resources, to save water and energy and promote recycling through the catchword *mottainai*, "What a waste!" Similar to Zen Buddhism, they justify their campaign through reference to the Buddhist chain of causes and conditions, and the idea that "mountains and rivers, plants and trees, all attain buddhahood" (*sansen sōmoku shikkai jōbutsu*) [29,30].

Among the denominations of traditional Buddhism, the Honganji branch of Shin Buddhism (Jōdo Shinshū Honganji-ha) has also been promoting energy-saving and renewable energy, as well as the construction of a national database of forests (Honganji no Mori) [31,32]. In this case, too, environmentalism is broadly related to the basic Buddhist teaching of interdependence, and, on the sectarian side, to the other-power of Amida Buddha, which is believed to embrace all forms of life [31,33].

The two largest Buddhism-based new religious movements, Sōka Gakkai and Risshō Kōseikai, have also promoted environmentalist action. The former has supported various activities since the early 1990s through Soka Gakkai International (SGI). In particular, SGI collaborates with the Earth Charter Initiative and the United Nations for the promotion of sustainable development [34]. In Sōka Gakkai, too, environmentalism is legitimized through reference to basic Buddhist teachings such as interdependence, the universality of the buddha-nature, and the control of desires [35,36].

Risshō Kōseikai certified its headquarters according to the International Organization for Standardization (ISO) environmental management system in 2010 [37], soon after it issued its Environmental Policy. The guidelines of this official document are imbued with Buddhist ideas such as the equal dignity of all forms of life, their interdependence, and the exhortation to be "contented with few desires" (*shōyoku chisoku*) [38,39].

After the Tōhoku earthquake and tsunami that caused the accident at the Fukushima nuclear power plant in March 2011, several Buddhist organizations issued official statements against the civil nuclear power program. Among these, the Japan Buddhist Federation issued in December 2011 an "Appeal for a Lifestyle without Dependence on Nuclear Power" (*Genshiryoku hatsuden ni yoranai ikikata o motomete*) [40,41], in which, for the first time, the Japanese Buddhist world as a whole took a critical position against this issue. In this appeal, it was argued that the way out of the nuclear problem toward sustainability is through a lifestyle centered on "knowing satisfaction" (*taru koto o shiri*), which aims to protect all forms of life [40,41].

In September of the same year, the Myōshinji branch of Rinzai Zen Buddhism (Rinzaishū Myōshinji-ha) had issued a declaration for the "Realization of a Society Not Dependent on Nuclear Power Generation" (*Genshiryoku hatsuden ni izon shinai shakai no genjitsu*), in which reference is made to the Buddhist ideal of "knowing satisfaction" (*chisoku*) and the creation of a "harmonious society" (*kyōsei shakai*) [42]. Two months later, Sōtō Zen also made public the statement "Sōtō Zen's Opinion on Nuclear Power Generation" (*Genshiryoku hatsuden ni tai suru Sōtōshū no kenkai ni tsuite*), which proposes a cautious transition to sustainable sources of energy [43]. Within Shin Buddhism, the Ōtani branch (Shinshū Ōtani-ha) has been very critical of nuclear power plants since the late 1990s, and after the Fukushima accident has issued several anti-nuclear statements. In these documents, considerable emphasis is placed on the idea of "life" (*inochi*), which refers to the immeasurable life of Amida Buddha and his salvific vow that is believed to embrace all living beings [44,45].

The two new religious movements mentioned above, Sōka Gakkai and Risshō Kōseikai, have also been quite active in this regard. Sōka Gakkai's charismatic leader Ikeda Daisaku has urged "a rapid transition to an energy policy that is not reliant on nuclear power" based on the dignity of all forms of life, present and future [46]. In its statements of protest, Risshō Kōseikai maintains that Japan should abandon nuclear power, cultivate the spirit of *shōyoku chisoku*, and strive to live in harmony with nature [47].

This generalized greening of Japanese Buddhism of recent years should not lead us to overestimate its impact. In most cases, Buddhist environmentalism remains an educational endeavor that hardly reaches out to the masses of lay practitioners, traditionally interested as they are in memorial rites and worldly benefits of various kinds. However, this religious environmentalism is quite relevant for the understanding of the interplay of the local and the global in contemporary Japanese Buddhism. In fact, there are strong indications that we are not simply dealing with local dynamics.

To start with, the greening of Japanese Buddhism follows both chronologically and thematically the development of environmentalism worldwide and the discussions about global warming, which led to the establishment of the Intergovernmental Panel on Climate Change (IPCC) in 1988, and the adoption of the Kyoto Protocol in 1997. More specifically, it can be considered as an outcome and integral part of the "religious environmentalist paradigm" postulated by Poul Pedersen [48]. This expression refers to the increasing worldwide tendency to frame ecological issues in religious terms that can be traced back to the work of the historian Lynn White in the late 1960s, and to various initiatives such as the Assisi Declarations (1986) and the conferences on religion and ecology held at Harvard University since the late 1990s, which involved Buddhism and other religious traditions [49].

The impact of the global ecological discourse on Buddhist environmentalism is also revealed by the language used by Buddhist institutions. Not only do they make reference to the ongoing worldwide debate on ecology, but in many cases, they also show their aspiration to be an active part of such debate. In Sōtō Zen, for example, practitioners are admonished to protect the environment because "the Earth is the home of life" [50]; one of the main priorities in Tendai Buddhism's ecological agenda is to persuade its adherents that we must "transmit our precious Earth to the next generation" [51]; Sōka Gakkai's collaboration with the Earth Charter Initiative is justified in terms of global interdependence and global responsibilities by local actors [52]; and Risshō Kōseikai claims that Japan needs to shut down all nuclear power plants as a step toward the "transformation of contemporary civilization" [47].

It is interesting to note that the emergence of such global consciousness does not necessarily amount to the superimposition of global ideas on local religion. Rather, the appropriation of these ideas seems to be dependent on the extent to which they can find their echo in aspects of Japanese Buddhism. From the discussion above, it is apparent that ideas such as interdependence, the control of worldly desires, and the presence of the buddha-nature in all beings are often used by Japanese Buddhist institutions as the lenses through which they view the issues of sustainability and environmental protection. In this sense, it is possible to speak of a resonance factor that plays an important role behind the local adaptation of global ecological themes.

Another important factor in this process of repositioning is represented by decontextualization. That is, selected aspects of the religious tradition are not just reframed against the background of compelling external ideas, but also with reference to the tradition as a whole, as they come to be seen in isolation from their original context. In this way, the selective reading of the tradition can lead to the absolutization of Buddhist ideas that resonate with global environmentalism. This helps to explain why, within the greening of Japanese Buddhism, this religious tradition is often presented as inherently ecological, and its historical responsibilities in the exploitation of nature are obliterated.

As one may expect, decontextualization can be meaningfully related to power issues. In fact, the common self-representation of Japanese Buddhism as a timeless "green Dharma" (cf. [27]; [13], pp. 67–97) is generally coupled by the depiction of Western thought as anthropocentric and nature-dominating, which exposes a distinctive longing for global legitimation. This is apparent, for example, in Sōtō Zen's claim to be morally superior to other forms of environmentalism because its original spirit lies in the harmony with nature [53]; and in Shin Buddhism's understanding of its own environmentalism as a response to the exploitation of nature promoted by an increasingly westernized society (cf. [54]). Indeed, this eco-nationalism [55] is not just a contemporary issue. Rather, it is well rooted in modern Japanese culture, as may be seen in the work of Suzuki Daisetsu [56] and Nakamura Hajime [57], and, much earlier, in the wartime ideology of imperial Japan, in which the contraposition of the "nature-friendly" Japanese and the "nature-subjugating" Westerners served the scope of shaping a national consciousness [58].

However, it should be noted that the search for power in Buddhist environmentalism and the emergence of cultural chauvinism are not necessarily intertwined. As a matter of fact, the greening of Buddhism can also be seen by religious leaders as a way of contesting the claims of authority of other secular social systems, and reassert the indispensability of religion as a force for the solution of the global environmental crisis.

The discussion above indicates that the relativization induced by the global idea of sustainability affects the constellation of goods the access to which is regulated by Japanese Buddhism. The combined effect of the factors illustrated above leads to the inclusion of sustainability among those very goods, that is, to the glocalization of Japanese Buddhism through the issue of ecology. In this connection, it is possible to distinguish at least two types of glocalization (with a grey zone between them): the generic creative adoption of sustainability (glocalization), and a glocalization coupled with the revitalization of wartime ideological structures, which leads to the emergence of forms of eco-nationalism (chauvinistic glocalization).

4. Meditation in Hawaiian Shin Buddhism

Shin Buddhism (Jōdo Shinshū) is a mainstream form of Japanese Buddhism belonging to the Pure Land tradition. It was established in medieval Japan by the monk Shinran (1173–1262), although it gained institutional strength only a few centuries later especially under the leadership of Rennyo (1415–1499). Shin Buddhism is characterized by the centrality of the *nenbutsu* practice (the repetition of Amida Buddha's name) and the reliance on Amida's salvific "other-power" (*tariki*) which is believed to lead practitioners to the Pure Land, the last station before final awakening in this Buddhist tradition.

From a perspective based on the concept of authority, Shin Buddhism can be understood as a religious system that regulates the access to various goods through the authority of superempirical agencies such as the Buddhist Dharma and Amida. Among the goods mediated by Shin Buddhism, one finds not only the other-worldly goal of the Pure Land, but also worldly benefits. As in the general case of Japanese Buddhism, the structure of legitimation encompasses the various ways in which these superempirical agencies and the worldly/other-worldly goods are related to each other. This structure, which is generally (but not necessarily) managed by religious professionals, revolves around the Pure

Land texts, the writings of Shinran and a few other Shin Buddhist leaders, and a cluster of religious practices and rituals (notably the *nenbutsu*, chanting, and memorial rites). Whereas in other forms of Japanese Buddhism the precepts belong to this category, in Shin Buddhism, good behavior tends to be included among the constellation of worldly goods mediated by religion. In other words, it tends to be seen more as a consequence of religious liberation than a means to achieve it. This is because of the Shin Buddhist emphasis on Amida's other-power, which has also led to the abandonment of meditation and other practices characterized by self-effort or "self-power" (*jiriki*).

In Japan, the practice of meditation within a Shin Buddhist environment is very uncommon and generally not tolerated by the religious institutions (cf. [13], pp. 118–20). However, in other parts of the world where this tradition has spread through its missionary activities, there have been some attempts to reconcile Shin Buddhism with the practice of meditation. This strategy is related to the increasing worldwide popularity of meditation which is apparent in phenomena such as the mushrooming of publications on meditation, its commercialization and popularization through the media, and the creation of meditation centers related to *vipassanā*, Tibetan Buddhism, and other traditions. Following this general trend, and the emergence of what Jeff Wilson has termed a "Mindful America" [59], meditation has been adopted by various Shin Buddhist priests and lay practitioners in Canada and the United States who are attempting to reach out to the wide community of spiritual seekers interested in alternative practices. The presence of a similar phenomenon in South American Buddhism has also been documented (cf. [12,60]).

During my ethnographic fieldwork in Hawaii (January–June 2013), I researched the interplay of meditation and Shin Buddhism within the Hawaii Kyodan, the local branch of Honganji-ha Shin Buddhism, which was established there in 1889 following the arrival of Japanese workers for the sugar cane plantation industry. Shin Buddhism in Hawaii was rather successful until the closure of the plantations in the 1980s, which caused a considerable shrinking of the religious community. Various attempts to disentangle this tradition from the label of ethnic religion have been made ever since by members of the Hawaii Kyodan, including the adoption of meditation by various groups of Shin Buddhist practitioners.

As of 2013, there were at least five active groups of Shin Buddhist meditators in Hawaii, while another seven groups had been discontinued. In the two groups operating on the island of Oahu, the practice of meditation is very informal, although in one of them the facilitators have a background in Siddha Yoga, and participants are free to adopt their own personal style while sitting in chairs or pews. Two groups, one of which is still active on the Big Island, are related to the tradition of mindfulness meditation developed by Thich Nhat Hanh. In the past, there have been two instances of meditation sessions promoted by Shin Buddhist ministers who followed the Zen Buddhist style or a modified form of it. In another group on Oahu, Zen meditational techniques (*zazen*) are blended with *vipassanā* and yoga. In at least three cases, meditation sessions have been conducted based on the *seiza* (quiet sitting) style developed by Okada Torajirō (1872–1920), or Kawahata Ayoshi's (1905–2005) Universal Meditation method, both of which emphasize proper sitting and breathing and were developed in modern Japan at the intersection between local traditions and Western medical/bodily practices.

Such groups of Shin Buddhist meditators, which include lay people and priests, are thus characterized by the considerable variety of global sources on which their practices rely. For the participants in these sessions, meditation can indicate things as diverse as a simple moment of reflection during the day, the practice of mindfulness, Buddhist meditational techniques, *seiza*, and yoga. The global dimension of this practice also emerges from my in-depth interviews. Several practitioners, for example, understand meditation as something that makes one feel closer to other Buddhists in other parts of the world, and as the unifying practice of all Buddhists worldwide, while others insist on the benefits that Buddhism can offer to the entire world. Similar to the case of the greening of Japanese Buddhism, here, too, one can notice the emergence of a global consciousness, which allows for the understanding of the Shin Buddhist religious practice within a broader global framework.

Another important factor behind the adoption of meditation in Hawaiian Shin Buddhism and its glocalization is the resonance between global ideas about meditation and local practices. Most practitioners do not unreservedly incorporate meditational techniques of different sorts in their daily practice. On the contrary, this process of adoption is most often accompanied by the active search for correspondences between meditation and aspects of their religious background and preexisting practices. For some Shin Buddhist meditators, this means a return to the basic ideas of Buddhism and the Eightfold Path preached by Śākyamuni, which included meditation. For others, the abandonment of the self that characterizes meditation is nothing but the expression of the idea of other-power, which is prominent in Shin Buddhism. For Shin Buddhist meditators with a weak sectarian identity, meditation is often understood as a means to rediscover the buddha-nature within themselves. In not a few cases, the perceived affinity of meditation with the practice of observing some moments of silence during Shin Buddhist services can also provide the motivation for joining a meditation group. As a result of this process of creative adaptation, ideas about meditation originally foreign to Shin Buddhism that circulate in global culture are selected and made to resonate with aspects of the Shin Buddhist tradition. Otherwise, aspects of Shin Buddhism are made to resonate with various forms of meditation by practitioners coming from different religious traditions.

It is interesting to note that the creative adaptation of meditation in Shin Buddhism generally requires that practitioners place the orthodox opposition between self-power and other-power in the background. In this way, the meaning of practice in Shin Buddhism can be reconsidered within a more flexible framework. This parallels the decontextualization factor illustrated above in the case of Buddhist environmentalism.

Still, another important factor underlying this globally-oriented religious change in Hawaiian Shin Buddhism is the quest for power. From the perspective of the central Shin Buddhist institutions in Japan, the issue of meditation in Shin Buddhism is related to power mainly because of its implications in terms of doctrinal orthodoxy. According to the headquarters in Kyoto, although birth in the Pure Land and final awakening can only be achieved through the salvific power of Amida, ministers are allowed to use meditation as an auxiliary non-religious practice in order to attract new members. This official position of the Honganji branch was recently reiterated during a symposium held in 2011 at the headquarters in Kyoto [61], thus apparently bringing an end to a controversy with the US branch, the Buddhist Churches of America, which had introduced the practice of meditation in various temples as early as the 1980s. It should be specified that this policy applies in practice only to overseas ministers. In Japan, the adoption of meditational practices by Shin Buddhist priests of the Honganji branch is seen with suspicion and can lead to extreme disciplinary measures such as excommunication (cf. [13], pp. 117–22).

The attitude of the Hawaii Kyodan toward meditation is less strict but nonetheless rather cautious. The incumbent and former religious leaders of this religious organization broadly agree that meditation can be used as a preparation to Shin Buddhism. However, the practice of meditation in a Shin Buddhist context has occasionally provoked some controversy, and open discussions to explore the suitability of meditation to Shin Buddhism are not promoted.

From another perspective, the adoption of meditation is related to power issues because it is seen by many religious professionals and lay practitioners as a strategy to counter the current decline in membership and attract new members. Moreover, it is related to the issue of ethnicity, since meditational activities seem to be less successful when they are promoted by non-Japanese-American members. Last but not least, the practice of meditation is a matter of personal empowerment especially for lay practitioners, who can thus bypass to some extent the mediation of religious professionals and their perceived overemphasis on the ritualistic sphere.

The discussion above indicates that the global appeal of meditation is capable of directly relativizing the structure of legitimation within Shin Buddhism. That is, the religious narrative concerning birth in the Pure Land and final awakening is subject to adjustments, through which meditation becomes eligible as a practice along the Shin Buddhist path and is thus adopted within the structure of legitimation of the religious system of Shin Buddhism.

Moreover, my interviews with Shin Buddhist meditators indicate that glocalization as such is not an undifferentiated block. Rather, this case study allows for the distinction between at least two main configurations of glocalization, based on the place occupied by meditation within the structure of legitimation.

For some of the interviewees, either priests or lay practitioners, meditation remains peripheral to the core of their religious commitment. These meditators clearly state that meditation is a non-religious practice and relate it to the psychological well-being that it brings about. In this case, the practice of meditation appears to be simply juxtaposed to other doctrinal and practical elements in the structure of legitimation. Nonetheless, it still makes sense to define this as a glocal form because of the role played by the four factors illustrated above, and because meditation is still seen by those meditators as compatible with a fully Shin Buddhist lifestyle and the practice of the *nenbutsu*.

At the other end of the spectrum, one finds the experiences of those interviewees who have successfully integrated the practice of meditation into the structure of legitimation. This is especially apparent for those who have come to Shin Buddhism from other religious traditions and do not value strict sectarianism. These meditators, who can be broadly classified as belonging to the category of middle-class spiritual seekers and rarely include priests, typically establish a meaningful connection between meditation, the buddha-nature, the practice of the *nenbutsu*, and gratitude (to Amida). As a consequence, they view meditation as a full-fledged religious practice.

However, in the practices of most of the interviewees, meditation is less tightly integrated into the structure of legitimation. Members of this category, which also includes many priests, generally understand meditation as a preparatory practice without necessarily denying its religious value. For many of them, meditation is a useful tool for overcoming the hindrances of the ego and approaching the core of Shin Buddhism. Within this configuration of glocalization, meditation can implicitly occupy a meaningful, though peripheral, place in the structure of religious liberation.

5. Conclusions: Japanese Buddhism and Glocalization

The two case studies illustrated in the previous sections expose the complexity of the processes of glocalization taking place within the context of Japanese Buddhism. While at a superficial glance, Buddhist environmentalism and the adoption of meditation in Hawaiian Shin Buddhism might appear unrelated to each other, they actually provide evidence of the structure of Japanese Buddhism's (in Japan and overseas) repositioning within a global society characterized by the unprecedented availability and pervasiveness of worldwide-circulating ideas. Even more importantly, these two case studies reveal the presence of similar patterns that underlie the entire process of glocalization.

The increasing availability of the ideas of ecology and meditation within the global cultural network carries the potential to relativize different parts of the religious system. In the case of ecology, relativization affects primarily the constellation of goods mediated by Japanese Buddhism. In the case of meditation, what is mainly relativized is the structure of legitimation that relates the superempirical source of authority to the constellation of worldly/other-worldly goods. The relativization induced by discrete religious/non-religious elements (ecology and meditation) puts in motion a process of repositioning through which Japanese Buddhism attempts to attune itself to global society. There are at least four major factors underlying this process (cf. [13], pp. 170–77).

First, the material analyzed shows the emergence of a global consciousness. By global consciousness, I mean here the perception of the unity of the world and a certain desire to be part of global communication. This idea was first clarified by Robertson in terms of "globality," that is, the "consciousness of the (problem of) the world as a single place" ([62], p. 132), and plays an important role in Arjun Appadurai's theory of -scapes and the work of other globalization scholars [16,63]. Global consciousness is not necessarily a noble sentiment, since it can be embedded in public relations strategies. It more generically indicates the extent to which Japanese Buddhism is pressed by globalization to familiarize with the idea of the world as a single place.

Second, the adoption of discrete elements circulating in the global cultural network is dependent on their resonance with aspects of the local tradition. This affinity allows Japanese Buddhism and Shin Buddhism to look at the issues of environmentalism and meditation, respectively, through the lenses of their own tradition. Throughout this process, traditional ideas and practices such as interdependence, the control of desires, the *nenbutsu*, and gratitude can become the catalysts in the production of glocal forms.

Third, the extent to which selected aspects of the tradition are placed into the foreground can lead to their decontextualization from the overall tradition. The case of the greening of Japanese Buddhism indicates that this can be accompanied by the idealization of tradition and the systematic obliteration of problematic aspects of it.

Fourth, the creative adoption of external elements and the glocalization of Japanese Buddhism is related to the issue of power. Glocalization can be viewed by local actors not only as a means to self-empowerment, but also as a way of countering the current decline and marginalization of Japanese Buddhism. By presenting itself as a force for the solution of pressing global problems, Japanese Buddhism shows an aspiration to global legitimation. This aspiration can also be combined with the revitalization of past ideologies, which are then used as external sources of legitimation in the quest for global (and local) power.

All this indicates that it is possible to approach glocalization analytically and shed light on the factors that constrain the overall process. Moreover, as the case of Hawaiian Shin Buddhism strongly suggests, the focus on the authority structure of the religious system allows a more nuanced understanding of the resulting glocal forms. Discrete elements adopted by Japanese Buddhism from global culture can undergo a thorough process of integration but also be simply juxtaposed to the preexisting religious system.

As the case study on Japanese Buddhism's environmentalism and the emergence of eco-nationalism shows, there is also the need to distinguish between two types of glocalization: a) generic glocalization and b) chauvinistic glocalization characterized by the presence of elements of cultural chauvinism. It is tempting to see an analogy between chauvinistic glocalization and the idea of "glocalism," which has been illustrated by Roudometof in terms of "an overall perspective or worldview that transforms glocalization and glocality into future visions of a utopia or dystopia" ([25], pp. 75–78). Indeed, both terms have important implications for the understanding of glocalization as an ideology and for the analysis of the power relations underlying this process. However, I should also clarify that by chauvinistic glocalization, I refer to a very specific kind of power issue. In my interpretive model, the quest for power in concrete social practice characterizes glocalization as such, and can basically assume four different shapes, which can have a global or local relevance: the pure concern for institutional strength; the preservation/consolidation of religious legitimation; the pursuit of external legitimation to strengthen the authority structure of the religious system; and the search for individual empowerment. It is only when external legitimation is pursued by relying on Japanese cultural nationalism that I use the term chauvinistic glocalization to describe these dynamics ([13], pp. 170–77).

The idea of chauvinistic glocalization can provide a useful corrective to a certain tendency within academia to polarize the relationship between "native" Japanese culture and cross-cultural hybridity in mutually-exclusive terms. That is, Japanese culture is often seen either as naturally inclined to hybridization (cf. [5,64]) or as almost immune to hybridization because of the important role still played in Japan by theories of uniqueness (*nihonjinron*) and cultural homogeneity (cf. [65]). As the analysis above and previous research [66] indicate, hybridization and glocalization can actually go hand in hand with the emergence of cultural chauvinism.

It is worth mentioning here that glocalization and chauvinistic glocalization are not the only products of such processes of global repositioning. The relativization induced by discrete elements circulating in the global cultural network can also be seen by Japanese Buddhism as a threat and thus be rejected (cf. [12], pp. 122–28). And yet, this defensive attitude is still partially dependent on the global context, that is, on the availability of new alternative global options and modalities of interaction. Moreover, homogenization or the passive adoption of external elements should be taken into account as a potential option, although it is rarely seen as such in the context of Japanese Buddhism (for a more extensive discussion on this topic and two more forms of global repositioning occurring at the inter-religious and inter-systemic level, respectively, cf. [13]).

Finally, it is important to emphasize that the glocalization of Japanese Buddhism does not refer to the interplay of two distinct locations, and namely, the world at large and Japan. Rather, the global and the local are understood here as processes. This point was already made by Robertson when he explained that there is no antinomy whatsoever between the local and the global [2], and has been further clarified by other theorists. Among them, J.K. Gibson-Graham and Arif Dirlik have convincingly argued that the global and the local should not be reified, but rather be understood as analytical tools, as "interpretive frames" and terms that "derive their meaning from each other" [67,68]. This is why, as suggested by Roudometof, it is possible and perhaps even necessary to distinguish between local and "locale", the latter being "the entity that is responsible for sending (or resisting) waves of cultural influence, authority, or power" ([25], p. 74).

In this connection, a focus on the rhizomatic nature of globalization seems to provide a particularly suggestive framework for understanding the interplay of the global and the local. If one takes the global as the totality of cultural networks available worldwide, and the local as a specific configuration of nodes within it (cf. [69,70]), the flesh and bone of globalization cannot but consist at any given moment of interactions and connectivity at the level of particular configurations of nodes. Seen from this perspective, the glocalization of Japanese Buddhism turns out to be nothing but an aspect of the very busy daily routine of globalization.

Acknowledgments: This study was funded by the German Research Foundation (DFG) through the research project "Japanese Religions in the Context of Globalization and Secularization" at the Institute for the Study of Religion, University of Leipzig (March 2012–September 2015). I would like to thank the guest editor of this special issue and three anonymous reviewers for their valuable comments and positive feedback.

Conflicts of Interest: The author declares no conflict of interest.

References

1. Roland Robertson. "Globalization and Societal Modernization: A Note on Japan and Japanese Religion." *Sociological Analysis* 47 (1987): 35–42. [CrossRef]
2. Roland Robertson. "Glocalization: Time-Space and Homogeneity-Heterogeneity." In *Global Modernities*. Edited by Mike Featherstone, Scott Lash and Roland Robertson. London: Sage Publications, 1995, pp. 25–44.
3. Kashimura Aiko. "Nyū eiji, seishin bunsekiteki bunka, ai: Rakan-ha seishin bunsekigaku kara mita aidentiti kuraishisu." In *Gurōbaruka to aidentiti kuraishisu*. Edited by Miyanaga Kuniko. Tokyo: Akashi Shoten, 2002, pp. 183–205.
4. Inoue Nobutaka. "Gurōbaruka kara mita kindai Nihon shūkyō." *Tokyo Daigaku shūkyōgaku nenpō* 6 (1990): 1–18.
5. Maruyama Tetsuo. "Toward the Universal Ethics and Values in the Age of Globalization: With Reference to Japanese Religions Compared to Modern Rationalism." *Politics and Religion* 2 (2008): 165–80.
6. Sanda Ionescu. "Adapt or Perish: The Story of Soka Gakkai in Germany." In *Japanese New Religions in Global Perspective*. Edited by Peter B. Clarke. Richmond: Curzon Press, 2000, pp. 182–97.
7. Ugo Dessì. "Shin Buddhism, Authority, and the Fundamental Law of Education." *Numen* 56 (2009): 523–44. [CrossRef]
8. Ugo Dessì. "Shin Buddhism and Globalization: Attitudes toward the Political Subsystem and Pluralism at the Organizational and Individual Levels." In *The Social Dimension of Shin Buddhism*. Edited by Ugo Dessì. Leiden: Brill, 2010, pp. 241–66.
9. John K. Nelson. "Global and Domestic Challenges Confronting Buddhist Institutions in Japan." *Journal of Global Buddhism* 12 (2011): 1–15.

10. Christal Whelan. "Religious Responses to Globalization in Japan: The Case of the God Light Association." Ph.D. Dissertation, Boston University, Boston, MA, USA, 2007.
11. Cristina Rocha. *Zen in Brazil: The Quest for Cosmopolitan Modernity*. Honolulu: University of Hawaii Press, 2006.
12. Ugo Dessì. *Japanese Religions and Globalization*. London and New York: Routledge, 2013.
13. Ugo Dessì. *The Global Repositioning of Japanese Religions: An Integrated Approach*. London and New York: Routledge, 2016.
14. Galen Amstutz, and Ugo Dessì, eds. "New Research on Japanese Religions under Globalization." Special issue, *Journal of Religion in Japan* 3 (2014).
15. Nestor Garcia Canclini. *Hybrid Cultures: Strategies for Entering and Leaving Modernity*. Minneapolis: University of Minnesota Press, 1995.
16. Arjun Appadurai. *Modernity at Large: Cultural Dimensions of Globalization*. Minneapolis: University of Minnesota Press, 1996.
17. Revathi Krishnaswamy. "The Criticism of Culture and the Culture of Criticism: At the Intersection of Postcolonialism and Globalization Theory." *Diacritics* 32 (2002): 106–26. [CrossRef]
18. Marwan M. Kraidy. "Hybridity in Cultural Globalization." *Communication Theory* 12 (2002): 316–39. [CrossRef]
19. Ronen Shamir. "Without Borders? Notes on Globalization as a Mobility Regime." *Sociological Theory* 23 (2005): 197–217. [CrossRef]
20. Manuel A. Vásquez. "The Limits of the Hydrodynamics of Religion." *Journal of the American Academy of Religion* 77 (2009): 434–45. [CrossRef]
21. George Van Pelt Campbell. *Everything You Think Seems Wrong: Globalization and the Relativizing of Tradition*. Lanham: University Press of America, 2005.
22. Max Weber. *Economy and Society: An Outline of Interpretive Sociology*. Berkeley: University of California Press, 1978.
23. Mark Chaves. "Secularization as Declining Religious Authority." *Social Forces* 72 (1994): 749–74. [CrossRef]
24. Benson Saler. "Supernatural as a Western Category." *Ethos* 5 (1977): 31–53. [CrossRef]
25. Victor Roudometof. *Glocalization: A Critical Introduction*. London and New York: Routledge, 2016.
26. Duncan Ryūken Williams. "Buddhist Environmentalism in Contemporary Japan." In *How Much Is Enough? Buddhism, Consumerism, and the Human Environment*. Edited by Richard K. Payne. Somervill: Wisdom Publications, 2010, pp. 17–37.
27. Ugo Dessì. "'Greening Dharma': Contemporary Japanese Buddhism and Ecology." *Journal for the Study of Religion, Nature and Culture* 7 (2013): 334–55. [CrossRef]
28. 'Sōtōshū Danshinto Hikkei' Kaitei Iinkai, ed. *Sōtōshū Danshinto Hikkei*. Tokyo: Sotoshu Shūmuchō, 2008.
29. Ichigū o Terasu Undō. "Ningen no Toribun." 2006. Available online: http://ichigu.net/pillar/life02.html (accessed on 26 November 2015).
30. Ichigū o Terasu Undō. "Inochi o Kangaeru Mittsu no Shiten." 2006. Available online: http://ichigu.net/pillar/life03.html (accessed on 26 November 2015).
31. Jōdo Shinshū Honganji-ha. *Honganji no mori*. Kyoto: Jōdo Shinshū Honganji-ha, 2011.
32. Jōdo Shinshū Honganji-ha. "Jūten Purojekuto Kihon Keikaku." 2012. Available online: http://www.hongwanji.or.jp/source/pdf/jis_2012_jyuten-project_kihon_keikaku.pdf (accessed on 25 November 2015).
33. Jōdo Shinshū Honganji-ha. *Honganji shinpō*. Kyoto: Jōdo Shinshū Honganji-ha, 2005.
34. Soka Gakkai International. "Soka Gakkai International: NGO Activity Report." 2011. Available online: http://www.sgi.org/assets/pdf/SGINGO_activity_report2010.pdf (accessed on 26 November 2015).
35. Yamamoto Shūichi. "Kankyō shisō e no Bukkyō no kiyo." In *Daijō Bukkyō no Chōsen: Jinruiteki Kadai e Mukete*. Edited by Tōyō Tetsugaku Kenkyūsho. Tokyo: Tōyō Tetsugaku Kenkyūsho, 2006, pp. 135–69.
36. Kawada Yōichi. "Chikyū kankyō to no kyōsei: Bōsatsu to shite no raifu sutairu." In *Chikyū Kankyō to Bukkyō: Daijō Bukkyō no Chōsen 3*. Edited by Tōyō Tetsugaku Kenkyūsho. Tokyo: Tōyō Tetsugaku Kenkyūsho, 2008, pp. 21–47.
37. Risshō Kōseikai. "ISO 14001." 2012. Available online: http://www.kosei-kai.or.jp/environment/iso (accessed on 26 November 2015).
38. Risshō Kōseikai. *Kōsei shinbun*. Tokyo: Risshō Kōseikai, 2009.

39. Risshō Kōseikai. "Kankyō hōshin." 2015. Available online: http://www.kosei-kai.or.jp/environment/policy (accessed on 27 November 2015).

40. Zen-nihon Bukkyōkai. "Appeal for a Lifestyle without Dependence on Nuclear Power." 2011. Available online: http://www.jbf.ne.jp/english/earthquake.html (accessed on 25 November 2015).

41. Zen-nihon Bukkyōkai. *Zenbutsu*. Tokyo: Zen-nihon Bukkyōkai, 2012.

42. Rinzaishū Myōshinji-ha. "Genshiryoku Hatsuden ni Izon Shinai Shakai No Jitsugen." 2011. Available online: http://www.myoshinji.or.jp/about/post_9.html (accessed on 25 November 2015).

43. Sōtōshū. "Genshiryoku Hatsuden ni tai Suru Sōtōshū no Kenkai ni Tsuite." 2011. Available online: http://jiin. sotozen-net.or.jp/wp-content/uploads/2011/11/20111101aboutapg.pdf (accessed on 25 November 2015).

44. Shinshū Ōtani-ha. "Genshiryoku Hatsuden ni Izon Shinai Shakai No Jitsugen ni Mukete." 2011. Available online: http://www.higashihonganji.or.jp/news/declaration/419 (accessed on 25 November 2015).

45. Shinshū Ōtani-ha. "Subete no Genpatsu no Unten Teishi to Hairo o Tōshite, Genshiryoku Hatsuden ni Izon Shinai Shakai No Jitsugen o Motomeru Ketsugi." 2012. Available online: http://www.higashihonganji.or.jp/news/declaration/798 (accessed on 25 November 2015).

46. Ikeda Daisaku. "Human Security and Sustainability: Sharing Reverence for the Dignity of Life (2012 Peace Proposal)." 2012. Available online: http://www.sgi-usa.org/newsandevents/docs/peace2012.pdf (accessed on 26 November 2015).

47. Risshō Kōseikai. "Makoto Ni Yutakana Shakai o Mezashite: Genpatsu o Koete." 2012. Available online: http://www.kosei-kai.or.jp/infomation/070/post_46.html (accessed on 26 November 2015).

48. Poul Pedersen. "Nature, Religion and Cultural Identity: The Religious Environmentalist Paradigm." In *Asian Perceptions of Nature: A Critical Approach*. Edited by Ole Bruun and Arne Kalland. Richmond: Curzon, 1995, pp. 258–76.

49. Arne Kalland. "The Religious Environmentalist Paradigm." In *Encyclopedia of Religion and Nature*. Edited by Bron Taylor. London and New York: Continuum International, 2005, pp. 1367–71.

50. Sōtōshū. "Five Principles of Green Life." 2015. Available online: http://global.sotozen-net.or.jp/eng/what/environment/index.html (accessed on 26 November 2015).

51. Tendaishū. "Ima, Chikyū Wa." 2006. Available online: http://ichigu.net/pillar/symbiosis02_01.html (accessed on 27 November 2015).

52. Soka Gakkai International. "SGI and the Earth Charter." 2015. Available online: http://www.sgi.org/resources/ngo-resources/education-for-sustainable-development/sgi-and-the-earth-charter.html (accessed on 26 November 2015).

53. Sōtōshū. *"Gurīn puran": Seimei to kankyō no chōwa o mezashite*. Tokyo: Sōtōshū, 1996.

54. Ugo Dessì. "The Critique of Anthropocentrism and Humanism in Present-day Shin Buddhism." *Japanese Religions* 31 (2006): 111–25.

55. Tessa Morris-Suzuki. "Concepts of Nature and Technology in Pre-Industrial Japan." *East Asian History* 1 (1991): 81–97.

56. Suzuki Daisetsu. *Zen and Japanese Culture*. Princeton: Princeton University Press, 1959.

57. Nakamura Hajime. *Ways of Thinking of Eastern Peoples: India, China, Tibet, Japan*. Honolulu: East-West Center Press, 1964.

58. Julia Adeney Thomas. *Reconfiguring Modernity: Concepts of Nature in Japanese Political Ideology*. Berkeley: University of California Press. Los Angeles: University of California Press, 2001.

59. Jeff Wilson. *Mindful America: The Mutual Transformation of Buddhist Meditation and American Culture*. Oxford: Oxford University Press, 2014.

60. Regina Yoshie Matsue. "The Glocalization Process of Shin Buddhism in Brasilia." *Journal of Religion in Japan* 3 (2014): 226–46. [CrossRef]

61. Jōdo Shinshū Honganji-ha Sōgō Kenkyūsho, ed. *Namo Amida Butsu: Sekai ni hibiku o-nenbutsu*. Kyoto: Honganji Shuppansha, 2013.

62. Roland Robertson. *Globalization: Social Theory and Global Culture*. London: Sage Publications, 1992.

63. Jan Aart Scholte. *Globalization: A Critical Introduction*. Basingstoke: Palgrave Macmillan, 2005.

64. Yui Kiyomitsu. "Globalization." In *Routledge Companion to Contemporary Japanese Social Theory: From Individualization to Globalization in Japan Today*. Edited by Anthony Elliot, Katagiri Masataka and Sawai Atsushi. London and New York: Routledge, 2013, pp. 227–45.

65. Bryan S. Turner. "Prelude: Japanese Uniqueness versus Globalization. A Reply to Professor Yui." In *Routledge Companion to Contemporary Japanese Social Theory: From Individualization to Globalization in Japan Today*. Edited by Anthony Elliot, Katagiri Masataka and Sawai Atsushi. London and New York: Routledge, 2013, pp. 227–45.

66. Rumi Sakamoto. "Japan, Hybridity and the Creation of Colonialist Discourse." *Theory, Culture & Society* 13 (1996): 113–28.

67. Julie Katherine Gibson-Graham. "Beyond Global vs. Local: Economic Politics outside the Binary Frame." In *Geographies of Power*. Edited by Andrew Herod and Melissa W. Wright. Oxford: Blackwell, 2002, pp. 25–60.

68. Arif Dirlik. "Globalism and the Politics of Place." In *Globalisation and the Asia-Pacific: Contested Territories*. Edited by Kris Olds, Peter Dicken, Philip F. Kelly, Lily Kong and Henry Wai-chung Yeung. London and New York: Routledge, 1999, pp. 39–56.

69. Ash Amin. "Spatialities of Globalisation." *Environment and Planning* 34 (2002): 385–99. [CrossRef]

70. Erik Swyngedouw. "Globalisation or 'Glocalisation'? Networks, Territories and Rescaling." *Cambridge Review of International Affairs* 17 (2004): 25–48. [CrossRef]

religions

MDPI

Article

Glocal Religion and Feeling at Home: Ethnography of Artistry in Finnish Orthodox Liturgy

Tatiana Tiaynen-Qadir

Faculty of Social Sciences, University of Turku, Turku 20014, Finland; tatiana.tiaynen@ttaq.fi

Academic Editors: Victor Roudometof and Peter Iver Kaufman
Received: 19 December 2016; Accepted: 9 February 2017; Published: 13 February 2017

Abstract: This paper adapts a glocalization framework in a transnational, anthropological exploration of liturgy in the Orthodox Church of Finland (OCF). It draws on long-term ethnographic fieldwork and interviews with participants of liturgy from Finnish, Russian, and Greek cultural and linguistic backgrounds. The main argument of the paper is that generic processes of nationalization and transnationalization are not mutually exclusive in practitioners' experiences of liturgy in OCF, but rather generate a glocal space that incorporates Finnish, Russian, Karelian, and Byzantine elements. Individuals artistically engage with glocal liturgy on sensorial, cognitive, social, and semantic levels. What is important for the participants is a therapeutic sense that comes from a feeling of 'being at home', metaphorically, spiritually, and literally. People's ongoing, creative work constitutes Orthodoxy as their national *and* transnational home.

Keywords: glocal religion; Orthodox Christianity; glocalization; transnational anthropology; artistry; liturgy; home; therapeutic

1. Introduction

Most contemporary Orthodox churches across the world are divided into national or diasporic churches; the latter of which is often organized alongside ethno-national and linguistic lines. National churches include, for example, those of Greece and Cyprus, where histories of entanglement between Orthodoxy and nationalization date back to the 19th century. In Russia, Orthodox Christianity emerged as a signifier of individual and collective national identity after the Soviet collapse [1]. On the other hand, Orthodox churches in the USA are mostly diasporic churches, where this religion functions as a 'cultural marker' that implies belonging to a certain national or ethnic group, whether Greek, Serbian, or Russian versions of Orthodoxy ([2], p. 122). This is also the case in Western Europe, for instance, in Switzerland, Denmark, Sweden, and Norway [3,4]. This situation led to the scholarly categorization of national vs diasporic Orthodox churches in contemporary research [2,4–6].

Such categorizations are analytically useful for examining the social aspects of religion. Yet, they tend to brush aside cross-sectional and cross-cutting processes that cannot be easily captured by the division between national and diasporic. In many ways, 'religious transnationalism' becomes evident in hybrid or minority identities *within* Orthodox diasporas, through the experiences of migration in the modern world of nation-states ([6], p. 213). The Orthodox Church of Finland (OCF), for example, is an interesting case, suggesting that the processes of nationalization and transnationalization are not mutually exclusive, but together constitute a glocal manifestation of Orthodoxy in Finland. This paper unpacks this argument by focusing on individual experiences of liturgy in the OCF, a Eucharistic church service of the Byzantine rite that has been central to Eastern Christian practices since the time of late antiquity, and remains so today amongst Orthodox populations across the globe [7,8].

In general, many approaches to questions of lived religion are bound within a methodological nationalist approach, restricted to exploring phenomena within one national realm or church. However, the author's ethnographic fieldwork in Finland paints a different picture, of the Orthodox Church as a multi-sited space transcending national borders. The findings are grounded in a glocalization framework [2] and in transnational anthropology [9–11], which challenges methodological nationalism and accentuates multi-sited selves and lives. A transnational anthropological approach helps to yield new interpretations of people's narratives and experiences of liturgy.

Another, key, theoretical axis of the paper is material religion, which emphasizes the holistic character of mind-body experiences [12,13]. The term 'religious aesthetics' is employed to address people's 'embodied and embedded praxis' of religion, in which the process of making meanings and knowing is understood as a holistic experience of the mind, as well as of the bodily emotions and experiences [14]. Religious aesthetics enable us to see that individuals' experiences of, for instance, liturgy, are often sensorially and corporeally felt, in addition to being consciously articulated and apprehended. Following a people's perspective shows the 'work' they do, their 'vernacular' artistry, which is often overlooked in academic accounts of institutionally-based religiosities [15].

The paper draws on the author's long-term ethnographic fieldwork in one of the parishes of the OCF, a dynamic site of multicultural and multilinguistic interaction. Ethnographic interviews were conducted with 22 practitioners from Finnish, Russian, and Greek backgrounds, who either regularly or occasionally attend liturgical services. The main argument presented here is that Finnish Orthodox glocal liturgy incorporates both nationalization and transnationalization, and thus creates and enables practitioners from different backgrounds to experience a feeling of 'home', both metaphorically and literally. Individuals creatively and artistically engage with glocal liturgy on sensorial, cognitive, and semantic levels.

The paper unfolds as follows. The next section provides a brief background to Finnish Orthodox Christianity from a glocal perspective, focusing on liturgy. This is followed by a section discussing the theory and method. The ensuing three empirical sections discuss individual experiences of liturgy through senses, the language, and shifting lens. The paper concludes with a section that summarizes the findings, as well as opens avenues for future exploration.

2. Orthodox Church of Finland

Orthodoxy in Finland dates back to the eleventh century: it was indigenized in the region of Karelia[1], under the influence of the Novgorodians, who adopted this religion from the Byzantines through Kiev at the end of the tenth century ([16], p. 153). Throughout history, Orthodox Christianity remained a religion of minority, mainly concentrated in the eastern part of Finland. Where religion had been evident in Finland under the centuries-old Swedish rule, culturally or institutionally, that religion had been Lutheranism. There had been some spread of Orthodox Christianity into other parts of the country in the nineteenth century due to the Russian Orthodox Church, when the Grand Duchy of Finland was part of the Russian Empire. After Finland gained independence in 1917, the OCF became an autonomous Finnish Orthodox archdiocese of the Patriarchate of Constantinople in 1923. The histories of Finnish Orthodoxy embraced numerous people's dislocations, resettlements, and enforced and voluntary moves, as well as the alleged tensions between Karelian and Russian Orthodox identities (for a detailed historical accounts of these moves see [16]).

The first half of the twentieth century was marked by the process of nationalization or *Finnicisation*, i.e., deliberate attempts of the OCF to disassociate Orthodoxy from its Russian heritage [16,17]. The national popularity of the OCF started to grow in the 1970s among Finnish intellectuals, due to the 'Romantic movement' that appreciated the Byzantine art of icons and music, which enhanced the oriental and exotic image of Orthodoxy in Finland [16,18,19]. In general, any attentive

---

[1] Occupying an intermediate position on the Russian-Finnish border, Karelia has historically been an area of warlike conflicts or peaceful interactions between Sweden and Novgorod, the Swedish Kingdom and the Russian Empire, Finland and the Soviet Union, and the centuries-old coexistence and interconnectedness of Slavonic and Finno-Ugric cultures.

observer will be overwhelmed by the visibility of Eastern Orthodox materiality—icons of Mary, Jesus, or saints—throughout the country, and the intense activity surrounding them. Many Finns with wide-ranging beliefs, including Lutherans, keep Orthodox icons in their homes, attend icon-painting courses, or enjoy Orthodox choir singing. This situation is also due to 'good ecumenical relationships' and multiple interactions between the OCF and the Evangelical Lutheran Church of Finland (ELCF), 'the two folk churches' that have a legal status as national churches in the country ([20], p. 7). Indeed, there is hardly any sense of resentment between these two branches of Christianity in Finland, and in many cases, there is a continuum for those who convert from Lutheranism to Orthodoxy, or vice versa. Similarly, some Lutherans appreciate and apply elements of Orthodoxy, without feeling any compulsion to join the OCF.

From the 1990s onwards, the OCF started to undergo the process of transnationalization, mainly due to an influx of migrants from Eastern European countries. The share of foreign-born members increased from 3 per cent in 1990, to 11 per cent in 2009 ([16], p. 166). In 2015, the Church's official membership amounted to 60,877, approximately 1.1 per cent of the total population in Finland [21]. However, these official numbers do not include those practitioners who are not officially registered, but share some form of commitment to Orthodoxy. There are most likely many individuals among Russian-speakers (presently the largest migrant minority in Finland, roughly estimated at 78,000), who consider themselves Orthodox, but may not have officially joined the OCF. Practitioners from this and other linguistic minorities (Greek, Romanian, Ukrainian, Serbian, Tigrinya, etc) also attend church services in the parish where the fieldwork research was conducted, but not all of them are registered members of the OCF.

A central component of the regular Orthodox Church service is the Divine Liturgy or, simply, liturgy. Liturgy stands for the recreation and celebration of the Kingdom of Heaven, as well as the symbolic and actual reliving of the mystery of the Last Supper. The term derives from the Ancient Greek 'leitourgia', translated as 'public works' to emphasize the communal character of this rite ([22], p. 190). As a 'synthesis of arts' [23], liturgy has been a 'unique source of aesthetic, intellectual, music, poetic and visual enjoyment' [24]. According to Orthodox theology, its 'sorrowful joy' manifests in the re-enactment of the sacrifice of Jesus's body and blood, but also in the glorious resurrection and glad thanking (*Eucharistia*), as well as the glorifying of the life-giving Trinitarian God [7,22]. Although theological research into liturgy has been substantial, there is little scholarly understanding of the ethnographic reality surrounding this service in the lives of Orthodox practitioners ([25], p. 12).

In particular, scant attention has been paid to how liturgy in the OCF embeds *both* the processes of nationalization *and* transnationalization. In the course of the twentieth century, Finnish has become the main liturgical language, as well as the medium of social interaction in the OCF. The translation of liturgical texts from Church Slavonic into Finnish—liturgies by John Chrysostom and St. Basil the Great, the two most frequently used in the church service—signifies a process of nationalization through vernacularization. Although the first translation was made in 1862 in Saint Petersburg, that carried out by Sergei Okulov became the most commonly used translation from 1910 ([26], p. 9). Composing music specifically for the Finnish text of the liturgy also depicts the process of nationalization, and was first completed by Peter Akimov (published under P. Attinen, 1936) ([26], p. 10). Yet these attempts at nationalization had in fact relied on a strong transnational component. First, there had been a great deal of effort placed on reviving the Byzantine art of icon-painting and the eight-mode system of chanting [27] and, thus, on establishing a direct connection to the Greek heritage. Second, in its religious aesthetics, Finnish Orthodoxy has also retained Russian Orthodox elements (albeit it has been less articulated in Church public rhetoric [16]). In particular, the Finnish liturgical practice has continued to follow the Russian Orthodox tradition of multi-vocal choir singing. Many hymns and chants composed by Russian composers (such as the famous 'Cherubim hymn' by G. Lvovski), have been adopted for choir singing in the Finnish language, and continue to be sung during liturgies (Figure 1). Compositions of the Finnish composers Aleksei Krasnostovski, Leonid Bashmakov, Pasi Torhamo, and Timo Ruottinen, incorporate both Byzantine and Slavic influences [26,28]. Likewise, the church architecture, church interior, and icons—indispensable parts of the religious aesthetics of the liturgy—variably integrate Byzantine, Russian, and Karelian features [19,29].

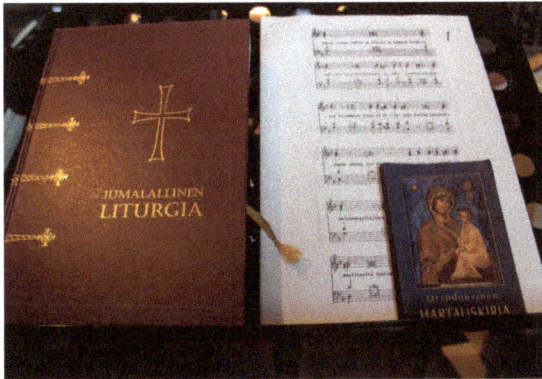

Figure 1. The Liturgy used by the choir during services. Photo by the author.

The church in which the fieldwork research was conducted is located in a major urban centre of the country. In its architecture and interior, including icons, this church incorporates 19th-century Russian 'academic classicism' ([29], p. 289). The 'western' style of iconography within the church is not always appreciated by scholars of art, as it diverges from the Byzantine and Old Russian art of icons [19]. Yet, the fieldwork research illustrates that both old and new iconographic styles 'speak' to individuals, and practitioners venerate icons, irrespective of their artistic and theological 'correctness'. Most clubs and groups in the church are run in both Finnish and Russian languages, and as one of the Finnish interlocutors puts it: 'it is great that one can hear many languages spoken'. Although Finnish is the main language of liturgy, church services are also occasionally conducted in Church Slavonic, Greek, Romanian, Serbian, and English languages. There is a multi-vocal choir and a one-vocal choir: both sing a diversity of choral music during liturgies, ranging from traditional (Neo) Byzantine chant and Russian 'znamenny chant', to various Finnish compositions, which may also integrate traditional and modern Nordic music influences.

3. Theory and Methods

Growing research has attempted to address the global and transnational character of Orthodox Christianity [4,6,25]. The argument here draws on Roudometof's account of Orthodox Christianity, as historical glocalization that comprises processes of indigenization, vernacularization, nationalization, and transnationalization [2]. These glocalizations of Orthodoxy emerge as concrete historical processes involving a fusion between religious universalism and local particularism. The expression 'transformations of a religious tradition' in the book's title points to the diversity of manifestations of Orthodoxy in local contexts, in particular its different responses to nationalization and transnationalization. Roudometof's theorizing on glocalization is an excellent framework for understanding the historical and contemporary dynamic in the OCF.

The contribution of this paper is that it incorporates an anthropological perspective into the sociological glocalization framework [30]. First, this paper applies transnational anthropology, which challenges methodological nationalism and accentuates multi-sited histories, lives, and senses of belonging [9–11]. An ethnic group or a nation can no longer be viewed as being self-evidently fixed with a certain locality and state, as 'the structures of feeling that constitute nationalism need to be set in the context of other forms of imagining communities, other means of endowing significance to space in the production of location and "home"' ([31], p. 331). In the increasingly interconnected global realm, many individuals share *transnational subjectivities* that refer to a 'trajectory that combines living in different places, and makes mobility a historical trajectory of one's own, always connecting to where one is located but simultaneously keeping oneself solidly anchored in one's own story and oneself' ([11], p. 170). This anthropological perspective helps to illustrate people's agency in renegotiating their transnational subjectivities, where nationalization and transnationalization may in fact be simultaneously at work.

Second, this paper approaches Orthodoxy as a vernacular, lived religion that necessarily entails an experiential component, an individual's creativity and artistry in interpretation, and a unique engagement with liturgy [15]. In this respect, it expands on Roudometof's concept of 'vernacularization' to go beyond linguistics and into the artful and creative way in which people relate to religiosity. Most approaches to the important questions of lived religion build on a cognitive approach to religious materiality (icons, music), which stresses how believers relate to the theological meaning of an image or appreciate its aesthetics, in more or less theoretical terms. However, ethnographic fieldwork offers a different view, namely significant evidence of sensorial and corporeal experiences of religious art [13,32].

The argument presented here draws on the long-term ethnographic fieldwork research [33–35]. The fieldwork research was conducted amongst Orthodox Christians in Finland (2014–2016), which included participant and non-participant observation in a church setting,[2] as well as 22 ethnographic interviews. The church serves as the spiritual and social environment of a vibrant multicultural community within the parish in western Finland. Following the premises of transnational anthropology the purpose of approaching interlocutors was to interact and interview individuals from various linguistic and cultural backgrounds, in order to address the multicultural dynamic of the OCF. Thus, the ethnographic interviews were conducted with individuals of Russian, Finnish, and Greek origins. The interviewees were mostly women aged between 26 and 69, all but two had a university degree, and most were teachers, university lecturers, accountants, researchers, and doctors. The findings presented here should be seen as the result of the long-term immersion in the studied phenomenon and engagement with the interlocutors.

4. Transnational and National Experiences of Liturgy: 'Being at Home'

4.1. Liturgy and Senses

What unites the interlocutors of this research is that none of them (except two women from a Greek background), for various reasons, could be seen as 'cradle' Orthodox. Despite all of the differences between the cultural and political situations of the Orthodox Churches in Finland and Russia, there are some obvious parallels in their interrelated histories. Due to the decades of Soviet suppression of religion, Orthodoxy was rather passively present in people's lives, and was mainly transferred through elderly women or babushkas (grandmothers in Russian) [35,36]. In Finland, Orthodoxy was the religion of a 'stigmatized minority' up to the 1970s [18] and, therefore, many Finnish interlocutors also only had passive experiences of Orthodoxy. This tangible experience of Orthodoxy formed a 'latent religious affiliation' [37] that many individuals built on in their rediscovery of Orthodox spirituality in their adult lives. Corporeal and emotional experiences of liturgy have been important in their pursuit of the Orthodox path.

This is how Maija, who was raised as a member of the (Protestant) Free Church of Finland, recollects her first experience of liturgy in the New Valaam Monastery in Finland, in her early twenties:

> I found Orthodoxy after I finished high school. I went to the Valaam Monastery, and it was more about how I felt [tunneasia in Finnish] there during the liturgy, and the monks

---

2 The name and the location of the church are omitted to enhance anonymity of the interlocutors. Naturally, their real names are not mentioned in the paper, and certain other details have also been anonymized.

singing. When I came home and went to the service [at the Free Church of Finland], it was not the same. Yes, it was a liturgy in a parish, and all the elements were there, but I was thinking that it was not the same as in Valaam. The service [in Valaam] was very intense, and it was alive, and this affected me. Many people say that there is a powerful energy in the Valaam Monastery... And there was something very moving in that icon [the Valaam icon of the Mother of God]. I felt it that very first time I went there. When I was close to the icon, I felt peace inside, and it stayed deeply in my memories [38].

Johanna, too, recollects that she felt like 'being at home' when she visited the Valaam Monastery, also in her early twenties. Marja compares 'joining the church' with 'coming home', while Minna says that she found her 'spiritual home' in Orthodoxy. The word 'home' frequently appears in people's narratives, irrespective of their linguistic backgrounds. There are multiple meanings of 'home', ranging from a place that one physically inhabits, to various subjective experiences of home [39], and the use of the term in the interviews captures these different levels. Shifting experiences of home may signify 'movement within the constitution of home' ([40], p. 341). Various situated and changing experiences of home(s) reveal that being at home is always a matter of 'how one feels or how one might fail to feel', rather than a marker of one specific abode [40]. Upon her return to what used to be her home church, Maija failed to feel that way after she faced another kind of church service. Liturgy with flickering candles, icons, incense, and choir singing, was experienced as welcoming, and home-like. In other women's narratives, the first encounters of Orthodox materiality are also often recollected as experienced on a sensory and intuitional level, connecting to something familiar and seemingly known, that one had been longing for.

Such a sensorial component remains significant throughout years of participation in the liturgy. Many emphasize that they 'like the smell' in the church, that choir singing 'touched my very soul', or that they were 'moved to tears'; they talk of the feeling of 'trembling' or 'gooses bumps' in the body. This is how the sensorial effects of liturgy are described in the words of Vera, a Russian-speaking practising psychiatrist, in her early thirties:

Solemnity. Sometimes there is such moment in life, some kind of breakdown. Not like some kind of quarrel, but some serious stress. Somebody got sick or some problems, for instance, at a work place. And there is a feeling [oshchushchenie] of tearfulness, a feeling that it is bad. And then it is gone. And there is a peak of bliss. And tears stream down, I don't know...I don't know how to explain it as it is well difficult to do it. Well you know, when you say that you are extremely deeply moved. There is this very feeling [oshchushchenie]...well you know, it is actually overwhelming you, and there is a lump in the throat...I don't know, it is difficult to explain [41].

Vera applies the Russian word *oshchushchenie*, which does not have any direct translation into English. Yet, its use is important, as this term implies a 'subjective image' of the world and encompasses the whole range of senses and sensations, tangible and emotional experiences, and perceptions [42]. Vera and her family have stayed in different places in Finland and attended church services in local churches. She mentions that, although 'she has been always attracted by the Orthodox church', she did not really attend church in Russia, where one's behaviour and clothes could be easily misjudged. Instead, she says that the OCF is more 'democratic', explaining that she 'found her church in Finland, not in Russia'. This is also important to sensorial experiences of liturgy, as it stands for the comforting feeling of being at home.

However, most of the Russian-speaking interlocutors appreciate the multi-locality of Orthodoxy. They do not draw a particular difference between Russian and Finnish Orthodox churches, but rather their Orthodox journey takes place within the constitution of their transnational home. Anfisa, for instance, points out that she has never been disconnected from the church, and always liked the music, the smell, and the entire 'atmosphere' during the liturgy. She used to attend church services, but later apprehended Orthodoxy with 'awareness' when she was in Finland, through her brother who stayed in Russia and acted as her spiritual mentor. Yet, she notes: 'It all started in Russia, and the first Eucharist I also received in Russia.' Only somewhat later, she came to the Eastern service in Finland, started regularly attending liturgies, and joined the choir.

The feeling of being at home is not necessarily rationally apprehended. It is often a non-cognitive, sensorial, and embodied connection that evokes a comforting feeling of being at home. When Russian-speakers or Greek-speakers participate in the liturgy in the OCF, they also connect to the religious aesthetics of glocal liturgy in Finland; the art of icons and music that incorporate Russian and Byzantine features (and often are not fully familiar within the complex, ambiguous histories of Finnish Orthodoxy). They encounter the same images and familiar melodies that connect them with their homes, where they were born. This is why many Russian-speakers, when entering an Orthodox church in Finland, may have a feeling of 'very home', as Elena puts it (Figure 2).

Figure 2. Church interior (iconostasis) in the Uspenski Cathedral in Helsinki. Photo by the author.

During liturgies, they also face and contemplate icons of Mary, Jesus, and other saints. In their eyes, these figures do not belong to one single national realm, but rather transcend national borders. Victoria notes that, upon her first visit to a Finnish Orthodox church, she was pleasantly surprised to view what seemed to be an exact image of the Virgin that she had seen at the Valaam Monastery in Russian Karelia[3], a copy of which she had also brought with her to Finland.

A similar effect of Orthodox religious aesthetics can be observed among so-called transnationals, who have moved and stayed in different places due to their work. For instance, Marta, a woman of Greek origins, is a researcher who came to Finland 10 years ago. She notes that, with age, she has realized the spiritual depth of the Orthodox tradition, but participation in liturgy has also meant that she has joined with something that she has been 'missing, maybe part of the identity I had in Greece'. Individual artistry manifests in the various sensorial ways individuals from different backgrounds engage with the Orthodox materiality of liturgy. These engagements often generate a therapeutic feeling of being at home, in both metaphorical and literal senses. The glocal character of Finnish liturgy—its national and transnational religious aesthetics—enables this artistry, and this feeling amongst people from both Finnish and non-Finnish backgrounds.

---

3   The existence of the two Valaam Monasteries, one in Russia and one in Finland, is another example of transnational Orthodox entanglements [43].

4.2. *Liturgy and Languages*

Individual artistry also shapes the various ways in which participants experience liturgy on a semantic level, and how these experiences change over a period of years. As mentioned above, although the main language of the liturgy is Finnish, liturgies are also held in Church Slavonic, Ancient Greek, Romanian, Serbian, and English. Some parts may be sung in Finnish, Swedish (the second official language of Finland alongside Finnish), and Church Slavonic during a single liturgy. When services are conducted in Church Slavonic, there are many Russian-speakers, including those who come from out of town, who attend the liturgy. Some don't understand Finnish well enough to follow the service in Finnish, and as physiotherapist Slava expresses: 'Of course, it is easier to follow in Church Slavonic, and the liturgy unfolds better'. Although many understand liturgy in Finnish, some also note that liturgy in Church Slavonic is particularly moving and, in the words of Ivan, 'sounds smoothly', 'probably because this tradition is hundreds of years old'. Others simply say that it is so 'touching' because it is in Russian. Similarly, Marta and Evgenija, women of Greek origins, make efforts to attend liturgies in Greek, which is usually followed by a gathering, and by talking over coffee with a Greek priest and other Greeks living in Finland. This points to the therapeutic effect of feeling at home amongst non-Finnish Orthodox through the language of the liturgy, but also through the broader social interaction with people from similar cultural backgrounds.

The language of liturgy is not simply a medium for transmitting the meaning of the words, but is irrevocably inscribed in the holistic experience of liturgy, and evolves over years. For instance, Johanna, a Finnish-speaking woman, has been singing in a church choir for more than twenty years, and she points out that not a single liturgy has ever been the same: it has also varied across different life stages, and even the season and weather affects the ways in which liturgy has been experienced. She describes that, in her earlier years of engagements, perfecting the singing technique, enjoying the physical and emotional sensations, and hearing oneself in the harmony with others, were what she enjoyed most. She notes that, when the singing technique was improved, she started paying more attention to the texts of the hymns and verses. Some texts have been familiar to Johanna since her childhood, during which time she was studying the Bible in her Lutheran school classes. Yet, those texts come alive with music in her liturgical experience:

> I have known some [texts] as I was attending religious classes, and heard what the Bible says. But when you sing those texts yourself, almost the same texts or related to the same matter, then in these verses the matter starts to come alive. Some texts have been translated from Russian in such a way that Old Finnish was preserved. So when some unusual word comes, then you start thinking of its deeper...Of course, a person lives through different life phases, and at some point I stopped being stressed during liturgy. I did not think only of singing, but I started to listen to what a priest had to say, very excitingly [44].

Other interlocutors, too, point out that, during liturgy, hymns and verses 'open' texts in different ways. Some also underline the special power of archaic prayers, especially in Ancient Greek and Church Slavonic. For instance, Victoria, a Russian-speaking Orthodox, mentions that as she immersed in the Orthodox tradition and prayers, she learnt to appreciate Church Slavonic more as a 'deeply poetic' and 'metaphorical' language, with weighty words and subtle meanings. Similarly, Marta mentions that one ancient prayer in Ancient Greek is especially powerful and beautiful to her, although when translated into English, 'it does not make sense at all'. The prayer that Marta refers to is a prayer that is addressed to the Holy Ghost 'O Heavenly King', which begins all prayers, and Liturgy in particular:

> Yes, it is beautiful to read and makes sense in old Greek. But as I was going to translate it, there is no sense. It is like that 'You, that you have all the power in the world, and let Your Kingdom become true also not in heaven, but here, and empower us to do the good and show us, if possible, to which way to follow, and make us wise and come and live inside us as the good of the eternal good to help us do these things. You are the treasure of the poor

and the Giver of life to everyone. Come and relieve us from many siC.' Something like that, but it makes no sense, you know [45].[4]

Thus, cognitive engagement with aspects of the language of the liturgy is linked to sensorial and embodied experiences. Some attend liturgy in archaic languages that they don't understand, but nevertheless feel connected to the church service through the 'beauty' of the language. Multiple engagements with the ancient Trisagion prayer, which includes triple recitation 'Holy God, Holy Mighty One, Holy Immortal One, have mercy on us', and is sung during liturgy, is a good example. The fieldwork and interviews show that this prayer 'reaches' individuals through the medium of different languages and varying music arrangements. For Minna, the Trisagion 'reaches' when performed in Finnish as a 'Slavic melody'; for Marta, when it is in Ancient Greek or Church Slavonic as a Byzantine chant; and for Polina, it is in Finnish as a Byzantine chant, adopted for Finnish choral singing. In some cases, it is not one single configuration of the language and the music, but its multiple variations and engagement over time, that makes it work. As Victoria notices: 'Sometimes I get the deep meaning of a certain word when I hear and sing it in both Finnish and Church Slavonic languages and during many services'. Many interlocutors find that archaic words generate different experiences and meanings. It seems that archaic words tend to be more poetic and deep, thus offering an alternative to the instrumental language of modernity. These various experiences and dynamic work on the languages illustrate people's creativity and artistry in participation during liturgy. Words seem to carry and interplay with the "authentic' inner life experiences of individuals' ([30], p. 50). These engagements disclose that the semantic diversity of glocal Finnish liturgy enables this artistry, and allows a connection to Orthodoxy as a metaphorical, spiritual, and actual home.

4.3. Shifting Experiences of Liturgy

As evident, the nature of individual experiences of liturgy is intrinsically dynamic and shifting. Experiences may change across one's life span and under various life circumstances. Many Russian-speakers who sing in the choir, for instance, point out that joining the choir helped them better understand and immerse in liturgy in the Finnish language. Minna, a Finnish-speaking singer, on the contrary, points out that temporary withdrawal from the choir due to her motherly duties, positively affected her prayer concentration, and eventually helped when she started singing during liturgies again:

> There are of course many church songs, which open texts in a completely different ways. It was also good for me that I had not been singing in a church choir for a long time as I had to be with the children and other stuff. And during this time, my concentration on prayers gradually somehow improved, when I didn't sing in the choir. Especially when there are new melodies and other things, then one has to concentrate more on that you sing correctly, rather than what you sing. But when the melody is well-known, then singing becomes a prayer [46].

This narrative illustrates that liturgical experiences are tightly intertwined with people's home practices, and are subject to change. Natalia's case is also an interesting example of that. Natalia recollects one episode from her life, that took place when she had recently moved to Finland, and as an art teacher, had difficulties in finding a job. She had applied for a highly competitive course, organized for teachers who had earned degrees in other countries, to allow them to teach in the Finnish schooling system. By that time, Natalia had received an answer that she would be able to attend, only if two other participants cancelled their participation. It was at that moment in her life that she happened to be in Helsinki and came to the liturgy in the Uspenski Cathedral:

---

[4] One of most common translations of this prayer, used in Liturgy in English is: O Heavenly King, the Comforter, the Spirit of Truth, You are everywhere and fill all things, Treasury of blessings and Giver of Life, Come and abide in us, cleanse us from every impurity. And save our souls, O Good One.

I came to the big icon of Jesus Christ. The icon depicted Jesus—that icon is near the altar—and the children surrounding Jesus. I approached that icon and said: 'Lord, I don't know which path I am to take in Finland, which profession, what to do? You', I am saying 'help me and guide me. I don't know what to do'...'Lord, if it is meant to be, and you want me to become [find myself] in Finland...If the society needs that I would be a teacher, help me please find my path'. And the miracle happened. That autumn, during the first days of September, a secretary from the institute called me and said: 'You are accepted, come and study' [47].

Natalia successfully completed the course and has been working as an art teacher since, 'surrounded by children'. Natalia's story shows that experiences of liturgy are necessarily embedded in an individual's everyday life, and evolve accordingly. It also discloses both a national and transnational dynamic: she turns to Jesus, the transcendental figure depicted in the icon, in her attempts to find her place in the new national realm. Her narrative highlights the general observation that each individual may have a unique experience of icons during liturgy, and in different life situations.

Similarly, Ivan, a Ukrainian Russian-speaking transnational, who has worked and lived in Canada, England, and now in Finland, talks about the personal significance of the figures and icons of St Nicolas and Mary. For him, Mary (or Mother of God as the Virgin is referred to in Orthodoxy) is associated with 'cosmic wisdom' and 'all-acceptance', and St Nicolas with indulgence and kindness. In the midst of transnational moves, the figure of St Nicolas, known as the protector of travellers, has become especially close to Ivan. Again, Ivan says that a realization of, and closeness to, these figures have come with age. Ivan attends church services whenever possible, which often produces the feeling of 'being in Russia or Ukraine' for him. It can also be assumed that, given the importance of Mary and St Nicolas, a unique space opens up through Ivan's personal engagement with their icons during liturgy. Notably, the figure of St Nicolas is much venerated in Finnish Orthodoxy, and many churches are devoted to this saint. Below, a photograph (Figure 3) shows the icon of St Nicolas, framed by elaborate floral arrangements carefully made by two regular participants of liturgy, as yet another example of individuals' artistry and creativity.

Figure 3. The icon of St Nicolas decorated with flowers. Photo by the author.

Anfisa's story (above) provides another illustration of shifting experiences of liturgy. According to her, she was raised in an ordinary Soviet family, where most family members were atheists. She started attending church services as an adult, enjoying the smell of incense and the music. It took her several years to receive her first Eucharist in Russia, with the help of her brother, who guided and supported her. Soon, she started attending liturgies in Finland as well. The major shift in her experience of liturgy is evident in an extract from the interview with Anfisa that took place half a year after she had joined the choir in the Finnish Orthodox parish:

> This is such a great blessing to be there, breath that air, be able to sing to the glory of God. It is not possible to describe it. One has to really merely stand there and feel it. And there is always some trembling [in the body]. And when you leave the temple, and everything went well. And then you understand that it is not because of us, it is not our merits, that everything went well. But everything went fine, and there were less mistakes, and the sound was beautiful, and you feel it, and other people feel it...and then people come and thank you. But how can you explain people: 'It is not me, understand me. It is not me. I am the instrument' [48].

5. Discussion

This paper has adapted Roudometof's glocalization framework for a transnational anthropological exploration of liturgy in the Orthodox Church of Finland. The paper has shown that the OCF is a specific example of the entanglement of nationalization and transnationalization. It does not readily fit in the mainstream categorization of national vs. diasporic churches; rather, its glocal manifestation occupies an in-between position. On the one hand, OCF went through intense nationalization in the 20th century, and has become a national church of a religious minority. On the other hand, since the 1990s, it has gone through a dynamic process of transnationalization, incorporating migrants from the Eastern European heartlands of Orthodoxy, especially Russian-speakers. In contrast to diasporic churches, where both hybrid and minority identities are constructed through orientation to the past and an external national homeland ([4], p. 219), OCF enables a space for transnational subjectivities. The space is activated in many church practices, including that of liturgy. The complex nature of such subjectivities is best captured through the metaphor of 'home'; the term that most interlocutors frequently activate to channel its various modalities. Individuals from migrant backgrounds (Russian, Ukrainian, or Greek) may develop their home-relatedness to Finland, while at the same time retaining their cultural sense of identity and belonging with their origins. Individuals with Finnish backgrounds also contribute to the making of transnational subjectivities, as participants of glocal liturgy and a multicultural parish.

The processes of nationalization and transnationalization are not mutually exclusive in the Finnish liturgy, but rather generate a glocal space that incorporates Finnish, Russian, Byzantine, and Karelian elements. Liturgy emerges as a 'synthesis of the arts' that encompasses the 'art of fire' or burning candles, the 'art of smoke' or the incense dissolved in the air, the art of icons, singing, church poetry, and priestly conduct ([23], p. 109). People's own artistry is essential in making the national and transnational nature of the church, and these experiences evolve across one's life span, and in response to different life situations. Individuals creatively and artistically engage with the glocal Finnish church artistry of liturgy on a sensorial, cognitive, social, and semantic level, and create a connection with 'home', metaphorically, spiritually, and literally. More importantly, this therapeutic feeling is in the nature of the artistry by the people. All of these individual efforts constitute movement within the constitution of Orthodoxy as their national and transnational home. This home-feeling is another aspect of therapy (curing, health) of the soul and the body, to which references are numerously made in the prayers and texts sung during liturgies. As many pointed out, the ultimate joy and effect of liturgy is going beyond the self, and such a therapeutic feeling of home may also transcend the very idea of national belonging and a modern nation-state.

Of course, the liturgy is only one aspect of the OCF that enables glocality. More research is needed into other practices, such as the Church's ecumenical and outreach work, for instance through organising icon-painting courses or summer camps, or employing multilingual clergy. All of these may contribute to the glocality of the Church. Yet, the prime movers in generating this hybrid nature are the participants themselves. They engage in all manners of artistry, to find a 'spiritual home' in the liturgy in the OCF. This feature complicates simple divisions of nationalization vs. transnationalization, or national vs. diasporic, in the OCF. However, further research is needed to determine whether such cross-overs also exist elsewhere, for instance in traditionally diasporic churches, where Orthodoxy is not afforded state encouragement.

It must also be noted that discovery of this spiritual home also signified the beginning of yet another journey of 'spiritual transformation' ([49], p. 190). 'To be on a journey', according to Bishop Kallistos Ware, is metaphorically applicable to each Orthodox Christian, as it emphasizes the practical character and spiritual depth of the living tradition, through the 'inward space of the heart' ([50], p. 7). Likewise, Durre Ahmed points to the archetypal significance of the journey as 'a symbolic trope signifying discovery or knowledge, not only of the physical world but more so of the psychological and spiritual' ([51], p. 3). The scope of this paper did not allow an illustration of the intrinsic dynamism which is pertinent to experiences of liturgy. The complex and productive nature of the tension between the modalities of home and journey, in experiences of liturgy, remains to be addressed in forthcoming research.

Acknowledgments: Foremost, sincere thanks are due to the interlocutors of this research, who generously entrusted the author with their life stories and shared their views and experiences. The author also expresses gratitude to all those in the parish for their discussions. In keeping with guidelines of research ethics, and requests of some interlocutors, names and locations have been carefully anonymized. The author also gratefully acknowledges Ali Qadir, University of Tampere, for his insightful comments on the paper. Research for this paper was financed by the project 'Tracking the Therapeutic: Ethnographies of Wellbeing, Politics and Inequality' at the University of Turku [grant number 289004, Academy of Finland, Suvi Salmenniemi PI].

Conflicts of Interest: The author declares no conflict of interest.

References

1. Kathy Rousselet, and Alexander Agadjanian. "Individual and Collective Identities in Russian Orthodoxy." In *Eastern Christians in Anthropological Perspective*. Edited by Chris Hann and Hermann Goltz. Oakland: University of California Press, 2010, pp. 265–79.
2. Victor Roudometof. *Globalization and Orthodox Christianity: The Transformations of a Religious Tradition*. New York and London: Routledge, 2014, p. 228.
3. Maria Hämmerli. "How Do Orthodox Integrate in their Host Countries? Examples from Switzerland." In *Orthodox Identities in Western Europe: Migration, Settlement and Innovation*. Edited by Maria Hämmerli and Jean-François Mayer. Farnham: Ashgate, 2014, pp. 115–32.
4. Victor Roudometof. "Orthodox Christianity as a transnational religion: Theoretical, historical and comparative considerations." *Religion, State and Society* 43 (2015): 211 27. [CrossRef]
5. Maria Hämmerli, and Jean-François Mayer, eds. *Orthodox Identities in Western Europe: Migration, Settlement and Innovation*. Farnham: Ashgate, 2014, p. 320.
6. Victor Roudometof, Alexander Agadjanian, and Jerry Pankhurst, eds. *Eastern Orthodoxy in a Global Age: Tradition Faces the Twenty-First Century*. Walnut Creek: Alta Mira Press, 2005, p. 290.
7. Robert H. Taft. *Liturgy in Byzantium and Beyond*. Varioum Aldershot: Variorum, 1995, p. 352.
8. Miguel Arranz. "Oko Tserkovnoe. Pererabotka Opyta LTD 1978 g. Istoriya Tipikona." Available online: http://www.miguel-arranz.net/files/oko_tcerkovnoe.pdf (accessed on 19 January 2017).
9. Arjun Appadurai. *Modernity at Large: Cultural Dimensions of Globalization*. Minneapolis: University of Minnesota Press, 1996, p. 248.
10. Steven Vertovec. *Transnationalism*. London: Routledge, 2009, p. 205.
11. Ulla Vuorela. "Meeting Sophia Mustafa—A Transnational Encounter." In *The Tanganyika Way. A Personal Story of Tanganyika's Growth to Independence*. Edited by Sophia Mustafa. Toronto: TSAR Publication, 2009, pp. 169–80.
12. Birgit Meyer. "Introduction: From Imagined Communities to Aesthetic Formations: Religious Mediations, Sensational Forms, and Styles of Binding." In *Aesthetic Formations: Media, Religion and the Senses*. Edited by Birgit Meyer. New York: Palgrave Macimillan, 2009, pp. 1–28.
13. David Morgan. *Sacred Gaze: Religious Visual Culture in Theory and Practice*. Berkeley: University of California Press, 2005, p. 333.

14. Birgit Meyer, and Jojada Verrips. "Aesthetics." In *Key Words in Religion, Media and Culture.* Edited by David Morgan. New York and London: Routledge, 2008, pp. 20–30.
15. Leonard Norman Primiano. "Vernacular Religion and the Search for Method in Religious Folklife." *Western Folklore* 54 (1995): 37–56. [CrossRef]
16. Tuomas Martikainen, and Teuvo Laitila. "Population Movements and Orthodox Christianity in Finland: Dislocations, Resettlements, Migrations and Identities." In *Orthodox Identities in Western Europe: Migration, Settlement and Innovation.* Edited by Maria Hämmerli and Jean-François Mayer. Farnham: Ashagate, 2014, pp. 151–78.
17. Juha Riikonen. "The Nationality Question in the Orthodox Church of Finland." In *The Two Folk Churches in Finland. The 12th Finnish Lutheran-Orthodox Theological Discussions 2014.* Edited by Tomi Karttunen. Translated by Rupert Moreton. Helsinki: National Church Council, Department for International Relations, 2015, pp. 96–104.
18. Helena Kupari. "'Remembering God' through Religious Habits: The Daily Religious Practices of Evacuee Karelian Orthodox Women." *Temenos* 47 (2011): 197–222.
19. Katariina Husso. *Ikkunoita Ikonien ja Kirkkoesineiden Historiaan: Suomen Ortodoksisen Kirkon Esineellinen Kulttuuriperintö 1920–1980-Luvuilla.* Helsinki: Suomen Muinaismuistoyhdistys, 2011, p. 256.
20. Tomi Karttunen, ed. *The Two Folk Churches in Finland. The 12th Finnish Lutheran-Orthodox Theological Discussions 2014.* Translated by Rupert Moreton. Helsinki: National Church Council, Department for International Relations, 2015, p. 105.
21. Väestökatsaus. "Ortodoksisen Kirkon Keskusrekisteri." Available online: https://www.ort.fi/keskusrekisteri (accessed on 16 December 2016).
22. John Anthony McGuckin. "Divine Liturgy. Orthodox." In *The Encyclopedia of Eastern Orthodox Christianity.* Edited by John Anthony McGuckin. Malden, Oxford and Chichester: Blackwell Publishing Ltd., 2011, vol. 1 (A–M), pp. 190–96.
23. Pavel Florensky. "Church Ritual as a Synthesis of the Arts." In *Pavel Florensky. Beyond Vision. Essays of the Perception of Art (1922).* Edited by Nicoletta Misler. Translated by Wendy Salmond. London: Reaktion Books, 2002, pp. 95–111.
24. John Meyendorff. "Liturgia, ili Vvedenie v dukhovnost' Vizantii." Available online: http://aliom.orthodoxy.ru/arch/004/004-meyend.htm (accessed on 15 December 2016).
25. Chris Hann, and Hermann Goltz. "Introducton. The Other Christianity? " In *Eastern Christians in Anthropological Perspective.* Berkeley: University of California Press, 2010, pp. 1–29.
26. Wilhelmiina Virolainen. "Suomenkielisen liturgian kehitys." *Ortodoksia* 52 (2013): 7–21.
27. Hilkka Seppälä. "Maan Tomu ylistää Luojaansa. Eräs lähtökohta Ortodoksisen Kirkkolaulun." *Ortodoksia* 52 (2013): 103–16.
28. Isä Hariton. "Tutuista tilkuista uusi vaate. Kirkkomusiikki tunnistaa kirkon perinteen." *Analogi* 2 (2012): 4–9.
29. Heikki Hanka. "Ortodoksinen kirkkoarkkitehtuuri Suomessa." In *Uskon tilat ja Kuvat. Moderni Suomalainen Kirkkoarkkitehtuuri ja –Taide.* Edited by Arto Kuorikoski. Helsinki: Suomalainen Teologinen Kirjallisuusseura, 2008, pp. 281–301.
30. Terhi Utriainen. "Language, Presence and Transforming Christianities Through the Anthropology and Sociology of Religion. Comment to John Bialecki." *Suomen Antropologi* 40 (2015): 47–51.
31. Akhil Gupta. "The Song of the Nonaligned World: Transnational Identities and the Reinscription of Space in Late Capitalism." In *The Anthropology of Space and Place: Locating Culture.* Edited by Setha M. Low and Denise Lawrence-Zuniga. Malden: Blackwell Publishing, 2003, pp. 321–36.
32. Birgit Meyer. "Mediation and Immidiacy: Sensational Forms, Semiotic Ideologies and the Question of the Medium." *Social Anthropology* 19 (2011): 23–39. [CrossRef]
33. Allaine Cerwonka, and Lisa Malkki. *Improvising Theory: Process and Temporality in Ethnographic Fieldwork.* Chicago: University of Chicago Press, 2007, p. 224.
34. Charlotte Aull Davies. *Reflexive Ethnography: A Guide to Researching Selves and Others*, 2nd ed. London: Routledge, 2008, p. 320.
35. Tatiana Tiaynen. *Babushka in Flux. Grandmothers and Family-making between Russian Karelia and Finland.* Tampere: Tampere University Press, 2013, 297p.
36. Nadieszda Kizenko. "Feminized Patriarchy? Orthodoxy and Gender in Post-Soviet Russia." *Signs: Journal of Women in Culture and Society* 38 (2013): 595–621. [CrossRef]

37. Juliet Johnson, Marietta Stepaniants, and Benjamin Forest, eds. *Religion and Identity in Modern Russia. The Revival of Orthodoxy and Islam.* Burlington: Ashgate Publishing Company, 2005.
38. Maija (woman of Finnish origins, aged 42), interviewed by Tatiana Tiaynen-Qadir, 3 March 2016, Finland.
39. Tatiana Tiaynen-Qadir. "Transnational Grandmothers Making Their Multi-sited Homes between Finland and Russian Karelia." In *Rethinking Home. Transnational Migration and Older Age.* Edited by Kati Walsh and Lena Näre. New York and London: Routledge, 2016, pp. 25–37.
40. Sara Ahmed. "Home and Away: Narratives of Migration and Estrangment." *International Journal of Cultural Studies* 2 (1999): 329–47. [CrossRef]
41. Vera (woman of Russian origins, aged 33), interviewed by Tatiana Tiaynen-Qadir, 31 January 2016, Finland.
42. Nikolay Sergeevich Mansurov. *Oshchushchenie—Subjektivnyi obraz Objektivnogo Mira.* Moskva: Vysshaya shkola, 1963, p. 117.
43. Tatiana Tiaynen-Qadir. "Orthodox Icons of Mary Generating Transnational Space between Finland and Russia." *Lähde Historiallinen Aikakauskirja*, 2016, 138–71.
44. Johanna (woman of Finnish origins, aged 50), interviewed by Tatiana Tiaynen-Qadir, 25 February 2016, Finland.
45. Marta (woman of Greek origins, aged 43), interviewed by Tatiana Tiaynen-Qadir, 15 March 2016, Finland.
46. Minna (woman of Finnish origins, aged 34), interview by Tatiana Tiaynen-Qadir, 7 September 2016, Finland.
47. Natalia (woman of Russian origings, aged 43), interview by Tatiana Tiaynen-Qadir, 5 January 2016, Finland.
48. Anfisa (woman of Russian origings, aged 35), interview by Tatiana Tiaynen-Qadir, 12 February 2016, Finland.
49. Rene Gothoni. *Tales and Truth. Pilgrimage on Mount Athos. Past and Present.* Helsinki: Helsinki University Press, 1994, p. 222.
50. Kallistos Ware. *The Orthodox Way*, New Rev. ed. Crestwood: St Vladimir's Seminary Press, 1995, p. 165.
51. Durre S. Ahmed. "The Journey. Buraq, Ihuley Lal and Zulljinnah." In *Mazaar, Bazaar. Design and Visual Culture in Pakistan.* Edited by Saima Zaidi. Karachi: Oxford University Press, 2011, pp. 2–9.

religions

MDPI

Article

Glocalization and Transnationalization in (neo)-Mayanization Processes: Ethnographic Case Studies from Mexico and Guatemala

Manéli Farahmand [1,2]

[1]   Institute for Social Sciences of Contemporary Religion, University of Lausanne, UNIL-Dorigny, Anthropole-Desk 5065, Lausanne 1015, Switzerland; maneli.farahmand@unil.ch; Tel.: +41-21-692-2738

[2]   Department of Classics and Religious Studies, University of Ottawa, Pavillon Desmarais, Laurier Ave. East, Ottawa, ON K1N 6N5, Canada

Academic Editors: Victor Roudometof and Peter Iver Kaufman
Received: 14 October 2015; Accepted: 30 December 2015; Published: 15 February 2016

Abstract: In this article, the author focuses on the field of neo-Mayanity and its current transformations. She analyzes these transformations using a historico-ethnographic approach, which includes two phases. The first one consists in reconstructing the historical development of the "Mayan" category in two different social contexts. The second one focuses on current narrative and imageries produced around this category, stemming from ethnographic fieldwork in Mexico and Guatemala. Since the "2012 phenomenon", in both countries, the accelerating transnationalization of the religious leaders has triggered a resignification of contents through various logics of rearrangement, innovation, cohabitation and glocalization. Finally, she demonstrates that the variations in the different ethnographies are linked with the religious leaders' biographies and the modes of signification of the "Mayan" category—influenced by the socio-historical contexts of production.

Keywords: glocalization; transnationalization; Central America; neo-Mayanity; 2012 phenomenon

1. Introduction

In his public conference about the "Mayan calendar", the Californian author Xan Xel Lugold[1] answers the question: "Where did the Mayans get their information from in the first place?"[2]:

"We do not precisely know. They have their own legends. The legends are all we actually know about it. Their legends tell that a person, or a god, named Itzamma, came down to the Mayan people and delivered information about language, writing, mathematics and the calendar. So they received this information as a gift. Where Itzamma came from, and where he went, we do not really know. And frankly, it is none of our business to know where they got it. It is much more important what we do with this information now. [. . .]. We have added to this information, with all the science we now have, and it's come more to complete the circle[3]."

This quote reflects the approximation of Westerners' representations of the Mayans as distant people with mysterious legends and prophecies whose history and mythological tales we do not really know. This definitional blur around the Mayans echoes the controversy about the circulation

---

[1]   This independent author is close to a U.S. stream that emerged between 1980 and 2000, called "Mayanist," and composed of independent researchers connected with Californian New-Age circles, which proposes a new reading of the Mayan calendars [1,2].
[2]   His most famous public conference is published in eighteen parts on YouTube. See [3].
[3]   [3], part 9, 3 min.

of representations into the context of cultural globalization. This blur is consistent with the current spread of decontextualized, dehistoricized, recycled and wrongly re-attributed information. The "neo-colonialist" attitude behind these inter-cultural appropriations troubles an entire generation of activist natives; however, some of the natives also contribute to the transnationalization of their representations. This controversy mainly drives the debates about "authenticity" [4]. The "2012 phenomenon"[4] is an example: the Mayans and their "prophecies" found a strong resonance in our Western cultures, thanks to an audience that has been in search of alternative visions since the 1980s. This quote also reminds us of a Gregory Lassalle documentary film *From Art Drifts to Oil Drifts* (2012). The movie denounces the culturalist and capitalist attitude behind the organization of the 2011 exhibition "Mayan—from Dawn to Dusk" hosted at the Museum of Quai Branly in Paris (see, [5]). The exhibition opened under the patronage of Perenco, a multinational oil company working near the archaeological sites where the exhibited pieces were found. It displays "the Guatemalan Mayan civilization", highlighting the aesthetics of "cosmovisions"[5] and traditional expertise such as weaving without any social or political contextualization regarding the "contemporary Mayans." An awkward silence remains concerning the living conditions and the daily struggles of Mayan people [6]. In his article "We Are *Not* Indigenous!" [7], Quetzil Castañeda endeavors to deconstruct the Western stereotypes and beliefs around the word "Mayan." Tourists, NGOs, media, politicians and New Agers are among the many agents who participate in the construction of a fantasized and romantic image of the "Mayans." Their image vacillates between excessive victimization, hyper-spiritualization, militance and aestheticization emptied of its political contents ([7], pp. 36–38). "Mayan" has thus become a transhistorical, homogeneous and abstract category existing in another dimension outside space and time.

The age of globalization enhances inter-cultural exchanges and interactions, enabling articulations between different symbolic systems. Connections between "New Age"[6] and Mayan cosmovisions have been particularly fertile since the 1990s, evident in the many products of imagination inspired by the "2012 phenomenon." The kitsch aesthetics of the ceremonies and their apparently artificial splendor make the journalists smile. Some anthropologists avoid studying neo-Mayan groups because they challenge conventional disciplinary assumptions about authenticity and tradition. In secularized contexts such as Switzerland, these Mayan-New-Age representations are overlooked in the media as figures of kitsch exoticism. Leaders of Mayan-New-Age groups are depicted as socially non-integrated. In reality, fieldwork shows that the activities of Westerners who simultaneously propagate and revise "Mayan wisdom" are not peripheral. Instead, they are socially integrated, urban and upper-middle-class, with unlimited access to postmodern technologies. The activities take place in city centers where they can purchase high quality audio-visual accessories to accompany their practice and downloadable meditation guides that are accessible from iPhone devices. Overall, neo-Mayan perfectly fit the economic model of neoliberal societies, without necessarily adopting its values. Meanwhile, American pan-Indian movements denounce the non-native economic exploitation of their symbolic resources and participate in the international legal struggle for gaining recognition and protection of their cultural and intellectual property rights (see, [8]). The field of neo-Mayanism is therefore filled with global challenges that extend beyond the frameworks of national borders.

As Peter Beyer writes, in studying contemporary transformations of religious phenomena, we question current expressions of social changes ([9], p. 428). Unlike the Mayan-New-Age, the formerly pejoratively connoted word "Mayan" today enjoys a mainly positive connotation in the public sphere

---

[4] By "2012 phenomenon", we mean here the different narratives about the "end of the world" or "end of a world", the mythological origins of which have often been attributed to the "Mayans". The date 12 December 2012, essentially, would have been finding, from the 1980s on, various millenarianist echoes in some circles linked with the North-American New-Age *milieu*, before circulating through new spiritual globalized networks ([1], p. 25).

[5] An indigenous understanding of the world centered on the interrelation between human beings, nature and the cosmos.

[6] The notion of "New Age" will be defined later. In a broad sense, we mean here the vast spiritual movement born in California between 1970s and 1980s, characterized by hope in the succession of a new era called "Aquarius".

as a fashionable ethnic category. In my ethnographic fieldwork this notion is revisited in terms of spirituality, gender equality and harmonious relationship with nature. It is synonymous with "universal love", "peace", "unity" and "interconnectedness of all the elements." This ethnic category has been currently updated within the same cultures that once condemned its symbolic aspects. Although some "Mayans" in certain regions such as Yucatan in southeast Mexico Hispanicized their names in the 1950s to avoid social and ethnic stigmatization ([10], p. 466), bearing a "Mayan" label is now a source of social pride and cultural capital [11]. The "Mayan" category is becoming a tool for making political demands, a place for spiritual creativity and a mode of identification that extends far beyond the traditional criteria of ethnicity and native family ties.

2. Research Questions and Ethnographic Methods

2.1. Research Questions

The general goal of this article is to analyze the contemporary transformations of the symbolic field of Mayanity through two cases taken from fieldwork in Guatemala (Quetzaltenango) and Mexico (Yucatan)[7]. Central to this mutation process, this field will be referred to as "neo-Mayanism" to designate its contemporary "transnationalized" and "glocalized" manifestations. Mayanism and its "neo" expressions are geographically multi-localized. Personally, I have observed them in Guatemala, Switzerland and various areas of Mexico and Germany. The concept of "field" is to be understood here as defined by P. Bourdieu [12], according to a semantic acceptation as a "structured space" composed of sub-fields and traversed by conflicts, power struggles, struggles for symbolic legitimacy and other specific issues that will be covered by this article.

Theoretically, the main purpose of this article is to demonstrate one of the specificities of this symbolic field, namely, that it has been growing in a "glocal" manner since the "2012 phenomenon", which has been affecting the traditional ways of identifying "Mayan ethnicity". More than a tension or a contradictory dynamics between particularization and universalization, my perspective integrates the dimension of the production of local meanings through transnationalization. Following the work of Sophie Bava, Stefania Capone [13], Renée de la Torre, Kali Argyriadi [14] and André Mary [15], I differentiate the concepts of "globalization" and "transnationalization". I write about the effects of "transnationalization" rather than "globalization" to refer to the local reproductions linked with the flux of people, knowledge, practices and information coming from Central America to the hegemonic extra-continental poles, in the political meaning of a shift of cultural axis of influence. Not merely affecting the traditional ways of identifying "Mayan ethnicity", the "glocal" construction of the symbolic field of Mayanity shall be seen as the very condition of its innovation by the rearrangement of contents.

By means of this neologization, I mean significations and new uses of images, contents, objects and ritual practices that are undergoing the process of social legitimization, which are not yet recognized as "new historical purities" [9]. The "2012 phenomenon" has been one, if not the only, source of the transnationalization of the field of Mayanity. It has intensified the leaders' mobility and accelerated the circulation of contents. Since "2012", the recuperation movements of Mayan traditions have been pluralized. Nowadays, the field is even more heterogeneous than in the past, driven by a variety of actors, views and trajectories, varying among regions and groups. Despite this great internal diversity, and following the analyses of the anthropologist Stefania Capone on common references to Yoruba culture in Orisha religion [16], the Mayanity field distinguishes itself by the claim of "Mayan" origin by all its actors, and/or by the common acceptance, on a partial or integral level, of discourses and practices emically attached to this category. This diversity does not prevent its actors from being guided by precise logics, either. Among these dynamics, we can point out, along

---

[7]   I shall return to the "Mayan" category.

with glocalization and transnationalization, logics of gender, revitalization, therapeutization, spiritual politicization-depoliticization, innovation of contents and new forms of "religious *butinage*" (religious picking). *Butinage*, in the religious field, is a mobile and creative way to develop and fertilize one's symbolic universe and enhance it by bringing each element gathered (the "fruit") from the other universes to it, following a multi-directional movement ([17], p. 30). The *butineur* produces new "hybrid" elements in its process [18]. All these processes are interconnected, producing an internal coherence. This article will focus on the first processes—glocalization and transnationalization—that will be illustrated by ethnographic examples from fieldwork in Mexico and Guatemala.

Broadly, revitalization is the logic predominating over all the others. It is shown at the individual level by forms of auto-identification, nuanced by exogenous attributions, and/or "identitary appropriations"[8], both intra-cultural and inter-cultural. Among these appropriative forms, the assembled ethnographic material brings into contrast two general movements: "Mayanization" and "New-Ageization". The ethnographic material enables us to distinguish different types of Mayanization and New-Ageization. Literature and empirical data allow me to list the following variety of forms:

(1) The processes of intra-national "Mayanizations" (such as Mayan Yoga, Mayan Kung Fu, Mayan osteopathy promoted by Mexican mixed-race or the Mayanization of the identity of a mixed-race group). These processes are accompanied by a discursive Mayanization of origins.

(2) The intra-ethnic "Mayanizations" (such as the discourses of revitalization in activist terms delivered by the K'iche' of Quetzaltenango or the Tsotziles[9] from Chiapas).

(3) New Age appropriations of all kinds (for instance, the spiritualization and millenarianization of the 2012 phenomenon in Switzerland, or the New-Ageization of the Mayan sweat lodge).

(4) An intra-ethnic New-Ageization (for example, natives who integrate a New Age reinterpretation of their communitarian practices).

These various forms are the results of the first analyses. The notion of "Mayanization" must be understood here as the concept developed by S. Bastos in order to analyze the symbolic extent of "Mayan movements" in Guatemala and their modalities of reception and reformulation among *outsiders* (the state, the Catholic churches, the cooperative agents and private authorities) ([20], p. 9). For Bastos, this process means the action of spreading Mayan discourses and symbolic systems beyond the organizational borders, among actors who are located outside the structures that generate these discourses ([20], pp. 11–12). These actors appropriate and reinterpret those symbolic systems, which are therefore being transformed ([20], p. 12). For this research, I extend Bastos's interpretation to the appropriation of diverse practices and objects coming from distant cultures, accompanied by a discursive Mayanization of origins (e.g., Mayan Yoga, Mayan Kung Fu or Mayan osteopathy). Another dynamic that emerges in the field and acts as a factor of differentiation is the dichotomy between the politicized and activist Mayanity on the one hand and the non-politicized Mayan New-Age on the other hand. This dichotomy is also illustrated by regional oppositions between, first, the militant Mayanities of Guatemala and Chiapas (Mexico) and, second, the less militant Mayanities of the Yucatan peninsula (Mexico).

2.2. Ethnographic Methods

On the ethnographic level, I have opted for mobility within mobility, since I traveled from one research site to another according to exterior events, and independently of the actors' movements. This model of "itinerant ethnography" ([14], p. 21) made me "pick" [17] into different places of production of Mayanity. I have brought back with me every element picked from the various research sites in a single frame of study to develop my own ethnographic viewpoint.

---

[8] The expression is borrowed from Christina Welch, which she uses in her analyses of the inter- and intra-cultural reappropriations of the Native-American *sweat lodge* and Aborigine *didgeridoo* [4].

[9] Here in its historical meaning as an ethnolinguistic designation linked to a territory [19].

In my interview sample, all the interviewees had a common denominator: a shared sense of proximity with the "Mayans"—the common feeling of "Mayanity"—which varied according to their relationship to the broader category of "Mayan", ranging from imaginary lineages [21] to real territorial and linguistic rooting, all of these being subject to particularisms. Thus, my sample is not randomly developed; it is inductive, thematic and cumulative. The character of the "Mayanity" claimed by various actors reflects the existence of a field, with borders, linking people into a network between Switzerland, Mexico, Germany and Guatemala, as many particular cases that fall within a transnational space. Therefore, while "2012" contributed to transnationalization, it converted me to the logic of "multi-site" ethnographic mobility, following the work of George E. Marcus [22].

For data collection, I have used direct participant observation, paying particular attention to the contents of the discourses and practices. In the tradition of qualitative research, I have also used biographic open-ended "narrative interviews"[10], mainly that of "life histories", a tool of ethno-sociology [23,24]. The life histories focused on the interviewees "spiritual and therapeutic journeys" [25], in order to sort out the different levels of discourses, similarities or differences among them, and therefore assist with understanding the interviewees' patterns and logics of participation. In-depth interviewing with a loose thematic discussion guide wasalso used to supplement participant observation, especially when focusing on contextual and synchronous elements or organizational aspects rather than on individual life-journeys [26]. A total of fifty-two interviews were conducted between 2012 and 2015.

The interviews' content analysis used the Nvivo qualitative analysis software program in order to analyze and code the collected empirical data (interviews, written sources, fieldwork journals and audio-visual sequences). This mode of categorization—based on empirical data—is similar to the approach recommended by *grounded theory* [27,28]. However, through a series of successive steps, conceptualization has also been adjusted, shaped and inspired by the author's broader theoretical framework. The codes used to classify the empirical data are therefore the fruits of a logic that is both inductive and deductive.

3. Mayan Ethnicity in Different Socio-Historical Contexts

3.1. The "Mayan" Category

In Latin America, the terms Mixed-Race, *Ladinos*, Indigenous, Natives and Mayan have no meaning on their own; they change according to times, points of view and situations. Behind this difficult question of ethnic designation, passionate historiographical debates question and deconstruct the notion of ethnicity, social classification and local policies of identity categorization. My ethnographic work took place between 2014 and 2015, mostly in the Yucatan peninsula, in Southeast Mexico.

The peninsula shelters the states of Quintana Roo, Campeche and Yucatan. The capital of Yucatan is Merida. Merida is a colonial city, which has experienced important urban growth since the nineteenth century. The city constitutes the main space framing most of my observations. The 1990 national censuses reveal that 30% of the peninsula population speak Yucatan Mayan ([10], p. 460). The data presented in this article also come from my exploratory research in Quetzaltenango, a state in southeast Guatemala mainly populated with "K'iche Mayans" [29].

From a historical point of view, the generic term "Mayan" constitutes a polysemic ethnolinguistic notion, which has been historically and socially elaborated ([30], p. 134). For anthropologists and archaeologists in the 1940s, it represents the "linguistic label of native populations" ([30], p. 143) living in southeast Mexico, Belize, Guatemala, western Honduras and Salvador. The exact definitions of the populations named by this category are to be found in the various national constitutions. Nowadays,

---

[10] More or less one hour and a half per interview.

the word has been widely recovered by movements, organizations and social actors as an identity category, enabling the formulation of political claims and the struggle for recognition ([30], p. 143). If one looks at this category as a state designation, in Mexico, for example, it identifies "ethno-linguistic communities" linked to a certain territory: the Yucatan Mayan (Yucatan peninsula), the Lacandons (eastern Chiapas), the Chols (northeast of Chiapas), the Tzeltales and Tzotziles (center and North Chiapas), the Tojolabales (southern Tzeltales Chiapas), the Mames (southern Chiapas, near the border with Guatemala), and the Chontals (Tabasco) ([19], pp. 46–78). If one considers this category under the angle of "indigenous people", the well-known political and legal expression in institutional discourses, it is also related to territorial, linguistic and lineage rooting ([31], p. 31).

3.2. Mayan Ethnicity in Yucatan (Mexico)

Yucatan is prominent in *Mayan Studies*. In this area, the uses and ways of identifying the "Mayan" category differ from those of Chiapas or Guatemala, notably because of the specificity of its history, from colonization to the Mexican revolutions ([7], p. 38). For example, the Yucatan "Mayan" have never been the objects of transnational media effervescence, which the Zapatista and Guatemalan social movements have known [7]. The anthropologist Quetzil Castañeda showed that, in this peninsula, the Mayan-speaking people have even distanced themselves from the category, declaring: "we are *not* indigenous" ([7], p. 38). This dis-identification makes one think about the "Mayan ethnicity" category, for this sole example challenges linguistic criteria of ethnic differentiation, reminding us of the importance of Frédéric Barth's contribution to the debate about ethnicity and his effort to define it as a mobile, unfixed category whose borders are endlessly reshaped by social actors according to specific strategies [32].

The historico-anthropological analyses in the collection *The Maya Identity of Yucatan, 1500–1935: Re-Thinking Ethnicity, History and Anthropology?* [33] address the question of "Mayan ethnicity" and its historical mutations between 1500 and 1935. Specifically, these studies adopt a critical perspective on the issue of Maya's ethnic boundaries. These studies show that, in the peninsula, the term "Mayan" has been coined with regard to public policies and not in response to a dominant-subordinate relationship. People designated in this way have used the term in a selected, re-conceptualized and calculated manner, responding to the colonial and state "interpellation" in order to negotiate specific modes of governance ([33], p. 46). These authors demonstrate that, unlike in Guatemala, the elaboration of ethnicity has been mutual between the state and the social group in question, and has not been horizontally defined against other ethnic groups (mixed-race, *ladinos*). Quetzil Castañeda draws the conclusion that, substantially speaking, in Yucatan, "Mayan" does not exist. The texts of this collection break off from the scientific paradigms of continuity, notably approved by the North American literature. Despite the spatial continuity with the pre-Hispanic civilizations, the socio-cultural developments since colonization have created, for these authors, temporal and socio-demographic ruptures.

In his article about the development of ethnic categories in Yucatan and their individual uses in social interactions from the sixteenth century on, Wolfgang Gabbert [10] strongly criticizes the advocates of the continuity thesis. He also denounces the recent use of genetic and cultural criteria to argue in favor of categorical unity ([10], p. 462). He aims to analyze ethnicity not through "ethnic" lenses, but rather through its underlying logics and strategic uses, according to different social contexts ([10], p. 463). Following the work of F. Barth, this approach conceives ethnicity as the result of a historical process continuously reproduced by social actors in their ongoing pursuit of social specification and resource negotiation with the state. Moreover, there would be no empiric proof underlining any shared ethnic conscience between *indios* or *indígenas* of the colonial era and those of the end of the nineteenth century. This social category would have been vertically imposed on a genetic criteria basis, without any auto-identification from the people. Gabbert also points out the absence of ethno-linguistic differentiation criteria during colonial time, since people of mixed-race and some *ladinos* (the other social categories of the time) also spoke fluent Yucatan Mayan. According to him, it was after the resistance movements of the Caste War that the negative connotations of the term *indios* emerged, and that those perceptions were slowly adopted by the *indios*. It was only from the twentieth century on, after the ideological impact of the Mexican revolutions in Yucatan (1910–1917), that these categories would have seen a slight improvement together with the beginning of the Indigenist public policies, although they were still associated with the lower classes ([10], p. 474).

From the second half of the twentieth century, the expansion of the tourism industry and the policies of peninsular folklorization have given an elitist semantic impetus to the category: the "Yucatan Mayan" were then stereotypically associated with the pre-Hispanic civilization and its great advancements, without any concern for the day-to-day socio-economic realities of Yucatan workers and peasants. From the 1970s on, the native elite of Yucatan, from the educated milieu closely associated with or active in the indigenist movement, has brought a semantic change to the word in the public space, by initiating a process of revitalization and preservation (in the political meaning of cultural revitalization of language, folklore, *etc.*). Natives who, until then, had privileged the terms "*mestizo, mayero, campesino, gente del pueblo...*" have accepted those ethnicizing terms. Now, the identification of *Indio* with *Mayan* has become common and turned into a symbolic asset to claim negotiate state resources ([10], p. 466), but the revitalization movements have never gained the importance of the national Mayan movement in Guatemala. W. Gabbert reminds us of the importance of differentiating the social categories that shape Yucatan society, the groups based on them and the individuals that use them practically ([10], p. 479).

3.3. Mayan Movements in Guatemala

In contrast to the situation in Yucatan, in Guatemala the historiography of the Mayan movements' development focuses on the activist and socio-economic dimension of the people's identification with the "Mayan" label. In Guatemala, the close connection between religion and politics is obvious. That is because of the particularly violent history of conflicts. This history includes a series of authoritarian governments between 1821 and 1944; repeated agrarian conflicts; exploitation of the native work force; armed violent conflict between 1960 and 1996 accompanied by sexual violence; and criminalization of social protest [34]. The religious realm is analyzed as a "political space", a tool for identitary reformulations interacting with the public space and its modalities of intervention [35].

In Guatemala, it is within the internally fragmented "Mayan movements" that this revitalization and resignification of the "Mayan" category is most often found ([20], p. 19). Their principal leaders entered the public space in the 1960s, during the waves of protest against the agrarian reforms [29,36,37]. Their decisive appearance on the national stage took place during the 1992 commemoration of colonization and was marked by their radical willingness to distance themselves from Catholicism. These movements are politicized and seek revitalization, rediscovery and reaffirmation of "Mayan lore, values and beliefs" ([37], p. 13). They are organized around the promotion of cultural self-determination, reconstruction of the "Mayan identity" and political participation [36,38].

In Guatemala, this context of reformulation of the "Mayan identity" within Mayan movements—going through politicization, claims and cultural revitalization processes—is the one that supports the positive and fulfilling acceptance of the "Mayan ethnicity" within the frame of social interactions. This analysis allows Bastos to highlight the located and historically contingent aspect of ethnic classifications in Guatemala ([20], p. 16). For M. Macleod, this category implies a whole "cosmovision", that is, an understanding of the world centered on the interrelation between human beings, nature and the cosmos, which is also a resistance tool for contestation, redefinition of gender relations, and even, at some point, a resource for women's struggles for equality and emancipation [34]. In fact, my exploratory research in Guatemala and the time spent with a K'iche' Mayan human rights activist confirm this perception of cosmovision as an engine of secular conflicts; symbolic K'iche' references structure the contents of socio-political activities.

The difference between the activist and politicized Mayanity of Guatemala and the non-politicized Mayanity of Yucatan thus lies in the different relationships, socially and historically developed, with "Mayan ethnicity". The 2012 phenomenon is another indicator of these differences. In Guatemala, the date of 21 December 2012, has probably been the most recent source of blending between the religious and political registers for Mayan movements. In my view, this date has roots in two opposite poles: activist Mayanity and New Age Mayanity. The works of Santiago Bastos, Engel Tally and Marcelo Zamora [39], and Morna Macleod [40,41] about "2012" in Guatemala have shown that the phenomenon triggered the creation of a whole range of views and activities of a politico-spiritual type. In a recent comparative analysis on the same subject [42], I have demonstrated how "2012" has been generating various appropriations from one cultural context to another, according to the political angle. In the French-speaking part of Switzerland, in a secularized context, this date appears again in a chronology built by Judeo-Christian communications associated with an apolitical New Age vision of history. On the contrary, in Guatemala, it is mainly signified by Mayan activists, who revisit it through human rights discourses. The fieldwork conducted in Mexico among New Age Mayan groups also reveals the apolitical and therapeutic-spiritual relationship to "2012".

4. Toward a New Age Mayanity in Mexico?

4.1. Socio-Religious Contexts

In Mexico, the publication in 1988 of Arthur Velasco Piña's novel *Regina* [43] marks the beginning of the indigenous revivalisms in continuity with the student movements of 1968 [44]. This book announces the start of a "new era" in Mexico. It is inspired both by the prophecy announced in *La mujer dorminda debe dar a Luz* (1970)[11] and by the coming of the "Age of Aquarius" that, according to New Age philosophies, unfolds from the figure of Regina. Historically, Regina is a young Mexican student murdered during the student movements of 1968 in Mexico City. But the fictionalized part tells that she died in a sacrifice to her mission, activating the "cosmic energy" of two Mexican volcanoes to fulfill a prophecy. According to this prophecy, Mexico or its "chakra" represents the geographical axis of the new era, and its activation will happen through the restoration of pre-Hispanic traditions ([44], p. 105).

This myth is one of the pillars of "Mexicanity", a post-68 "cultural, political and spiritual movement", supported by foreigners or mixed-race middle-class Mexicans with a certain level of education who live in urban areas ([44], p. 187) and give themselves the goal of revitalizing the native identities in Mexico on the basis of an idealized reinterpretation of the past and an archetypal image of the native people ([44], p. 96). The streams of Mexicanity are heterogeneous, both on the ideological level (belief in the extra-terrestrial beings, New Age inspirations, apology of native culture's superiority, exclusion of any Western elements, *etc.*) and on the level of the activities (pre-Hispanic astronomy and mathematics, ritual dances, traditional medicine, conservation of the oral traditions, interpretations of the codices, handicrafts, Mexicanist arts, rituals in the public spaces, mainly in the archaeological sites, with commemorations of the historic dates of natural events such as equinoxes, *etc.*) ([44], pp. 97–98). Literature divides this movement into two tendencies: "radical Mexicanism" [44], also called "mexicayotl", and "neo-Mexicanism" [45]. The first one is politicized, anti-Western and anti-syncretic and praises the "purity of the Indian race" ([44], p. 101; [45], p. 183). The second one is more spiritualized and pluralistic, and is part of a global program of a New Age type.

American ethnologists A. Molinié and J. Galinier have observed a similar socio-religious phenomenon in Mexico, but describe it through the use of a different terminology [46]. The Mexican cultural-religious stage of the 1990s is seen as one in which "new forms of Indianity" emerge and become public during the celebration of the Fifth Centenary of colonization [1992] ([46], p. 27). They describe this new phenomenon as "new-Indianity" that builds itself by mirroring the images

---

[11] It consists of the adventure of a young Mexican initiated into the "sacred traditions of Mexico and Tibet". In Tibet, this young man is told of the existence of a prophecy foretelling that Mexico "is to become one of the most important places for the awakening of the new sacred culture" ([44], p. 103). Personal translation.

of Indianity that Westerners—mainly New Agers—provide. Like neo-Mexicanity, neo-Indianity paradoxically establishes itself between the "particularism inside the local" and a "worldwide message" of spreading "cosmic energy" ([46], pp. 9, 187). Its leaders are generally non-native ([46], p. 17), and consider themselves as "pure" as the rural Indians whose poor socio-economic conditions they deny. ([46], p. 9). As far as mythology is concerned, its origins could be traced back to the issue of V. Piña's *Regina*, while its historical premises would be placed in the nineteenth century, during the reconstruction of the national identity and the Indigenist programs ([46], p. 93).

The anthropologists Renée de la Torre, Cristina Gutiérrez Zúniga and Nahayeilli Juárez Huet link all these "neo-cosmovisionary" tendencies to the spread of the New Age in Latin America from the 1970s on, and to its effect on the processes of construction of the ethnic identities [47]. To them, the New Age is not to be defined in its substance, but as a "matrix of meaning" or a frame for "holistic reinterpretation", which was already hybrid in its own roots. In Latin America, this hybrid-holistic grid of reading provoked "new religious hybridizations" on a cultural ground already in a "syncretic" relationship with Catholicism. Therefore, there are three levels of syncretism—syncretism on the Mexican ground, New Age syncretism and New Age syncretization. In Latin America "popular actors" assimilated this matrix of meaning, which they re-signifiy and re-contextualize with a goal of cultural resistance to exogeneity. On the contrary, New Agers appropriated local traditions by essentializing them within a quest for Indianity, ancestrality and authenticity ([47], p. 15).

4.2. Toward New Identification Modes to Mayan Ethnicity: Ethnographic Examples

The personal names used in the following sections are fictional; the interviewees remain anonymous. In a café in Merida, Ricardo told me several times: "*no soy Maya . . . No lo necesitamos por ser en esta espiritualidad*" (in reference to the "SolarMayan Tradition") ("I am not Mayan . . . We don't need to be to enter this spirituality"). He said everyone follows their "*camino espiritual*" ("spiritual path") and let themselves be carried by the "*rueda de la vida*" ("the wheel of life") "*que te trae lo que tu ser necesita en el momento mismo*", ("which brings you what your being needs at the present moment"), "*cuando estas listo*" ("when you are ready") "*Fluye Manéli*" ("let it be, Manéli") [48]. The discussion with this painter from Quintana Roo, who uses a Mayan imagery, lasted several hours. He did not want a formal interview, nor to tell his life story. I asked no more than one or two questions, which he answered vaguely. He told me to "turn off my intellect" and said that I would remember the information "on a vibratory level", the memory of which would fully return when I awoke the next day. He tried to lead me in a form of hypnosis, showing me his Mayan paintings and telling me to feel them. He maintained the course of speech at a regular rhythm, but spoke few words.

The permanent members of the Solar Mayan Tradition (SMT) do not define themselves as an ethnic or cultural group; none of them has Mayan roots. The general coordinator speaks of "spiritual tradition born from a solar lineage", through a process of "reincarnation" [49]. The SMT is an organization whose seat is in Merida, led by the "Venerable Mother Nah Kin", a Mexican mixed-race woman who graduated with a degree in social psychology and studied with spiritual leaders from various traditions. The leaders of this particular movement, called "Ahaukanes", have given themselves the mission to "save the spirituality of pre-Hispanic Mayan civilizations", which they also call "Solar Mayan" or "Cosmic Mayanfrom the Golden Age". This reading of Mayanity is New Age, since a central place is given to millenarianism ("new paradigm" theorization), the therapeutic contribution and "personal transformation", accompanied by a rejection of the institutional religious models. One of the heirs of the movement also told me that one does not need to be "Mayan" to join this group [50]. However, most of the members—all of whom are non-native and many of whom are foreigners mostly upper-middle-class urban women who pursued higher education—consider themselves to be "reincarnations" of those "Cosmic Mayans". Personalized interviews with most of the members confirmed this personal conviction attached to the feeling of having been Mayan "in another life". In this group, the lineage is imagined, in reference to Danièle Hervieu-Léger's concept [21]; modalities of belonging to the category come from a spiritualized vision of lineage, accompanied by the Hindu philosophy of "reincarnation". From this deep conviction of being Mayan by reincarnation flows this idea of a "mission" that they should propagate an important and "cosmic" message to the world.

In 2015, Ricardo was the first young non-Mayan man to join the Council of Mexico Mayan Elders as an "initiated member" (with a voice and a vote inside the Council). The Council of the Elders is an association located in Merida with a long history of struggle for the promotion and defense of indigenous cultures of Mexico. The permanent members are traditionally from a masculine lineage of ethno-linguistic Mayan with a specific spiritual function within the tradition. Ricardo was born in Mexico City, but has Oaxacan Mixtec and Zapotec roots. During this long interview about his biographical narrative and his Mayan therapeutic practices ("Mayan acupuncture", "Mayan massage", "Pre-Hispanic Sound-Healing"), Ricardo told me that he "felt Mayan in his heart" [51]. His relationship with Mayan culture is internalized, affective, at the level of subjective feeling.

These examples illustrate the various relationships different people have to the Mayan label and the difficulty in determining a single common denominator capable of uniting the entire symbolic field. The individuals and the groups at the heart of this research are all "Mayan" in an arbitrary sense. They claim being "Mayan" in a unilateral manner in order to distinguish themselves at a social level, without necessarily adhering to the criteria of Indianity or ancestral descent, irrespective of whether these are construed in a genealogical, linguistic or territorial manner. But what about the exogenous dimension of social categorization (official historiography and discourse of public institutions)?

Here the issue of underlying social logics becomes an interesting one, because it is intertwined with various socio-historical processes. To capture this intertwining, I use the prefix "neo" in a twofold way. First, I use "neo-" to capture the chronological signification that is reflected in the expression "neo-Indian"—the emergence of new forms of Indianity that can be observed in Mexico since the nineties ([46], p. 7). Second, I use "neo-" in the way Renée de la Torre and Cristina Gutiérrez Zúñiga have used it: as a way to register the "new identitary generations" born from the encounter between "local specificities" and ideas related to New Age as these are circulated around the globe in worldwide networks ([47], p. 155). The prefix "neo" signals precisely this encounter between local and global and is reflected in the words neo-tradition, neo-religion, neo-Mexicanity, neo-Indian, neo-ethnic, and other words. These words imply the "re-characterization" of traditional practices ([47], p. 18).

5. Transnationalization and Glocalization

The social-scientific literature that analyzes the relationship between religion and globalization often includes under this heading the topic of religious transnationalization. However, while the concepts of "globalization", "glocalization", "internationalization", "transnationalism" and "transnationalization" are all inter-related, these terms also refer to different socio-cultural processes. Globalization is frequently discussed in terms of its impact upon the construction of individual and collective identities. Its effects are often described in terms of "*bricolage*, mixing, creolization and hybridization" ([52], p. 91). The debates about transnationalization stress the analysis of the processes of deterritorialization and reterritorialization, and the relationships of governance that cross the "transnational social field" [53] and its networks of actors.

The transnationalization of religion is also studied in terms of paradoxical logics or "trans-logics": those twin discourses that involve binary oppositions between homogenization and fragmentation, or between universalization and particularization ([15], p. 38). Anthrolopogists of religious transnationalization tend to prefer linguistic to biological metaphors in this context. Therefore, the term "resignification" is more appropriate here than the terms "mixing" and "hybridization" (in the organic sense) ([15], p. 39). The reception, reappropriation and resignification dynamics in cultural contexts of reterritorialization are analyzed as predetermined by presignified universes, in reference to Levi-Strauss's concept of "*bricolage*", of which the activity, applied to myths, "acts on the permutability of culturally structural elements historically predetermined" [54].

The word "globalization" now refers to the "the economic, political, social and cultural new logics" enabling the "circulation and consumption of material and immaterial goods" and the emergence of "transnational actors" ([55], p. 10). Globalization implies growing "inter-connections" beyond national borders, and covering long distances ([56], p. 17). The number of "inter-connections" is increased through new technologies—the Internet in particular—but also through "networks", structures linking places, crossed by fluxes of "persons, goods, information, significations, values, knowledge and ritual models" ([13], p. 244).

In the Anglo-Saxon literature, the term "transnationalism" was coined in the field of Migration Studies in the 1990s. The term represents the researchers' efforts to account for both the cross-border flows of people and cultural items, and for the social relationships that connect home countries and host nations by crossing over the physical borders of nation-states ([13], p. 237). The introduction of this concept allows us to focus on the links between "non-institutional actors" compare to the notion of "internationalization" that rather defines the (inter-)state relationships and activities ([15], p. 28) and [13], p. 237). "Transnationalism" supports an ideology describing both a political process opposed to the one of globalization and a "quality intrinsic to social phenomena", which reveals an anti-hegemonic and marginal posture ([15], pp. 27–28). It is later replaced by the concept of "transnationalization" in the religious realm, underlining the idea of a multidirectional process. This allows studying not only deterritorialization modalities, but also reterritorialization strategies and re-adaptation in different contexts ([13], p. 242). S. Capone thus postulates that the "process of deterritorialization rarely occurs without a subsequent reterritorialization". She adds that, while reference points, roots or boundaries may be dissolved or displaced, there is a concomitant production of discourse about origins, enabling what has been "deterritorialized" to be re-anchored in new real or symbolic spaces" ([25], p. 11). Therefore, transnationalization provokes a multiplication of "reference spaces" for a tradition and its roots, on a background of relationships of "power and prestige" ([25], pp. 16–17).

Because of the politicized dimension of the term transnationalism and of the reversed itineraries of transnationalization, contemporary anthropological literature stands apart from the notion of "globalization", and its evocation of an upward transnationalization, coming from the missionary neo-colonial societies, which is to say from the globalized centers to marginal peripheral areas ([14], p. 13). Another criticism is that the concept of "globalization" would not let us grasp all the phases of the process; it conceals, notably, the steps of appropriation and re-signification ([14], p. 13). Specifically, the bearing actors of (neo)-Mayanity come from Latin America to the Western centers. The tensions appear in the "transnational field" between subaltern proprieties and hegemonic appropriations. As a result, the concept of transnationalization is more relevant here. It allowed me, for example, to understand the spread of the "2012 phenomenon" from one continent to another in its different phases (delocalization, circulation, reappropriation, resignification) [42]. Nonetheless, other processes of Mayanization, such as "Mayan Yoga" in San Cristóbal de las Casas (México) practiced by mixed-race Mexicans, reveal transnational and multidirectional trajectories, which are more difficult to trace back. Rather, they indicate the effects of globalization in general.

In literature, globalization is often analyzed through its contradictory dynamics. In his book *Religion and Globalization* (1994) (see [57]), Peter Beyer shows the different means by which globalization generates both universalities and new particularisms ([57], p. 11). Chantal Saint-Blancat also underlines this tension between ethno-territorial identitary ostracisms, identitary recompositions and the development of "global solidarities", stressing the double dynamic structuring the relationship of religious actors to globalization ([58], p. 77). This tension is, moreover, the origin of the development of the word "glocalization" by Roland Robertson, writing in the Anglo-Saxon social science literature of the 1990s[12]. Robertson's "glocalization" seems to reconcile the tensions between the macro-sociology of globalization and the anthropological perspective of transnationalization. Roland Robertson explains that he introduced this notion to integrate the dimension of heterogeneity with the spatiality of

---

[12]   The debates concerning the origins of this notion are complex and dynamic (see, [59]).

Religions **2016**, *7*, 17

globalization, thus responding to the criticisms of globalization as a temporal process of cultural homogenization according to a model of unilateral domination ([60], p. 191). His argument is that we cannot deny that, today, the local is ultimately the product of globalization. He gives the example of the globalized promotion of "ethnicity", articulated in "global terms" while preserving its characteristic of producing difference and particularity ([60], p. 192). In this meaning, the local does not exist without the global; they interpenetrate and therefore cannot be opposed, since the global is the condition of a consciousness of the dimension of locality. As V. Roudometof emphasizes in his analyses of the scientific development of the term, the dimension of locality implies, more than a geographical dimension, the idea of a "social space" ever influenced by the global ([59], p. 5).

Despite the criticisms of this term within the social sciences, notably linked to its origins in business and economic studies, and to its neo-liberal influences, the term appears relevant to the analysis of my empirical data. The reason is that the glocalization process implies an idea of melting or hybridization[13]—and so, of creativity—useful for understanding the studied cases.

During my fieldwork, I observed tensions between the frequently mobile leaders and the less mobile ones. There are also some gaps between the discourses about purity and the multiple resignifications within practice, together with reversed dynamics between transnational mobility and ethnic particularization discourses. That tension emerges in their considerations of the processes of internal differentiation, auto-definition, designation and definition of the symbolic legitimacy. Such discussions generate hierarchization among leaders and a constant reformulation of the field. In the background, the question of "authenticity" is always an issue—an authenticity that is crucial in the eyes of actors to gain legitimacy. The following ethnographic examples offer empirical illustrations of the typologies developed in the previous discussion about glocalization and transnationalism.

The common argument is that, since "2012", the symbolic field of neo-Mayanity has been glocalized. This event has been the main engine of its actors' transnationalization. Transnationalization has been, in turn, an important symbolic resource both for the process of a rearrangement of content and in the paradoxical reinforcement of the discourses on "the purity of tradition". Since the acquisition of this global popularity, the neo-Mayanity networks have grown and the processes of Mayanization intensified. As far as I know, expressions such as "Mapuche Yoga" or "Inca osteopathy" do not yet exist; the current recompositions of Mayanity are singular.

6. Data Analysis

6.1. Glocalization in Quetzaltenango (Guatemala)

Into the context of the politicized Mayanity of Guatemala, the Xecam community, a little semi-urban zone of 8000 inhabitants located in the municipality of Cantel (Quetzaltenango state), the "globalocal" [60] represents an active dynamic within the discourse of the director of the *Centro Maya Para la Paz* ("Mayan Center for Peace"), an association promoting the K'iche' Mayan culture located in the center of this municipality. This tension appears in this director's discourses, practice and biography. In his mid-forties, Arcadio Salanic is a Guatemalan K'iche' Mayan who sees himself as a defender of human rights (*defensor de los derechos humanos*). In the area, he is known for his political involvement, as a member of the directing council of the "WINAQ[14] political movement". In parallel, and without any dissociation in his discourses, he practices activities linked with the K'iche' Mayan cosmovision, collaborating with Cantel "spiritual guides" (*guías espirituales*). From the 1990s on, he started to travel because he was invited by the solidarity networks of his center to lecture on the K'iche' Mayan situation. However, he also sought international protection because he was under a death threat at home. He began with the U.S. where he was in contact with different religious-cultural organizations such as

---

[13] On this subject, see the recent publication by V. Roudometof ([59], p. 8).
[14] "WINAQ" means "human being" in Mayan K'iche'. This Indian-led political movement was founded by Rigoberta Menchú, Nobel Peace Prize in 1992.

the Powderhorn/Phillips Cultural Wellness Centre, the Latin American-Multi-Ethnic Association for Networking & Opportunities and the Global Citizen Networks [61].

Then, shortly before 21 December 2012, he went to Switzerland, where he was invited for a series of conferences about "2012" and to act in the documentary film *"The Voice of the Mayan"* [62]. He returned to Switzerland in 2014, invited by his Swiss French network, composed both of alternative therapeutic groups with spiritual offerings (mainly women), claiming their closeness to Mayan cultures, and of Latino-American NGO members working in the realm of Indigenous people's rights. He led ceremonies between two U.N. meetings and sold his K'iche' embroidered fabrics. Because of the "2012 phenomenon", which he partly theorized, his transnational mobility has intensified and expanded. While following him—during his Swiss travels, in Guatemala, on Facebook, through written exchanges—I observed a tension between universalization and particularism in his messages. He works with the K'iche' popular version of *Pop Wuh* [63][15]. He expresses an intense attachment to his motherland, is deeply rooted in his locality and convinced of his mission to spread his ancestors' message. Despite the death threats and problems regarding the land's ownership, he refuses to leave the family house, where he performs ceremonies to his ancestors every day. He collaborates with locally rooted actors for the development of medicinal plant greenhouses in the Cantel region. He runs a local handicraft production and has communitarian commitments. Meanwhile, he uses global discursive registers about "native people" and "spirituality". He travels outside Guatemala once a year. He advocates pan-Mayanist solidarity, creating exchanges with other ethnolinguistic communities in Mexico and Guatemala, and among the Dakota people. He globally broadcasts his messages about "2012" and seeks international solidarity. Observed from the outside, his mobility generates some global and local tensions. It bothers local organization members, NGO actors based outside Guatemala and people engaged in Mayan revivalisms inside the country. Some people have qualified his spirituality as "New Age", synonymous with "non-authentic". The global dimension can also be seen in his local handicraft production.

The Mayan Center for Peace leader indeed collaborates with a cooperative of Cantel women that are collectively working for their rights, increasing self-esteem and self-empowerment. These women teach Cantel inhabitants the traditional Mayan techniques of weaving. The project of collaboration between this group of women and the Mayan Center for Peace is to reactivate some symbols from the K'iche' cosmovision to help the Cantel inhabitants to reappropriate this Mayan identity [64]. These fabrics conceal "codes" and "secrets"; each element hides a story, a meaning or the life of someone from Cantel. Arcadio defines the embroideries, in collaboration with the weaver and the "elders" of Xecam; they rely on the calendars, and on themes and symbols extracted from their mythological contexts. The colors also bear meanings. The number of threads usedcorrespond, for example, to the 5125 years of the Long Count. Also appearing on these fabrics is the "plumed serpent", the 0 restarting the Long Count at the end of the 13th *Baktun*, the "X" as the letter of the *Pop Wuh* gods, the image of the "sacred fire", "Mother Earth" (when the neck is round), the "4 cardinal points" and "4 directions" (when the neck is square), the "complementarity between man and woman" (birds facing each other), the "cloth goddess", "Xel", the symbol of lightning, various combinations of "positive vibrations" and "negative vibrations", the "earth and sky duality", and the number 13 (in reference to the 13 articulations of the K'iche' cosmovision that allow movement and action)[16].

Once the fabrics are woven, Salanic himself sews additional patterns inspired by Western fashion. He sells them in San Marcos (San Pedro department) and redistributes the money to the women of the cooperative. Other merchants buy them and sell them in additional marketplaces. The profit is

---

[15] The *Pop Wuh* or "Book of the Events" is a K'iche' poem relating the cosmogony and history of the K'iche' people. It was elaborated in K'iche' but written in Latin by an anonymous author in 1550 before being discovered and hispanicized in 1701 by Father Francisco Jiménez. It has since undergone five waves of translation. The most recent, by Adrían Chávez in 1978, seems to be the most thorough and valid. On this subject, see, [63].

[16] All these elements are based on my transcriptions of the exchanges with Arcadio Salanic [64].

then redistributed to the crafters. Arcadio keeps a low percentage. When asked to explain the choice of these new patterns, he says that it facilitates exporting to the U.S. and Europe. He would like to implant this art in an international market, purchase the threads in the U.S., discover new models, find more looms to develop the work and make it profitable. This is how this activity develops in the center of Xecam, in continuity with and in rupture from the past, under a glocal form, influenced by its director's biography. Here, local and global comingle within an activity both deeply rooted geographically and, because of the mobility of its leader, renewed by transnational influences.

6.2. Glocalization in Merida (Mexico)

Madre Nah Kin, leader and founder of the SMT (Mexico), has a far greater transnational mobility than the director of the *Centro para la Paz*; she frequently travels not only in North America, South America, Europe and Japan, but also in different regions of Mexico. She visits up to four countries each month [65]. Her organization *Casa del Sol*, whose headquarters is in Merida, includes five translators, and her books have been published in Spanish, German, French and English. The organization counts thousands of members around the globe. The relationship with the "Mayan" is told in spiritualized terms—"reincarnation" and "spiritual lineage of the Ahaukines", a "priestly" class from the past era of the "cosmic Mayan". The members identify with this conception, or rather with what they consider its "purest" version, by imagined genealogy and not ethnic or cultural identification.

These views are the main factors of differentiation from the other local entities. This original way of feeling Mayan flows from the transnational biography of Madre Nah Kin, who has lived next to spiritual leaders her whole life, notably some from Hindu traditions. The Solar Mayan Tradition was born into the post-68 context in Mexico, first in the shape of an unstructured "movement"[17] with undefined borders, gathered around Madre Nah Kin, the founding myth of the "Ahaukines" and the mythical hero "Kinich Ahau", guardian of the sun in the "traditional" Yucatan cosmovision [67]. In the Solar Mayan, this mythical character is resignified by a New Age reading associated with a eugenicist vision. He is seen as an "ascended master" who would have lived at the time of the "cosmic Mayan", a "superior Ahaukine". He is considered to be a superhuman character distinguished by "superior DNA" that he inherited from the "Atlantes", and the elevation and "purity of his heart". Nowadays, he would dwell on the archaeological site of Uxmal, Yucatan, under a non-organic form that only Madre Nah Kin could perceive. In the imagery produced by Nah Kin's team, Kinich Ahau is mainly distinguished by his Aryan physique. His skin is white; he is tall and thin. His hair and beard are golden and his eyes blue. He stands in a Christ-like aura, surrounded by a halo and a golden cape. This new iconography deracializes the classical Yucatan representation of Kinich Ahau: a dark-skinned man, with native features, sitting cross-legged in humble Mayan clothes. This is an example of the interpenetration between local and global.

Global influences are inserted in a local representation by resignification, according to pre-established logic. These logics are precisely those preaccepted doctrines, which Madre Nah Kin has been living with her whole life. Most of the doctrines have nothing Mexican at their origins. In that sense, they participate in the innovation of local representations. For instance, this visual representation of Kinich Ahau looks like one of Saint-Germain, a figure referred to as an "ascended master". Although this figure is also used in the New Age literature, it was initially developed in the "I AM" theosophical doctrines of Guy Ballard, who taught in the U.S. during the 1930s ([68], pp. 222–24). This North American figure is associated with a specific message, the Nah Kin's Solar Mayan Tradition; it stands out because of its insertion into a stream referring to a local ethnic tradition. Therefore, the innovation processes issued from Nah Kin's transnationalism maintain a strong link

---

[17] The notion of movement is related here to the concept of "social movements" involving "collective action" aimed at socio-cultural change, supported by people gathered around common interests ([66], p. 6).

with the local space. Paradoxically, however, it is not fully rooted in the local, since those processes differentiate the SMT from the "traditional" Yucatec representations.

Along the trips and encounters, Madre Nah Kin integrates new elements into the SMT. In 2014, the Japanese goddess *Amaterasu* became the female complement to Kinich Ahau, the "masculine deity". Considering both the de-ethnicized aesthetics of Kinich Ahau and the integration of the Japanese goddess, one can see a form of indigenization, the erection of a link between the imported representation and the pre-existing traditions. The story of this integration can be linked to the effects of "2012" on the group. In December 2012, Madre Nah Kin organized an international event in Uxmal. Non-Mexican spiritual leaders were invited; among them was Emoto Masaru, known in Japan for his research on how water and its crystal structure reacts to thoughts, prayer and music. Since then, a bond has been established with him and his Japanese team. Many meetings and inter-spiritual dialogues have been held in Japan with Madre Nah Kin's participation. A Mayan New Year celebration was even organized by the SMT on Mount Fuji in Japan during the summer of 2014. The place was viewed symbolicallyby the SMT as the "epicenter of the coming of a full and total love" [69]. But the sharing with this Japanese group was not without rules; it happened thanks to the compatibility of contents. In fact, Masaru's work on water echoes Madre Nah Kin's "initiations to water" that are inspired by a Yucatan Mayan representation of natural elements and their guardians.

Nonetheless, the message's aptitude for rearrangement is not enough to guarantee its transnationalization. In fact, other "trans-logics" act upstream such as the relationship with space and the mechanism of power reproduction ([13], p. 249). Therefore, inside the SMT, the relationship with space is central; Mount Fuji is seen as the Japanese equivalent of Uxmal, the ancient Mayan city of Yucatan. The question of power is also crucial. Before "2012", the SMT lived in peaceful and ecumenical cohabitation with national and local traditions, but afterward, it was pushed to the international stage, allowing Madre Nah Kin to dialogue on a multilateral inter-spiritual level with leaders from Japan, Europe and South America. Leaders recognize each other at the international level. Thus, they gain more social and symbolic legitimacy in the field of transnationality, whose issues remain tied up with the question of power. "2012" has been and remains an important factor in the process of legitimation of the SMT into the global system.

The general administrator of the organization tells the story of Madre Nah Kin's transnationality in spiritual terms, using notably the theory of "reincarnation":

> Her—at a very deep level of her soul—into one of her highest states of consciousness, since she was young, when she opens her eyes, she sees a Zen garden. It means that her soul—that is her soul at a certain point—lived a highly spiritual incarnation in the East. Therefore, since the beginning, in her highest states, she enters this garden and says that she understands it as if she had absorbed it, and not only had the meaning of it but also a great code of information. So in fact she has many soul links with Japan, so when they meet, they discuss those links and all […] [70].

The movement around Nah Kin has become increasingly institutionalized. The Kinich Ahau organization was created in the 1990s in Merida. From 2000 on, successive waves of change and restructuring took place. Madre Nah Kin has become increasingly famous for her representations around "2012"; her transnational mobility began a decade before 21 December 2012, in preparation for the date. More and more Westerners were attracted by her message and joined her activities in Merida. Numerous members told me that they had joined the movement out of curiosity. As a result, the network has expanded thanks to "2012". In 2008, the Casa del Sol Center was founded outside Merida as the place for formations and initiations. The eclecticism of the references is linked to Nah Kin's complex biography. She was, at a very young age, initiated to various New Age and esoteric streams that spread throughout Mexico in the second half of the twentieth century [71], such as the French stream of the Great Universal Fraternity of Raynaud de la Ferrière, where she practiced Yoga, meditation and vegetarianism, and the North American Metaphysic stream, influenced by the I AM theosophy. She was also trained in "psycho-astrology", "Reiki", "lithotherapy", "rebirthing", "neurolinguistics", "shamanistic trips and power animals", "past life regression", "Osho's active meditations" and more [72]. She is doubly mobile: her journeys outside national borders and her trans-spiritual circulation.

The transnationalization and the trans-spiritual curriculum of Madre Nah Kin, after "2012," have therefore brought changes and re-arrangement of contents. The integration, halfway through, of the goddess Amaterasu from the Shintoist mythology is explained by Madre Nah Kin in terms of "union", not "fusion": the two "deities" would unite without merging their contents [73]. The structural organization changes, not the cultural contents. However, this unity gives birth to a genuine message that integrates the dimension of gender, but also and above all, the prestige that comes from an association with an internationally recognized leader.

7. Conclusions

In this article, I began with an explanation of my field of research and the conceptual issues that it reveals, notably my choice of the term "neo-Mayanity" to define my subject and its frame. I defined it as being crossed by different social-religious processes, notably pointing out two opposing movements: "Mayanization" and "New-Ageization", which fall into a list of various forms such asintra-national Mayanizations, intra-ethnic Mayanizations, New Age appropriations and intra-ethnic New-Ageizations. I also made explicit both my investigation and my analysis methods.

Then, to understand the concept of neo-Mayanity, I presented the recent research historically deconstructing the "Mayan" category and its "weakly politicized" uses in the Yucatan peninsula in Mexico, together with the political signification given to the concept in the national context of Guatemala. This historical research allowed me to understand neo-Mayanity as a field crossed by two main categorical forms of revitalizations: one a collaborative type linked with New Age significations, the other highly politicized, crystallizing the collective struggles for recognition. Moreover, this work on the "Mayan" category allowed me to achieve two goals : to question "ethnicity" according to the new identifications observed in the fieldwork, thus enlightening my use of the prefix "neo", and to present, in the second part of this article, two cases corresponding to this binary typologization—politicized *vs.* New Age.

The analysis of the cases began with considering the effects of the "2012 phenomenon" as an initial engine. I showed that in Guatemala as in Mexico, the mobility of actors has increased since that date or just before, in preparation for it. The "2012 phenomenon" was even the trigger for the leaders' transnationalization beyond cultural and national borders. Rather than studying the global circulation of contents since that accelerated transnationalization, I opted to analyze its reversed effects, which are the transformation processes of contents at the local level. I referred to these effects through the notion of "glocalisation", a term coined by R. Robertson, but in light of the cases, I redefined it as characterized by a signification of contents through logics of rearrangement, innovation, cohabitation between local native influences and global inspirations, rather than analyzing them in term of "syncretism".

Regarding the variations in the ethnographic examples, they depend on the different socio-historical contexts and the leaders' curricula. These different historical contexts influence the production of narratives and imageries around the "Mayan" category. In this way, they affect the way the groups negotiate their recognition and legitimization. The national context factors are also crossed with this new context of a transnational social field, where symbolic objects, being uprooted, circulate, often via networks of spiritual offerings. This tension between universalization and socio-historical particularism is observable in both of the studied groups. The Guatemalan leader reveals a strong activist and associative biography, traveling within international human rights networks. His career is punctuated by social engagements, resignificated within the global language of human rights. Paradoxically, he expresses a deep attachment to the territory and claims a systematic local contextualization of K'iche Mayan practices and representations. His relationship to "Mayan" ethnicity is politicized and legitimized by his genealogical inheritance and public institutions, and their representations of "Indigenous people". Meanwhile, the life of Madre Nah Kin is characterized by a hyper-mobility across different transnational spiritual streams and an intra-national circulation through Mexican spiritual movements. Her relationship to Mayanity is simultaneously de-historicized, spiritualized and locally rooted. The biographies of these two leaders added to the differentiated revitalizations of the "Mayan" category from one cultural context to another (the Mayan movements in Guatemala and the less politicized Mayanity of Yucatan) show that, in the first case, the glocal views are used to support local cooperative work in favor of the K'iche' women and their fundamental rights, and more generally, in service of communitarian, collective goals. And, in the Yucatec one, the glocal views are, paradoxically, tools to claim the purity and singularity of the "Tradition" in a social context of Indigenous heritage revitalizations, spiritual tourism and merchandization of the Maya brand. In this last case, neo-Mayanization processes foster individual therapeutic journeys.

Abbreviations

SMT   Solar Mayan Tradition

Conflicts of Interest: The author declares no conflict of interest.

References

1. Robert K. Sitler. "The 2012 Phenomenon. New Age Appropriation of an Ancient Mayan Calendar." *Nova Religio: The Journal of Alternative and Emergent Religions* 9 (2006): 24–38. [CrossRef]
2. Robert K. Sitler. "The 2012 Phenomenon. New Uses for an Ancient Maya Calendar." In *2012 Decoding the Countercultural Apocalypse*. Edited by Joseph Gelfer. Oakville: Equinox, 2011, pp. 8–22.
3. Ian Xel Lungold. "The Mayan Calendar. The Evolution Continues." *YouTube*. Available online: http://www.youtube.com/watch?v=fPvC7dv-ROo&feature=relmfu (accessed on 10 October 2012).
4. Christina Welch. "Appropriating the Didjeridu and the Sweat Lodge: New Age Baddies and Indigenous Victims?" *Journal of Contemporary Religion* 17 (2002): 21–38. [CrossRef]
5. Quai Branly. "Mayas, de l'aube au crépuscule." Available online: http://www.quaibranly.fr/fr/programmation/expositions/expositions-passees/maya.html (accessed on 16 October 2012).
6. Gregory Lassalle. *Des Dérives de L'art aux Dérives du Pétrole*. Paris: Collectif Guatemala, 2012.
7. Castañeda Quetzil. "'We Are *Not. Indigenous!*' An Introduction to the Maya Identity of Yucatan." *The Journal of Latin American Anthropology* 1 (2004): 36–63.
8. Docip. "Declaration of the International Symposium—Indigenous Peoples at the United Nations: From the Experience of the First Delegates to the Empowerment of the Younger Generations." 2013. Available online: http://eaford.org/wp-content/uploads/2014/04/Declaration-of-the-International-Symposium-on-Indigenous-Peoples-at-the-UN.pdf (accessed on 4 January 2016).
9. Peter Beyer. "Au croisement de l'identité et de la différence: Les syncrétismes culturo-religieux dans le contexte de la mondialisation." *Social Compass* 52 (2005): 417–29. [CrossRef]
10. Wolfgang Gabbert. "Social Categories, Ethnicity and the State in Yucatán, Mexico." *Journal of Latin American Study* 33 (2001): 459–84. [CrossRef]
11. Pierre Bourdieu. *La Distinction Critique Sociale du Jugement*. Paris: Les Editions de Minuit, 1979.
12. Pierre Bourdieu. *Question de Sociologie*. Paris: Les Editions de Minuit, 1980.
13. Stefania Capone, and Sophie Bava. "Religions transnationales et migrations: Regards croisés sur un champ en mouvement." *Autrepart* 4 (2010): 3–16.
14. Kali Argyriadis, and René De la Torre. "Présentation générale et méthodologie: Les défis de la mobilité." In *Religions Transnationales des Suds Afrique, Europe Amériques*. Edited by Kali Argyriadis, Stefania Capone, René De la Torre and André Mary. Paris: Harmattan, 2012, pp. 13–25.
15. Stefania Capone, and André Mary. "Les translogiques d'une globalisation religieuse à l'envers." In *Religions Transnationales des Suds Afrique, Europe Amériques*. Edited by Kali Argyriadis, Stefania Capone, René De la Torre and André Mary. Paris: Harmattan, 2012, pp. 27–45.
16. Stefania Capone. "La religion des orisha: Les enjeux d'une transnationalisation religieuse ou le syncrétisme revisité." In *Colloque de Recherche de l'ISSRC, Enquêter en Sciences Sociales des Religions: Psychologie de la Religion, Sociologie des Religions, Sciences Sociales des Migrations*. Lausanne: University of Lausanne, 2014.

17. Edio Soares. *Le butinage Religieux Pratiques et Pratiquants au Brésil*. Paris and Genève: Editions Karthala and Institut de Hautes Etudes Internationales et du Développement, 2009.
18. Renée de la Torre. "Los Newagers: El efecto colibrí. Artífices de menús especializados, tejedores de circuitos en la red, y polinizadores de culturas híbridas." *Religião e Sociedade* 34 (2014): 36–64. [CrossRef]
19. Alfonso Villa Rojas. *Etnológicos. Los Mayas*. México: Universidad Nacional Autónoma de México and Instituto de Investigaciones Antropológicas, 1985.
20. Santiago Bastos, Aura Cumes, and Leslie Lemus. *Mayanizacioón y Vida Cotidiana. La Ideología Multicultural en la Sociedad Guatemalteca. Texto Para Debate*. Ciudad de Guatemala: FLACSO-CIRMA-Cholsamaj, 2007.
21. Danièle Hervieu-Léger. *La Religion Pour Mémoire*. Paris: Cerf, 1993.
22. George Marcus. "Ethnography in/of the World System: The Emergence of Multi-Sited Ethnography." *Annual Review of Anthropology* 24 (1995): 95–117. [CrossRef]
23. Daniel Bertaux. *L'enquête et ses Méthodes. Le Récit de vie*. Paris: Armand Colin, 2005.
24. Daniel Bertaux, and Martin Kohli. "The life Story Approach: A Continental View." *Annual Review of Sociology* 10 (1984): 215–37. [CrossRef]
25. Stefania Capone. "A propos des notions de globalisation et de transnationalisation." *Civilisations* 51 (2004): 9–22. [CrossRef]
26. Jean-Claude Kaufmann. *L'entretien Compréhensif*. Paris: A. Colin, 2011.
27. Barney Glaser, and Anselm Strauss. *La Découverte de la Théorie Ancrée. Stratégies. Pour la Recherche Qualitative*. Paris: Armand Colin, 2010.
28. Anselm Strauss, and Juliet Corbin. *Les Fondements de la Recherche Qualitative. Techniques et Procédures de Développement de la Théorie Enracinée*. Fribourg: Editions Saint-Paul, 2004.
29. Yvan Le Bot. *La Guerre en Terre Maya. Communauté, Violence et Modernité au Guatemala*. Paris: Karthala, 1992.
30. Carine Chavarochette. "L'Etat Guatémaltèque et les populations mayas: Stratégies d'identifications ethniques négociées chez les Chuj (1821–2011)." *Presses de Sciences Po* 3 (2013): 133–50. [CrossRef]
31. Anne Lavanchy. *Les Langages de L'autochtonie Enjeux. Politiques et Sociaux des Négociations Identitaires Mapuche au Chili*. Neuchâtel and Paris: Editions de l'Institut d'ethnologie and Editions de la Maison des sciences de l'homme, 2009.
32. Frederik Barth. *Los Grupos Étnicos y sus Fronteras. La Organización Social de las Diferencias Culturales Introducción*. México City: Fondo de Cultura Económica, 1976.
33. Quetzil Castañeda, and Ben Fallaw. "The Maya Identity of Yucatan, 1500–1935: Re-Thinking Ethnicity, History and Anthropology." Special Issue. *Journal of Latin American Anthropology* 9 (2004): 36–198. [CrossRef]
34. Morna Macleod. *Nietas del Fuego, Creadoras Del Alba: Luchas Politico-Culturales de Mujeres Mayas*. Guatemala City: Flacso, 2011.
35. Jesús García Ruiz, and Patrick Michel. *Et Dieu Sous-Traita le Salut au Marché. De L'action des Mouvements Évangéliques en Amérique Latine*. Paris: Armand Colin, 2012.
36. Jesús García Ruiz. "L'émergence politique des sociétés mayas dans le contexte de l'Etat-nation au Guatemala." *Civilisations* 42 (1993): 91–120. [CrossRef]
37. David H. Schelton. "Mouvement maya et culture nationale au Guatemala." *Journal de la Société des Américanistes* 90 (2004): 137–66.
38. Andrea Althoff. *Divided by Faith and Ethnicity: Religious Pluralism and the Problem of Race in Guatemala*. Berlin and New York: Verla Walter de Gruyter, 2013.
39. Santiago Bastos, Engel Tally, and Marcelo Zamora. "La reinterpretación del oxlajuj b'aqtun en Guatemala: entre el *new age* y la reconstitución maya." In *Variacones y Apropiaciones Latinoamericanas del New Age*. Edited by Renée De la Torre, Cristina Gutiérrez Zúñiga and Nahayeilli Juarez Huet. México City: Centro de Investigaciones y Estudios Superiores en Antropología Social, 2013, pp. 309–36.
40. Morna Macleod. "Mayan Calendrics in Movement in Guatemala: Mayan Spiritual Guides or Day-keepers Uniderstandings of 2012." *The Journal of Latin American and Caribbean Anthropology* 18 (2013): 447–63. [CrossRef]
41. Morna Macleod. *Tecnologías y Culturas. Diálogo Entre las Disciplinas del Conocimiento. Mirando al Futuro de América Latina y el Caribe*. Santiago: University of Santiago de Chile, 2013.
42. Manéli Farahmand. "Une date, deux discours? Le 21 décembre 2012 en Suisse et au Guatemala." *Religioscope* 12 (2014): 15–37.
43. Antonio Velasco Piña. *Regina*. México City: Editorial Punto de Lectura, 2013.

44. Francisco De la Peña. "Milenarismo, nativismo y neotradicionalismo en el México actual." *Ciencias Sociales y Religión* 3 (2001): 95–113.

45. Renée De la Torre, and Cristina Gutiérrez Zúñiga. "La neomexicanidad y los circuitos *new age*. ¿Un Hibridismo sin fronteras o múltiples estrategias de sintesis espiritual?" *Archives de Sciences Sociales des Religions* 1 (2011): 183–206. [CrossRef]

46. Jacques Galinier, and Antoinette Molinié. *Les Néo-Indiens: Une Religion du IIIe Millénaire*. Paris: Odile Jacob, 2006.

47. Renée De la Torre, Cristina Gutiérrez Zúñiga, and Nahayeilli Juarez Huet. *Variacones y Apropiaciones Latinoamericanas del New Age*. México City: Centro de Investigaciones y Estudios Superiores en Antropología Social, 2013.

48. Informal exchange with Ricardo, 21 April 2014, Merida, Mexico.

49. Formal interview with Suzana, 13 May 2014, Merida, Mexico.

50. Formal interview with Patti, 25 April 2014, Merida, Mexico.

51. Formal interview with Ricardo, 9 February 2015, Merida, Mexico.

52. André Mary. "Culture globale et religions transnationales." In *Réinventer L'anthropologie? Les Sciences de la Culture à L'épreuve des Globalisations*. Edited by Francine Saillant. Montréal: Liber, 2009, pp. 89–108.

53. Peggy Levitt, and Nina Glick Schiller. "Conceptualizing Simultaneity. A transnational Social Field Perspective on Society." *International Migration Review* 38 (2004): 1002–39. [CrossRef]

54. Claude Lévi-Strauss. *La Pensée Sauvage*. Paris: Plon, 1962.

55. Jean-Pierre Bastian, Françoise Champion, and Kathy Rousselet. *La Globalisation du Religieux*. Paris: L'Harmattan, 2001.

56. Ulf Hannerz. *Transnational Connections. Culture, People, Places*. London and New York: Routledge, 1996.

57. Peter Beyer. *Religion and Globalization*. London: Sage Publications, 1994.

58. Chantal Saint-Blancat. "Globalisation, réseaux et diasporas dans le champ religieux." In *La Globalisation du Religieux*. Edited by Jean-Pierre Bastian, Françoise Champion and Kathy Rousselet. Paris: L'Harmattan, 2001, pp. 75–86.

59. Victor Roudometof. "The Glocal and Global Studies." *Globalizations* 12 (2015): 1–14. [CrossRef]

60. Roland Robertson. "Globalisation or glocalisation?" *The Journal of International Communication* 18 (2012): 191–208. [CrossRef]

61. Formal interview with Arcadio, 24 March 2013, Guatemala City, Guatemala.

62. Christian Doninelli. "2012, La voix des Mayas." In *With the Participation of Samuel Dejardin and Jérôme Jeusset*. Neuchâtel: Nawalprod, 2012.

63. Adrián Inés Chavez. *Pop Wuj: Poema Mito-histórico K'iche'*. Quetge: Centro de Estudios Mayas TIMACH, 2001.

64. Informal exchanges with Arcadio, 14 March 2013, San Marco, Guatemala.

65. Formal interview with Nah Kin, 13 May 2014, Merida, Mexico.

66. Eric Neveu. *Sociologie des Mouvements Sociaux*. Paris: La Découverte, 2010.

67. Maria Montolíu Villar. *Cuando los Dioses Despertaron. Conceptos Cosmológicos de los Antiguos Mayas De Yucatán Estudiados en el Chilam Balam de Chumayael*. México City: Universidad Nacional Autonoma de México, 1989.

68. Fuller J. Overton. "Saint-Germain." In *Dictionary of Gnosis & Western Esotericism*. Edited by Wouter J. Hanegraaff. Leiden and Boston: Brill, 2005.

69. Kinich Ahau. "Año Nuevo Maya en Japón." Available online: http://www.kinich-ahau.org/ao_nuevo_maya_2014.html (accessed on 20 June 2015).

70. Formal interview with Rafaela, 12 May 2014, Merida, Mexico.

71. Cristina Gutiérrez Zúñiga, and Jesus García Medina. "La indianización de la nueva era en Guadalajara." *Cuicuilco* 19 (2012): 220–44.

72. Venerable Nah Kin. "Venerable Madre Nah Kin. Biografía." Available online: http://venerablemadre-nahkin.com/bio-ext.html (accessed on 25 June 2015).

73. Formal interview with Nah Kin, 13 May 2014, Merida, Mexico.

religions

MDPI

Article

Glocalization and the Marketing of Christianity in Early Modern Southeast Asia [†]

Barbara Watson Andaya

Asian Studies Program, University of Hawaii, Honolulu, HI 96825, USA; bandaya@hawaii.edu

† An earlier version of this paper was published as "The glocalization of Christianity in early modern Southeast Asia." In *Early modern Southeast Asia, 1350-1800*. Edited by Ooi Keat Gin and Hoang Anh Tuah. London: Routledge, 2015, pp. 233–49.

Academic Editors: Victor Roudometof and Peter Iver Kaufman
Received: 5 October 2016; Accepted: 30 December 2016; Published: 10 January 2017

Abstract: The expansion of European commercial interests into Southeast Asia during the early modern period was commonly justified by the biblical injunction to spread Christian teachings, and by the "civilizing" influences it was said to foster. In focusing on areas where Christianity gained a foothold or, in the Philippines and Timor Leste, became the dominant faith, this article invokes the marketing concept of "glocalization", frequently applied to the sociology of religion. It argues that the historical beginnings of the processes associated with the global/local interface of Christianity are situated in the sixteenth century, when Europe, Asia and the Americas were finally linked through maritime connections. Christian missionizing was undertaken with the assumption that the European-based "brand" of beliefs and practices could be successfully transported to a very different environment. However, the application of these ideas was complicated by the goal of imposing European economic control, by the local resistance thus generated, and by competition with other religions and among Christians themselves. In this often antagonistic environment, the degree to which a global product could be "repackaged" and "glocalized" so that it was appealing to consumers in different cultural environments was always constrained, even among the most sympathetic purveyors. As a result, the glocalization of Christianity set up "power-laden tensions" which both global institutions and dispersed consumers continue to negotiate.

Keywords: Christianity; globalization; glocalization; early modern; Southeast Asia

The literature on the nature of the processes we have termed "globalization" has expanded exponentially since the term began to gain currency in the 1970s. Much of the theoretical material has discussed globalization in terms of its connections to modernity, the dominating theme in studies of the 20th century ([1]; [2], pp. 138–45). Although academic debates about the fundamental characteristics of globalization are ongoing, and although there is a diversity of opinions, for the purposes of this article the early definition by Anthony Giddens is still useful. For Giddens, the essence of globalization lies in "the intensification of worldwide social relations which links distinct localities in such a way that local happenings are shaped by events occurring miles away and vice versa" ([3], p. 64). If we take this statement as a departure point, even with qualifications, it is quite possible to agree with those historians who argue that the foundations of twentieth century globalization were laid down in the period reaching from 1500 to about 1800, now increasingly termed "early modern".

This is not to equate such global connections with "modernity" per se, nor to ignore the scholarship which argues that the world had already been connected by flows of people, goods, technologies and ideas ([4], pp. 31–36; [5]). However, notwithstanding continuing debate, there is growing agreement that the sustained "interchange and interdependency" central to the concept of globalization did not begin to reshape world history until the sixteenth century ([6], pp. 418–21; [7], pp. 34–35; [8], p. 8). The circumnavigation of the globe and regular voyages across the Pacific meant that Europe, the

Americas, Asia and Africa were linked in what has been described as the "first" globalization [9]. Despite some reservations about the applicability of an "early modern" period in societies beyond Western Europe and the Americas, historians agree that this was a time of unprecedented and world-wide change ([10]; [11], pp. 5–10). Because of Southeast Asia's longstanding involvement in international trade, it follows that the region inevitably became a player in "a genuinely global periodization of world history" ([11], pp. 336–43; [12], p. 769). The expanding interactions that characterize this period are central to discussions of religious change in Southeast Asia because of the spread of Islam and Christianity. In tandem with increased trade networks, both faiths introduced new connectivities that scholars of contemporary religious plurality have characterized by the fashionable but inelegant amalgam, "glocalization" ([13], pp. 98–118).

Introduced by Japanese economists in the late 1980s, the concept of *dochakaku* ("global localization") became one of the "marketing buzzwords" of the late twentieth century, and in 1991 was added to the Oxford Dictionary as an acceptable "new word" ([14], p. 134). In business circles "glocalization" is used to describe a product or service that is developed centrally but distributed globally through a re-fashioning to accommodate consumers in different types of markets. Though its relationship with "globalization" continues to generate debate [15–17], "glocalization" has been adopted by sociologists to deepen discussions of the ways in which local contexts temper global pressures. It has also been incorporated into the sociology of religion, extending work on global modernities and helping to theorize the ways in which transnational networks can reach out to specific congregations ([18], pp. 32–43; [19,20]). Studies of various cultures have shown that religious "goods" were not necessarily consumed in the manner elite producers expected, and local actors appropriated the "product" in ways that often led to unintended consequences ([19]; [21], pp. 56–57). The concept of glocalization, Peter Ng argues, is preferable to terms such "inculturation" and "accommodation" because it recognizes both local and global perspectives and allows for more attention to interaction in a mutually beneficial and "harmonious" relationship ([18], pp. 6, 32, 222). Nonetheless, the marketing analogy reminds us that there are limits to the extent to which any product can be "glocalized", since a global brand must be internationally recognizable, and the extent of adaptation to a local environment is thus constrained. In the religious setting such constraints were reinforced by the fact that teachings presented as universally applicable were transmitted by agents of societies where religious praxis, aesthetics and modes of worship were regarded as intrinsically superior to those of the receiving culture.

In Southeast Asia these comments are particularly relevant to any regional analysis of the spread of Christianity in the early modern period. The ongoing process of localization is as evident among local converts as it is among followers of other world religions, but the transfer of influences from Southeast Asia to Europe that are implied in the "vice versa" of the Giddens definition is not easily tracked. For instance, in Southeast Asia we rarely see the type of missionary adaptation to local practices displayed by the Jesuits in China, Japan or India. While the situation in Vietnam is something of an exception, conversions in Southeast Asia were confined to areas where Europeans wielded economic and political power, so that the relationship between clerical authority and native Christians was fundamentally asymmetrical. This asymmetry was furthered by the dominance of what can be described as "alpha" cities, a term used in urban studies in reference to places like New York, London, Paris, and Tokyo that are considered nodes in the global economic system and purveyors of international culture. As Christianity moved out into the non-European world, the major sites of European control in Asia—Goa, Melaka, Manila, Macau and Batavia—developed to become the Christian "alphas" by acting as religious conduits and arbiters. From these new religious enclaves individuals and sacred objects moved and circulated as vehicles for the globalizing influences of Christianity, reinforcing the idea of an interlinked and supra-national community. The dominance of these European-controlled cities and the forms of Christianity they espoused remained an unsettling challenge to the mutuality of global-local interaction that some scholars of religion have seen as the basis of glocalization ([18], p. 43).

In sum, historians of religion have found the academic exchanges that highlight the global/glocal relationship particularly helpful in grounding theory in a specific cultural context. In today's business environment multinational companies are constantly alert to any attempt to counterfeit a product, or to change core elements such as the logo or a distinctive packaging that might dilute universal recognition. Similarly, in Asia, Africa and the Americas the concept of the essential universality of Christianity was repeatedly pitted against missionary beliefs that new Christian communities should as far as possible replicate the established practices of Europe. In Southeast Asia as elsewhere the idea that Christians were members of a potent "world religion" operated simultaneously to facilitate the conversion process while placing limits on the extent to which missionaries could enculturate themselves and their teachings. By applying the notion of glocalization to historical situations in early modern Southeast Asia, this article is thus concerned to demonstrate the very real ways in which Christian concerns to maintain their "brand" restrained patterns of local adaptation.

1. Christianity, Global Influences and "Alpha" Cities in Early Modern Southeast Asia

From the beginning of the sixteenth century, as the spread of Christianity became enmeshed in the European goal of commercial profit, religious networks in Southeast Asia were reshaped. European-controlled cities maintained much older trading connections, but also generated international links that transformed them into junctures for the dispersal of Christian influences. The development of a Portuguese seaborne empire, the Estado da India, for instance, resulted in new bonds of belief between world areas that had previously been linked only indirectly, if at all ([22]; [23], p. 121). Though frequently at odds with the Portuguese, the spread of Spanish colonialism into the Americas and the Philippines also created interlocking Catholic connections through which many different influences converged. The global mobility of the religious orders, especially the Jesuits, contributed to a shrinking world as missionaries moved between different zones of activity. In the early seventeenth century the arrival of the Dutch United East India Company (Verenigde Oost-Indische Compagnie, VOC) with its Protestant affiliation certainly disrupted or diverted some of these pathways. On the other hand, new chains of religious globality connected the Reformed Church hierarchy in the Netherlands to dimly imagined communities in far-off Indonesia, where native Christians appointed as "visitors of the sick" (*krankbezoekers*) symbolized the reach of the Christian network.

In Southeast Asia, Melaka, captured by the Portuguese in 1511, serves as an example of the global evangelism that characterized Catholicism in the sixteenth century. In commercial terms, economic continuities continued, for Melaka was still one of the richest entrepôts in the east, a highly cosmopolitan town in which the Portuguese were merely a new elite. The imprint of the new Christian presence was nevertheless dramatic and indisputable, since from the outset, the Portuguese saw their venture as a battle of Christians against unbelievers; indeed, the assault on Melaka was specifically launched on the feast day of the revered Santiago Matamoris—Saint James, the slayer of Moors (i.e., Muslims). The great mosque was destroyed, and much of Melaka was rebuilt to accommodate numerous convents, churches, chapels, and other religious establishments. Visiting priests may have railed against the lack of piety among its Catholic population, but in the eyes of Southeast Asians Melaka was indubitably Christian, a meeting place for Christians from all over the region and a nexus in the sixteenth-century global missionizing project. At the same time, it was infused with an architectural style and organizational forms that were "the defining marks of Portugal's colonial cities." ([24], p. 6).

Under the Portuguese, Melaka's primary connections with India were focused on Goa. Following its conquest in 1510, Goa became the hub of the Portuguese seaborne empire and from 1558 was made an archbishopric. Appointed by the Portuguese king, the archbishop administered a region that reached from Africa to Japan, while Goa itself functioned as the dissemination point for evangelism within India and to many other places in Portugal's overseas domains. As a religious and educational "alpha" city, seventeenth-century Goa could boast at least seventy Catholic establishments, including thirty-one churches, and by the eighteenth century the Jesuits were in charge of sixty parishes [25].

Although scholars have traced an Indo-Portuguese style in secular architecture, Goa's churches generally followed European models closely while infusing them with the glocalized message of Christian triumph. The Sé cathedral, for instance, was built with its counterpart in Valladolid in mind, but the high altar displayed a painting of the martyred Saint Catherine of Alexandria (on whose feast day Goa was captured) standing on the body of the Sultan of Bijapur ([26], pp. 36–43).

In the latter half of the sixteenth century Melaka gained additional religious importance as a half-way station between India, Japan, and Macau. The latter had been established as a Portuguese trading base in 1557, with the permission of the Ming Emperor. The connections made possible through this maritime route are well illustrated in the celebrated encounter between the Spanish Jesuit, Francis Xavier, and the Japanese Anjiro, a merchant from Kagoshima. When they met in Melaka, Anjiro expressed interest in conversion and was therefore sent to study in Goa. After his baptism, he accompanied Xavier back to Japan, again passing through Melaka ([27], pp. 1–9). Fostered by personal interaction, the networks traversing Portuguese Asia were so resilient that they survived the anti-Catholic fervour accompanying the Protestant Dutch capture of Melaka in 1641. By 1712, when the Dutch allowed greater freedom of worship, Melaka's Catholics outnumbered Protestants by six to one, and even though successive bishops had taken refuge in Flores and Timor, Melaka continued to be a diocesan town until 1818 ([28], p. 55).

However, the fact that after 1641 Melaka was controlled by a Protestant administration did mean a lessening of ties with Macau, which was under Goa but operated semi-independently. Although "a Catholic island in a Chinese sea", existing at the pleasure of the Ming dynasty, Macau developed into a centre for Portuguese operations in East Asia, most clearly evident in its multi-ethnic population. The Portuguese-born community was always small, and because of the lack of Portuguese women, the wives of European residents were variously Eurasian, Chinese converts, Christian Japanese exiles, or baptized former slaves from places such as Timor, Java, Makassar and India [29]. As a Catholic "alpha" in its own right, Macau was seen as the door to the Christianization of China and Japan, and thus the most suitable site for two Jesuit colleges similar to that already established in Goa. The Franciscan and Dominican friars, the Poor Clare nuns, and the Augustinians also established religious institutions in Macau. Missionaries hoping to spread Christianity in Vietnam, China and Japan viewed Macau as a bulwark of the faith and a source of financial support; donations from Macau even helped the Dominicans build a fortress on the distant Indonesian island of Solor ([30], p. 13).

The wealth that came to Macau's Lusitanian merchants and to the religious orders helped finance religious buildings and charitable foundations, transforming the town into a showcase of Catholic architecture and a critical point of connectivity as Catholicism moved to become a world religion. Begun in 1602, the impressive Madre de Deus Church (today only a façade) was probably modelled after the Gesú, a Jesuit church in Rome, but it also replicated artistic features common in the Iberian Peninsula while exhibiting aspects reminiscent of the architecture of Portuguese India. When Peter Mundy arrived in the early seventeenth century he expressed his admiration for the workmanship of the Chinese-made roof, the "spacious ascent [of] many steppes" and the "new faire frontispiece" ([31], pp. 162–63). It is nonetheless unlikely that he appreciated the symbolism of the façade, a "sermon in stone" that portrays the globalization project through depicting (as the Chinese characters inform us), and "The Holy Mother trampling on the dragon's head". In European art the dragon was a symbol of heresy, but in China it connoted benevolence and as such had been adopted as the Ming emblem. At a time when the Ming Empire was beginning to crumble, this could be read as the glocal expression of a triumphant and European-driven enterprise that would overwhelm the barbarism of the East. Nevertheless, artistic protocols were uncompromising. Even the three statues of Mary are in accordance with a Vatican-approved style. Mary should be represented as a young woman in a white robe and a blue cloak, with her hands in an attitude of prayer, or folded over the breast ([32], pp. 84–99).

While the final closure of the Japanese market in 1639 was a financial disaster for many Macau merchants, it did mean a revival of older links with Southeast Asia. The majority of Macau's traders were Luso-Asians who had close links with the "black Portuguese" diaspora in Southeast Asia, and a Malay chronicle from Borneo even mentions "Macau people" as a specific group ([33], p. 561). By the eighteenth century Catholic communities in eastern Indonesia were thus inclined to see Macau, rather than Goa, as the symbol of Portuguese power in Asia. In 1772 a French visitor to eastern Timor commented that most chiefs were Catholic, that he had seen a church in virtually all the coastal villages, and that trade with the Macau Chinese was thriving ([34], pp. 94–95, 97–98).

Rivalling Macau in the number of its religious buildings was another alpha centre, Spanish Manila. The walled centre, the Intramuros, enclosed the convents and churches of six major religious orders, and the opulence of its architecture aroused comments from many visitors. Though successive earthquakes necessitated modification to the towers and spires that typified Spanish Gothic cathedrals in Seville or Toledo, the town plan replicated typical arrangements in other Spanish colonies, laid down by royal orders in 1573 in an early attempt to "globalize" architecture [35]. Spanish repression of indigenous trade meant Manila never became an entrepôt like Melaka, but it attracted a highly cosmopolitan population and was a telling symbol of Spain's Asian presence. Most importantly, it was a key node in the new path of communication across the Pacific, a central point for the Acapulco-Manila-Macau-Nagasaki links by which Chinese silk and porcelain were exchanged for Japanese and American silver. The so-called Galleon Trade also established a pathway for religious interaction as well. A Jesuit mission was established on Guam in 1668 and for a hundred years became a significant point of connection on the Pacific route between Acapulco and Manila ([8], pp. 58–60; [36]).

Standing apart from these four Catholic-controlled centres was Batavia, taken by the VOC in 1619. The Dutch maritime empire arose in the context of commercial ambition and trade rivalries with the Iberian powers, behind which lay the legacy of Dutch conflict with Catholic Spain and the conviction that Calvinist Protestantism conveyed the true message of Christianity. The VOC charter of 1602 said nothing about the promotion of religion, but the company's directors instructed the first Governor-General not merely to determine which areas in the Indonesian archipelago were best suited for trade, but also to identify places where Christian evangelism was possible. The VOC did not formally accept responsibility for missionizing, but it was obligated to maintain "public belief", by which was meant support for reformed Calvinism ([37], pp. 21–22). Though rarely enforced, the statutes of Batavia thus laid down that only the Reformed Church had the right to propagate in Dutch-controlled areas and individuals found guilty of flouting this order, whether Christian, Moor or "heathen", could be put in jail, banned or even lose their lives.

As the centre for VOC operations, Batavia's commercial pre-eminence was confirmed by the extension of pre-existing trade routes and by linking previously unconnected places like the Cape of Good Hope and Java. For many Dutch Protestants, the VOC's global reach provided an unprecedented opportunity to take the gospel to remote nations and to combat the global spread of Papist "superstitions" and "blasphemies". Dutch gravestones still surviving in Melaka are a reminder of the new connections Protestantism established. Maria Quevelferius (1629–1664), we are told, was the wife of Johannes Riebeck, previously governor of the Cape of Good Hope and subsequently of Melaka. She was born at Rotterdam, educated in Leiden, married in Schiedam, and now lies "in this tomb [in Melaka]" ([38], p. 63).

2. Globalizing Connectivities

The Christian influences that moved through these alpha centres and globalizing networks were in the first instance carried by individuals. The most renowned is Francis Xavier, whose travels through Asia are memorialized in statues and shrines, in names attached to schools, and in his tomb in the Church of Bom Jesus, Goa. But there are other lesser known personalities whose peregrinations also had far reaching results. For example, at the age of 66, Mother Jerónima de la Asunción (1555–1630) left her birthplace, Toledo, to travel to Manila where she had permission to establish the first religious community for women. Her long journey by land and sea from Spain to the Philippines lasted over a year, and her "global renown" and reputation for saintliness created a public demand for her images not only in the Philippines but in Mexico and Spain itself. ([39], pp. 147–48; [40]). Another such traveller was François Caron (1634–1706), born in Hirado to a French father and a Japanese Catholic mother. Sent back to the Netherlands to complete his studies in theology, he arrived in the Indies as a Protestant minister in 1660. Caron spent thirteen years in Ambon before finally returning to the Netherlands where he published forty sermons that were recycled back to the Indonesian archipelago. His "Kitab Krong" (Caron book) became standard use in Protestant church services well into the nineteenth century [41].

For local converts these Christian connections fostered emotional attachments to distant religious hierarchies and to a heritage of saintly protectors, reminding believers of the global spread of this new faith. In Goa three of the four bronze reliefs around Francis Xavier's tomb depict the saint preaching and baptizing not in India but in far-off eastern Indonesia, where he is also shown escaping from hostile islanders ([26], p. 66). Filipinos celebrated the holy days of devout men and women who had lived long ago in far-away countries, Japanese boys took gifts to the Pope in Rome, and Timorese chiefs, baptized as Protestants, inserted orange flowers in their headdresses to celebrate the birth of a Dutch prince ([42,43]; [44], p. 93). Sometimes bestowed, sometimes personally selected, the baptismal names of converts proclaimed personalized and meaningful ties with the saintly figures of Christianity's larger world. The Japanese Christian Anjio was thus baptized as Paulo de Santa Fê (Paul of the Holy Faith), after the saint known as the Apostle to the Gentiles; in the Philippines, a well-born Hispanized Filipina accepted into the Manila convent of the Poor Clares in 1631 took the devotional name of Martha de San Bernardo, recalling Bernard of Clairvaux (1090–1153), a medieval theologian who was dedicated to the veneration of Mary ([27], pp. 1–9; [45], pp. 68–69). Protestantism, with its abhorrence of saint worship, had no such traditions, but converts were given new "Dutch" names, and a Ternate Sultan, anxious to demonstrate his loyalty to the VOC, called one son "Amsterdam" and another "Rotterdam".

The movement along these Christian circuits took many different forms. Catholic Indians and Eurasians were used by the missionary orders throughout much of Southeast Asia, and around 1741, when a seminary was set up in Timor, two members of an Indian order, the Oratorians, were sent as teachers ([46], pp. 42, 69, 422). Although the VOC employed only a very small number of Indians and Ceylonese as ministers, some Eurasians did go to the Netherlands for theological training ([37], p. 171; [47], p. 78).

As Christianized alpha cities became key points on a reshaped Asian landscape, places controlled by sympathetic believers became places of refuge when Christians faced banishment or persecution as in China, Vietnam and Japan. In 1614, for instance, a group of Japanese *beatas* sought protection in a convent in Manila to escape Tokugawa suppression [48]. The sectarian animosities that divided Catholics and Protestants could also create religious refugees, and Macau provided asylum for many Catholics who fled from Melaka and other areas taken by the Dutch in the seventeenth century. In Vietnam, where Christian communities were constantly under threat, wider missionary connections could be effectively employed to relocate institutions and personnel. Despite the rivalry between the Iberian-dominated religious orders and the French Société des Missions Étrangères de Paris (MEP), in 1769 the Franciscans in Vietnam helped MEP missionaries and eighteen students to escape to Dutch-controlled Melaka, and from thence to India, where their college was re-established at Pondicherry ([49], p. 117).

In many alpha cities the proliferation of Christian shrines, tombs and churches provided a meeting ground for people of very different origins, and encouraged travel to quite distant places. After their ship arrived safely in Acapulco around 1595, for example, Filipino sailors made the three-hundred kilometre journey to give thanks at the basilica of the Virgin of Guadalupe ([50], p. 374, n. 26). Nor did the individuals who travelled along these pathways come empty handed. Crucifixes, rosaries, bibles, psalm books, musical instruments, religious vestments, were all infused with multiple possibilities of imagining "globality", and most had the advantage of being light and easy to transport. Even the VOC, virulently opposed to "Popish" idolatry, found it profitable to trade in pictures of the Virgin and Mary Magdalene ([51], p. 103). Lifelike religious images were accorded a special place as sources of benevolence and protection, like the Virgin carried from Manila to south-eastern India's "fishery coast" in 1555 to become the Mother of the Parava fishing caste ([52], p. 52). The famed statue of Bunda Maria (Mother Mary) in Larantuka (Flores) is commonly believed to have miraculously arrived from Melaka, but it probably originated in late eighteenth century Manila, reaching Larantuka via Portuguese Macau [53]. The most well-travelled Marian image, the Virgin of Antipolo, was brought to Manila from Mexico in 1626. Because she was credited with special powers some captains gained permission to have her on board their ships, and over the next century she made eight voyages back and forth across the Pacific ([54], p. 14).

In the Catholic environment the distribution of relics provides another example of how religious belief could promote the sense of a global community. In 1572 the Bishop of Melaka, Gregorio de Santa Luzia, took to Goa a relic of the True Cross of Christ that had been sent from Rome. It was displayed in the procession inside a magnificent reliquary in the form of a golden cross ([55], p. 51). From 1633 the Tokugawa "closure" of Japan ended direct relations with Portuguese Melaka, but new emotional links were established through the bones of Christians martyred in Japan, and the distribution of these relics to other places. In Macau the remains of 72 martyrs (58 Japanese and 14 Vietnamese), including 15 women are still preserved in the crypt of St Paul's Church ([55], pp. 49–51; [56]). In the adjacent college a full length portrait of the martyrdom of the young catechist Andrew Phu-yen, executed in 1644, which was said to inspire great devotion among all who saw it ([55], p. 80; [57], p. 207). One of the most revered of these linkages again involves Francis Xavier. From the early seventeenth century his body, entombed in Goa, was treated as "a quarry of relics"; an arm was sent to Rome, and in 1619 three bones from the elbow to the shoulder were extracted; one was sent to the southern part of Vietnam, another to Melaka, and a third shipped to Japan, and then to Macau ([57], p. 205). Indeed, in the view of the writer Antônio Vieira (1608–1697), the distribution of Xavier's relics was a symbol that all Catholics occupied "the same world" ([26], p. 65). Newly converted Protestants whose religious talismans were now condemned as "papist", hungered for other tangible sources of protection. In the absence of crucifixes, rosaries and holy images, "permitted" products such as the Bible, psalters, books of sermons and catechisms, assumed a sacral status, in part because they were written in a "secret" (poor romanized Malay) language that few could read or understand.

Probably the most effective medium for the promotion of Christianity as a universal faith that could encompass all cultures was education. In the sixteenth century the Jesuit college of St Paul in Goa became a major site for the globalization project, and its reputation grew rapidly. Opened in 1542, the seminary included non-Portuguese boys from all over Asia and Africa, with the idea that the most promising would be trained as secular priests. Just three years after its opening a Portuguese merchant from Melaka brought "four brown boys" from Makassar to join a student body that was increasingly cosmopolitan, representing at least thirteen different ethnicities. By the early seventeenth century over two thousand pupils were enrolled ([58], pp. 45–46; [59], pp. 256–58; [60], p. 521). The Goa seminary formed the model for similar institutions in Melaka, which attracted students from various parts of the region, including a prince from Flores ([61], p. 95). One of the most well-known products of an "Asian" schooling was Manuel Godinho de Erédia (1563–1623), who was born in Melaka, his father Portuguese and his mother a Makassar woman of good birth who had adopted Christianity. Educated in Melaka and at the Jesuit seminary at Goa, Erédia became a cartographer of considerable repute and author of one of the best early accounts of the Malay Peninsula. It is likely that the French Société des Missions Étrangères had the Goa model in mind when two priests established a college in Ayudhya (Siam) in 1664, which trained students not only from Siam but from Tonkin, China, and Cochinchina ([22], p. 36; [49], p. 208).

Though Manila became a centre for post-primary education, the colleges that sometimes admitted well-born Filipinos were primarily intended to serve residents of the Philippines and were never envisaged as regional institutions like those in Goa, Macau, Melaka or even Ayudhya. The ambitions of the VOC-sponsored schools set up in Batavia and elsewhere in the archipelago were also more modest. In the first flush of enthusiasm, it was thought that a Christian education was best imparted in Europe, and in the early seventeenth century a number of boys from eastern Indonesia were sent to the Netherlands to learn Dutch and be introduced to Dutch life style. By the 1620s, however, the program was deemed unsuccessful and it was decided to teach students in their own country ([37], pp. 90, 95). Proposals to educate sons of traditional leaders as Dutch-speaking Protestant leaders saw few results, despite the establishment of a "Latin school" in Batavia and a short-lived seminary in 1745 ([62], pp. 44–45). The major contribution of the VOC's educational system was the training of a cohort of primary schoolteachers in Ambon, who were posted to Christian communities throughout the eastern areas to teach the basic elements of Protestant belief, the essential prayers, and to prepare students for examination by a minister when he made his annual visit ([37], pp. 35, 57).

Ironically, the very competition to gain converts exposed deep fissures in Christianity's touted universalism. In Southeast Asia the enmity between Protestant and Catholic was particularly evident, but internally both Christian streams were characterized by acrimonious disputes. Tensions within Catholicism that set the Jesuits (linked to Portugal) against Spanish Franciscans reflected the competition between Portuguese Melaka and Spanish Manila. The Jesuit-Dominican rivalry in Europe was transferred and re-enacted in the Philippines, where the hostility between the different religious orders often reached extreme heights. In mainland Southeast Asia national interests were similarly entangled with the missionizing enterprise. In Vietnam the priests of the Paris-based MEP, for instance, were highly critical of "Portuguese" Jesuit acceptance of baptizing "uninstructed" individuals, while the Jesuits accused their MEP rivals of ordaining Vietnamese clergy who were "ignorant and untrained" ([22], p. 137). These rivalries were intensified because descendants of liaisons between Portuguese men and local women formed the core of Christian communities in much of Southeast Asia outside the Philippines and the links between Catholicism and Portugal were consequently strong. A seventeenth-century account of Vietnam, for instance, describes a play performed in a public market place where a boy enacting the adoption of Christianity, asked whether he would "enter the belly of the Portuguese", crept under the robe of an actor depicting a missionary from Portugal. On this occasion a watchful Jesuit said the question should be changed to "will you enter into the Christian law?" to avoid implications that Christian conversion meant becoming "Portuguese" ([63], p. 139). However, the Universalist message was persistently undermined because converts to Catholicism saw even small differences in liturgical style or pronunciation of religious terms (for instance, when Spanish Dominicans replaced Jesuits in Vietnam) as a symbol of different loyalties and even a different religion ([22], p. 137). Though less intense, rivalries divided the Protestant denominations as well. In 1742, for instance, VOC authorities gave permission for the Lutherans to build a church in Batavia, overruling strong objections from the leaders of the Dutch Reformed Church. Determined to maintain their religious monopoly, Reformed ministers proceeded to oppose Lutheran efforts to conduct baptisms, marriages and even bury their dead in their own cemetery ([61], p. 123).

Arguably, the most divisive issue for both Catholics and Protestants concerned the degree to which Christian teachings—the "product"—should be "tailored" to be more compatible with local customs and practices. The debates surrounding the acceptability of ancestor veneration for Christians in China and Vietnam and the Papal interdiction have generated much academic discussion, but as Tara Alberts has shown, refusals to condone religious compromise resurfaced in a multitude of other contexts [22]. In tandem with the conviction that "true" Christianity could not condone any concessions to "heathen practices" was the belief in European superiority and its inevitable corollary, the spiritual inferiority of non-European converts.

3. Glocalization and Its Limitations

Debates about the degree to which Christianity should be adapted to the local environment represent a recurring theme in the history of Asian missions well into the twentieth century. In the early modern period the difficulty of amalgamating "global" and "local" in Southeast Asia is well documented in the Catholic context, but in the Indonesian archipelago Protestant attitudes were even more implacable. Without the accommodating influences of the Jesuits and the ritualistic features that could be linked to pre-Christian practices, Protestantism as a "product" was only weakly adapted to the environment in which VOC missionaries were working ([64], p. 365). The very architecture and interior décor of Protestant churches, resembling those in Europe, offered few opportunities for the kind of modifications that might appeal to local congregations. Though less ambitious than Batavia's imposing Kruiskerk, which was modelled after the Noorderkerk in Amsterdam, Melaka's Christ Church made minimal concessions to local aesthetics. Well over a hundred years later Isabella Bird described it as a "prosaic Dutch meeting house" and the only visible local touch is the moustachioed face of a Dutchman on the front door ([65], p. 152; [66], pp. 49, 296). The insistence on replication of Dutch prototypes caused major problems in timber-scarce areas like Kupang (Timor), where bricks and lime were the standard building materials. In 1761 the VOC resident was forced to abandon plans to construct a church similar to the one in Batavia because of the lack of wood suitable for beams [67].

At the end of the eighteenth century the never-completed Kupang church epitomizes nearly two hundred years of the Protestant presence in eastern Indonesia. Although several of the early ministers entered the field with enthusiasm, it was never easy to attract converts or transform individuals baptized as Catholics into faithful members of the Reformed Church. Clerical authorities were adamant that liturgy as practiced in the Netherlands should be followed as closely as possible, and any compromises were therefore concerned with minor matters, such as the celebration of communion with bread made of rice rather than wheat flour ([68], pp. 33, 47). At times, it is true, incentives could be held out for conversion. In 1677, when the entire population of a village on the island of Seram was baptised, the VOC governor uncharacteristically sponsored a feast and distributed textiles to the converts "in order to arouse jealousy amongst other heathens in the surrounding area" ([69], pp. 109, 115). However, it was more common to impose fines and other punishments for dereliction of Christian duties and poor church attendance. A seemingly never-ending succession of rules and ordinances flowed out from Batavia to VOC officials and Church personnel stationed in the eastern islands, addressing issues related to such matters as pre-baptismal instruction, criteria for admission as a church member, language use, marriage arrangements, administration, finances, ministerial dress, monitoring of religious practitioners. Local schoolmasters were given responsibility for preparing individuals to be examined during the minister's annual visit, but were not permitted to compose prayers or preach independently. In addition, the constant rotation of ministers, with very few staying for any length of time, meant that there was little familiarity with language or with local customs. A minister could even be fined if his sermon exceeded the prescribed limit, checked by an hourglass ([68], pp. 28–30). Lacking the processions, the rituals, the panoply, the holy objects of Catholicism, Protestantism had little to lure converts except musical participation, but even this was tightly controlled, with approval given only to the psalms of David and selected hymns. Because there was little room for innovation, Dutch church music did not adopt the alternating chanting more familiar to indigenous cultures, with one line read, and then people singing their response. This style was known to be an effective teaching method, but the VOC church hierarchy considered it too reminiscent of "heathen" practices and suggestions that the catechism be put into rhyme were rejected. Because indigenous musical instruments such as drums and gongs were similarly condemned, singing was normally unaccompanied, for although the main church in Batavia had an organ, none were available in eastern Indonesia ([68], p. 42). Musical instruction became part of the school curriculum, and a principal task of teachers was to guard the cupboard in hymnbooks were kept and to collect them after the lesson was over. In this sense, one could argue that musical notation and the accompanying words were effectively "owned" by the Church's agents in the form of ministers, *krankbezoekers*, and teachers.

It would be interesting to speculate how the "glocalization" of Protestantism in eastern Indonesia might have proceeded had it not been for the re-imposition of Dutch colonial control over Christian practice in the nineteenth century. As the VOC slipped into bankruptcy the Reformed congregations in larger centres such as Melaka and Batavia were maintained (their members, often poor women and former slaves, dependent on Church charity) but by the 1790s the Protestant presence in eastern

Indonesia had largely disappeared. In 1725 there had been 23 ordained ministers in the Indies, but by 1794 only 14 (7 of whom were in Batavia) served the entire area, and escalating raiding and piracy made clerical visits between islands increasingly unsafe ([61], pp. 87, 100, n. 55). As human resources and evangelical energies declined in company with the loss of trade and the Company's looming bankruptcy, small Protestant congregations were left on their own under the direction of local schoolteachers.

These developments had far-reaching implications for the oldest Protestant community on the island of Ambon, where permanent ministers were stationed, where conversion had been more successful, and where native teachers, employed by the VOC, had become key figures in Christian evangelism. When the English took control of Maluku in 1796, this group remained loyal to "old customs" (i.e., the worship style associated with Batavia and The Netherlands). Between 1794 and 1819, when Dutch ministers were completely absent, it was the schoolteachers who maintained the traditions and practices attached to baptism and church membership. At the same time, they were already staking out their own claim as guardians of a certain style of Christian ritual. The Dutch returned in 1817, only to face a rebellion in which schoolteachers played a leading role, believing that the Dutch planned to destroy "Malukan" Christianity, and seeing themselves as defenders of piety against an unwelcome secularization ([70], p. 385). It was their scriptural knowledge that provided the uprising with its religious justification and inspiration. When one of the rebel strongholds was taken, the church bible was open at David's great invocation, Psalm 17:

> I have called upon thee, for thou wilt hear me, O God . . . hide me under the shadow of thy wings, from the wicked that oppress me, from my deadly enemies, who compass me about. They are enclosed in their own fat: with their mouth they speak proudly ([61], p. 385).

The "glocalization" of early modern Catholicism would appear to be more successful, although in Southeast Asia it followed a number of different paths. On the one hand, there were areas where links to large "alpha" centres were so weakened over time that Catholic communities became independent "owners" of localized practices. For example, the expulsion of priests from Vietnam in the eighteenth century encouraged converts to assume a leadership role as mediators and interpreters of the Christian message. Two anonymous texts from the eighteenth century, "Treatise on True Religion" and "Conference of the Four Religions", were intended to prepare converts for baptism and answer the accusation that Christians neglected filial piety and were no longer loyal to their king [71]. Another example comes from Portugal's most distant territories in the Solor-Timor Archipelago, where Catholicism survived as a key marker of "Black Portuguese" (Topass) identity ([72], pp. 176, 183). When Dominican priests (often themselves of mixed Indian-Portuguese descent) were tapped for their spiritual powers, they also contributed to the Timorese domestication of Catholicism. Prior to a Topass attack on VOC-controlled Kupang in 1749, "a few priests of native complexion" baptized not only high-ranking Timor nobles, but also the soil and some sacred trees ([73], p. 142). Sponsored by the Dominicans, the Topass carried Christian banners and symbols into battle, but animal sacrifices and the drinking of blood were also performed to ensure success. Visitors to Timor noted that although local Catholics "knew little more than a few prayers", they never failed to wear a rosary or a cross around their necks as a form of protection and thus to affirm their adherence to the Christian faith ([74], pp. 8, 42).

Undoubtedly, the most effective "glocalization" of Christianity occurred in the Philippines, where the domestication of Hispanic Catholicism in virtually every aspect of Christian life has generated a corpus of historical studies. Emblematic of the manifold ways in which Catholicism was translated into a familiar cultural idiom is the Miag-ao church in Cebu. Built with the assistance of local Christians, its pediment is decorated with a bas-relief sculpture of St. Christopher—a universal Catholic icon, but here represented as a Filipino—who is carrying the Christ Child and planting a fully grown coconut palm (an attribute of the Immaculate Conception), with papaya and guava trees nearby [75]. Innumerable other conceptualizations and their tangible representations—revered images, all with their own specific histories, celebrations associated with a particular location, pre-existing "holy places" now transformed into pilgrimage sites, theatrical presentations of religious stories—show how the dynamics of Filipino cultures successfully tamed the behemoth of Spanish Catholicism. One study of religious music in the Philippines has demonstrated the complex processes by which Filipinos actively appropriated and reshaped a musical system rooted in a very different culture [8]. While the importation of Iberian religious music was "an explicit symbol of cultural universality...in the Hispanic World", these new styles could incorporate indigenous features and provide opportunities for local musicians to include elements that reflected the Filipino environment ([76], p. 364). The most well-known of these domesticated poetic and musical forms is the *Pasyon*, the account of the life of Christ, which established itself as an integral part of Filipino spiritual life beyond the confines of the church and fostered a sense of religious ownership through the use of indigenous languages ([8], pp. 147–53; [77]).

Nonetheless, the Philippines case shows that the very success of Catholicism's adaptation to "consumer" culture also exposed the limits of the global project. Like their VOC counterparts, the intrusion of the Catholic Church into the personal space of local Christians was a persistent reminder that Christianity required compliance with a certain lifestyle based upon what was considered "correct" not merely in Europe, but in the colonial alpha cities. In Goa, where the much-feared Inquisition was instituted in the mid sixteenth century, prohibitions against customs such as birth or marriage ceremonies that were seen as "heathen" could touch even the minutia of ordinary life. For instance, in 1736 the Goa Inquisition ruled that Christians could not eat boiled rice without salt, or bathe wearing clothes before cooking, as Hindus did ([78], p. 192; [79]). The prohibition against the use of Hindu musical instruments is echoed in the Philippines where there were complaints that the "localization" of religious music imparted incorrect doctrine and where the friars were concerned at the theatricality and burlesque that had crept into Filipino renditions of religious genres. Ecclesiastical occasions should be celebrated with solemnity and should not provide opportunities for entertainment, laugher and worldliness ([76], pp. 371–72). Underlying all these rulings was the ongoing debate about the extent to which the universal missionary enterprise should allow the continuation of practices and customs that originated from non-Christian traditions. Although the devout Filipino nun, Martha de San Bernardo, was among those sent to Macau in 1633 to establish a foundation ([45], pp. 68–69), there are many counter-stories as well. Lucia de Los Reyes, a *beata* (a member of the Third Order of pious lay women) reportedly experienced a state of ecstasy compared to that of Saint Teresa, but Church officials regarded this as dangerously close to the trances of indigenous spirit mediums. Lucia was accused of heresy and taken to Mexico to stand trial as a heretic ([80], pp. 120–21).

The chronological justification for different periodizations has long been debated, although most historians have cautiously accepted the idea of an "early modern" period characterized by increasing world-wide connections. Its boundaries, however, are fluid and in Southeast Asia there is a clear continuum between the global-local interaction of pre-nineteenth century missionizing and that which followed during the "colonial period". For example, the Spanish authorities and the Catholic hierarchy in the Philippines regarded, the leader of a locally-formed *Cofradia* de San Jose, Apolinario de la Cruz (1815–41), as a heretic because his Christianity incorporated many pre-Christian practices, such as the use of talismans and because his followers venerated him as Christ-like ([77], pp. 29–62). Captured after an anti-Spanish uprising, he was summarily executed. In a similar vein, Dutch reformed ministers denounced the "Apostle of Java," Kiai Sadrach (c.1835–1924) as a false teacher because he presented Christianity as a form of Javanese esoteric wisdom ([61], p. 642). In mid nineteenth-century Timor, returning Dutch Jesuits were appalled at the extent to which local communities, once under the Portuguese but left for two generations without priests, had reshaped Iberian Catholic rituals in accordance with their own Animistic culture. Measures were quickly put in place to bring these "baptized heathens" back to the fold and to foster the more restrained style of northern European Catholicism. In the history of Christian evangelism the definition of globalization proposed by Giddens thus requires some modification. The new relationships that European Christianity introduced undoubtedly contributed to the shaping of "local happenings" in Southeast Asia, but the "vice versa" of religious influences is difficult to discern. ([3], p. 64).

4. Conclusions

This article began by noting the expansion of the theoretical literature that has focused on the implications of globalization's penetration into local environments. Although the concept of "glocalization" has proved useful in the sociology of religion, it has been largely applied in relation to developments in modern times. By contrast, this discussion has moved chronologically backwards to consider the nature of Christian missionizing in the early modern period and the implications of elevating Christianity into a universal faith. The expansion of European commercial interests into Asia, the Americas and Africa was commonly justified by the biblical injunction to spread Christian teachings, and by the "civilizing" influences that would then be fostered. In his global project Christianization was underwritten by the belief that teachings and practices which had evolved in Europe could be successfully transported to very different environments. The early modern period was a critical period in Christianity's claim to be a "world" religion, but in Southeast Asia as elsewhere, responses to the missionizing endeavour varied from negotiation and acceptance to apathy and outright resistance. The transmission of what was seen as a universal message was complicated by the goal of imposing European economic control, by the opposition this generated, and by competition with other religions and among Christians themselves. In this often antagonistic environment, the degree to which a global product could be "repackaged"—i.e., glocalized—so that it was cross-culturally appealing was always constrained, even among the most sympathetic purveyors.

Within the framework of studies on religious globalization, Southeast Asia is particularly interesting because here we can compare different interpretations of Christianity, notably Catholicism and Protestantism, and contrast the boundaries that were imposed on glocalization. While it can be argued that Catholicism was generally more successful in this regard, we can also see continuing debates between the religious orders, and between Iberian Catholics and their northern European counterparts. Western imperialism and the imposition of colonialism over much of nineteenth–century Southeast Asia raised new questions about the extent to which a culturally-adapted Christian "brand" could be propagated by local congregations and the degree to which indigenous iterations were permissible. Arguments about the acceptability of what is often termed "inculturation" have continued into modern times, but the association with the West means that some societies still regard Christianity as a "foreign" religion, despite its long regional presence. An appreciation of the complex entwining of local and global, and the variety of different forms that this could take, must therefore underpin any study of Southeast Asia's religious history. Such an appreciation supports the proposition that the glocalization of Christianity in the early modern set up "power-laden tensions" which both global institutions and dispersed consumers continue to negotiate ([21], p. 57).

Conflicts of Interest: The author declares no conflict of interest.

References

1. Delanty, Gerard. "Europe in world regional perspective: Formations of modernity and major historical transformations." *The British Journal of Sociology* 66 (2015): 420–40. [CrossRef] [PubMed]
2. Robertson, Roland. *Globalization: Social Theory and Global Culture*. London: Sage, 1992.
3. Giddens, Anthony. *The Consequences of Modernity*. Stanford: Stanford University Press, 1990.
4. Hobson, John M. *The Eastern Origins of Western Civilisaton*. Cambridge: Cambridge University Press, 2002.
5. Pieterse Nederveen, Jan. "Periodizing globalization: Histories of globalization." *New Global Studies* 6 (2012): 1–25.
6. Held, David, Anthony McGrew, David Goldblatt, and Jonathan Perraton. *Global Transformations: Politics, Economics and Culture*. Stanford: Stanford University Press, 1999.
7. Holton, Robert J. *Globalization and the Nation State*, 2nd ed. London: Macmillan, 2011.
8. Irving, David. *Colonial Counterpoint: Music in Early Modern Manila*. Oxford: Oxford University Press, 2010.
9. Gunn, Geoffrey C. *First Globalization: The Eurasian Exchange 1500 to 1800*. Oxford: Rowman & Littlefield, 2003.

10. Andaya, Barbara Watson. "Historicizing 'modernity' in Southeast Asia." *Journal of the Economic and Social History of the Orient* 39 (1997): 391–409. [CrossRef]
11. Andaya, Barbara Watson, and Leonard Y. Andaya. *A History of Early Modern Southeast Asia.* Cambridge: Cambridge University Press, 2015.
12. Bentley, Jerry H. "Cross-cultural interaction and periodization in world history." *The American Historical Review* 101 (1996): 749–70. [CrossRef]
13. Beyer, Peter. "Globalization and glocalization." In *The Sage Handbook of the Sociology of Religion.* Edited by James A. Beckford and Nicholas Jay Demerath, III. London: Sage, 2007, pp. 98–118.
14. *The Oxford Dictionary of New Words.* Edited by Elizabeth Knowles and Julia Elliott. Oxford: Oxford University Press, 1991.
15. Roudometof, Victor. "Glocalization, space, and modernity 1." *The European Legacy* 8 (2003): 37–60. [CrossRef]
16. Roudometof, Victor. "Theorizing glocalization: Three interpretations." *European Journal of Social Theory* 19 (2016): 391–408. [CrossRef]
17. Roudometof, Victor. "Transnationalism, cosmopolitanism and glocalization." *Current Sociology* 53 (2005): 113–35. [CrossRef]
18. Ng, Peter Tze Ming. *Chinese Christianity: An Interplay between Global and Local Perspectives.* Leiden: Brill, 2012.
19. Robertson, Roland. "Glocalization: Time-space and homogeneity-heterogeneity." In *Global Modernities.* Edited by Mike Featherstone, Scott Lash and Roland Robertson. London: Sage, 1995, pp. 25–44.
20. Roudometof, Victor. "Forms of religious glocalization: Orthodox Christianity in the *Longue Durée.*" *Religions* 5 (2014): 1017–36. [CrossRef]
21. Vásquez, Manuel A., and Marie F. Marquardt. *Globalizing the Sacred: Religion across the Americas.* New York: Rutgers University Press, 2003.
22. Alberts, Tara. *Conflict & Conversion: Catholicism in Southeast Asia, 1500–1700.* Oxford: Oxford University Press, 2013.
23. Newitt, Malyn. *A History of Portuguese Overseas Expansion 1400–1668.* Abingdon: Routledge, 2005.
24. Brockey, Liam Matthew. "Introduction. Nodes of Empire." In *Portuguese Colonial Cities in the Early Modern World.* Edited by Liam Matthew Brockey. Farnham and Burlington: Ashgate, 2008, pp. 1–16.
25. Mascarenhas, Margaret. "The Church in eighteenth-century Goa." In *Essays in Goan History.* Edited by Teotonio R. de Souza. New Delhi: Concept, 1989, pp. 81–102.
26. Pereira, Jose. *Monumental Legacy: Churches of Goa.* New Delhi: Oxford University Press, 2002.
27. Higashibaba, Ikuo. *Christianity in Early Modern Japan: Kirishitan Belief and Practice.* Leiden: Brill, 2001.
28. Schumann, Olaf. "Christianity and colonialism in the Malay world." In *Christianity in Indonesia: Perspectives of Power.* Edited by Susanne Schröter. Munster: LIT Verlag, 2011, pp. 31–82.
29. Sá, Guimarães, and Isabel dos. "Charity, ritual and business at the edge of empire: The misericórdia of Macau." In *Portuguese Colonial Cities in the Early Modern World.* Edited by Liam Matthew Brockey. Princeton: Princeton University Press, 2008, pp. 149–76.
30. Pinto da França, António. *Portuguese Influence in Indonesia.* Lisbon: Calouste Gulbenkian Foundation, 1985.
31. Mundy, Peter. *The Travels of Peter Mundy in Europe and Asia, 1608–1667.* London: Hakluyt Society, 1919, vol. 3.
32. Miu Bing Cheng, Christina. *Macau: A Cultural Janus.* Hong Kong: Hong Kong University Press, 1999.
33. Ras, Johannes Jacobus. *Hikajat Bandjar.* The Hague: Nijhoff, 1968.
34. Lombard-Jourdan, Anne. "Un mémoire inédit de F.E. de Rosily sur l'île de Timor (1772)." *Archipel* 23 (1982): 75–104. [CrossRef]
35. Nuttall, Zelia. "Royal ordinances concerning the laying out of new towns." *The Hispanic American Historical Review* 5 (1992): 743–54.
36. Subrahmanyam, Sanjay. "Manila, Melaka, Mylapore . . . : A Dominican voyage through the Indies, ca. 1600." *Archipel* 57 (1999): 223–42. [CrossRef]
37. Koolen, Gijsbertus Marius. *Een seer Bequaem Middel: Onderwijs en Kerk onder de 17e Eeuwse VOC.* Kampen: J.H. Kok, 1993.
38. Bland, Robert Norman. *Historical Tombstones of Malacca.* London: Elliot Stock, 1905.
39. Cordova, James M. "Mexico's Crowned Virgins: Visual Strategies and Colonial Discourse in New Spain's Portraits of 'Crowned Nuns'." Ph.D. Thesis, Tulane University, New Orleans, LA, USA, 2006.
40. Ruano, Pedro. *Mother Jerónima de de la Asunción (1555–1630), A Biography.* Quezon City: Monastery of St. Claire, 1999.

41. Collins, James. "Studying seventeenth-century Ambonese Malay: Evidence from F. Caron's sermons (1694)." *Cakalele* 3 (1992): 99–122.
42. Cooper, Michael. *The Japanese Mission to Europe, 1582–1590: The Journey of Four Samurai Boys through Portugal, Spain and Italy.* Kent: Global Oriental, 2005.
43. General State Archives. The Hague. VOC 2761, Timor to Batavia 8 March 1751, folio 43.
44. Phan, Phat Huòn. *History of the Catholic Church in Viet Nam.* Los Angeles: Vietnamese Redemptorist Mission, 2002, vol. 1, pp. 1533–960.
45. Santiago, Luciano. *To Love and to Suffer: The Development of the Religious Congregations for Women in the Philippines during the Spanish Era (1565–1898).* Quezon City: Ateneo de Manila University Press, 2005.
46. Matos, Artur Teodoro de. *Timor Português 1515–1569: Contribuição para a sua História.* Lisbon: Faculty of Literature, University of Lisbon, 1974.
47. Lieburg, Fred. A. van. "Het personeel van de Indische kerk." In *Het Indisch Sion: De Gereformeerde Kerk onder de Verenigde Oost-Indische Compagnie.* Edited by Gerritt J. Schutte. Hilversum: Verloren, 2002, pp. 65–100.
48. Ward, Haruko Nawata. *Women Religious Leaders in Japan's Christian Century, 1549–1650.* Farnham and Burlington: Ashgate, 2009.
49. Lange, Claude. *L'église Catholique et la Société des Missions Étrangères au Vietnam: Vicariat Apostolique de Cochinchine, XVIIe et XVIIIe siècles.* Paris: l'Harmattan, 2004.
50. Curcio-Nagy, Linda A. "From native icon to city protectress to royal patroness: Ritual, political symbolism and the Virgin of Remedies." *The Americas* 52 (1996): 367–91. [CrossRef]
51. Ijzerman, Jan Willem. "Hollandsche prenten als handelsartikel te Patani in 1602." In *Koninklijk Instituut voor de Taal-, Land- en Volkenkunde van Nederlandsch-Indië. Gedenkschrift Uitgegeven ter Gelegenheid van het 75-Jarig Bestaan op 4 Juni 1926.* The Hague: Koninklijk Instituut, 1926, pp. 84–109.
52. Roche, Patrick A. *Fishermen of the Coromandel: A Social Study of the Paravas of the Coromandel.* New Delhi: Manohar, 1984.
53. Andaya, Barbara Watson. "Christianity, religion and identity in a Muslim environment: Mother Mary, Queen of Larantuka, Indonesia." In *Attending to Early Modern Women: Conflict and Concord.* Edited by Karen Nelson. Newark: University of Delaware Press, 2013, pp. 135–52.
54. Mercado, Monina A. *Antipolo: A Shrine to Our Lady.* Manila: Craftnotes/Aletheia Foundation, 1980.
55. Guillén-Nuñez, César. *Macao's Church of Saint Paul: A Glimmer of the Baroque in China.* Hong Kong: Hong Kong University Press, 2009.
56. Borschberg, Peter. "Ethnicity, language and culture in Melaka after the transition from Portuguese to Dutch rule (seventeenth century)." *Journal of the Malaysian Branch of the Royal Asiatic Society* 83 (2010): 93–117.
57. Bruce, Phillip. "A relic of St. Francis Xavier." *Journal of the Royal Asiatic Society Hong Kong Branch* 23 (1983): 204–7.
58. Alden, Dauril. *The Making of an Enterprise: The Society of Jesus in Portugal, its Empire, and Beyond, 1540–1750.* Stanford: Stanford University Press, 1996.
59. Gomes, Olivinho. *The Religious Orders in Goa (XVIth-XVIIth Centuries).* Goa: Konkani Sorospot Prakashan, 2003.
60. Schurhammer, Georg. *Francis Xavier: His Life, His Times: India, 1541–1545.* Translated by M. Joseph Costelloe. Rome: The Jesuit Historical Institute, 1977, vol. II.
61. Jan Sihar Aritonang, and Karel Steenbrink, eds. *A History of Christianity in Indonesia.* Leiden: Brill, 2008.
62. Groenenboer, Kees. *Gateway to the West: The Dutch Language in Colonial Indonesia, 1600–1950: A History of Language Policy.* Amsterdam: Amsterdam University Press, 1998.
63. Dror, Olga, and Keith Weller Taylor. *Views of Seventeenth-Century Vietnam: Christoforo Borri on Cochinchina and Samuel Baron on Tonkin.* Ithaca: Cornell Southeast Asia Program, 2008.
64. Beyer, Peter. "De-centering religious singularity: The globalization of Christianity as a case in point." *Numen* 50 (2003): 357–86. [CrossRef]
65. Bird, Isabella. *The Golden Chersonese and the Way Thither*, reprint of 1883 ed. Kuala Lumpur: Oxford University Press, 1967.
66. Haan, Frederik de. *Oud Batavia. Gedenkboek Uitgegeven door het Bataviaasch Genootschap van Kunsten en Wetenschappen naar Aanleiding van het Driehonderjarig Bestaan der Stad in 1919.* Batavia: Kolff, 1922–1923, vol. 1.

67. General State Archives. The Hague. VOC 3121 Missive van't opperhoofd en raad aan hun Hoog Eds., 15 October 1764, folio 23.

68. Abineno, Johannes Ludwig. *Liturgische Vormen en Patronen in de Evangelische Kerk op Timor*. Utrecht and The Hague: University of Utrecht, 1956.

69. Knaap, Gerrit. *Kruidnagelen en Christenen: de Verenigde Oost-Indische Compagnie en de Bevolking van Ambon 1656–96*. Leiden: KITLV Press, 2004.

70. Jong, Chris de. *De Protestantse Kerk in de Midden Molukken 1803–1900*. Leiden: KILTV Press, 2006.

71. Tran, Anh Q. "Inculturation, missions and dialogue in Vietnam: The conference of representatives of four religions." In *Beyond Conversion and Syncretism: Indigenous Encounters with Missionary Christianity*. Edited by David F. Lindenfeld and Miles Richards. Oxford and New York: Berghahn, 2011, pp. 167–94.

72. Dampier, William. *A Voyage to New Holland: The English Voyage of Discovery to the South Seas in 1699*. Edited by James Spencer. Gloucester: Alan Sutton, 1981.

73. Heijmering, Geerlof. "Bijdragen tot de geschiedenis van het eiland Timor." *Tijdschrift voor Nederlandsch-Indië* 9 (1847): 1–62, 121–42.

74. Pelon, Jean-Baptiste. *Description de Timor Occidental et des îles sous Domination Hollandaise (1771–1778)*. Edited by Anne Lombard-Jourdan. Paris: Association Archipel, 2002.

75. Reyes, Raquel. "Paradise in stone: Visual representations of New World plants and animals in eighteenth-century Philippine church architecture." Unpublished Paper presented at AAS Annual Meeting, Honolulu, HI, USA, 31 March 2011. Used with permission.

76. Irving, David. "Historical and literary vestiges of the *villancico* in the early modern Philippines." In *Devotional Music in the Iberian World 1400–1800: The Villancico and Related Genres*. Edited by Tess Knighton and Álvaro Torrente. Aldershot: Ashgate, 2007, pp. 363–98.

77. Ileto, Reynaldo Clemeña. *Pasyon and Revolution: Popular Movements in the Philippines, 1840–1910*. Quezon City: Ateneo de Manila University Press, 1979.

78. Gracias, Fátima da Silva. "Quality of life in colonial Goa: Its hygienic expression (19th–20th centuries)." In *Essays in Goan History*. Edited by Teotonio R. de Souza. New Delhi: Concept Publishing, 1989, pp. 185–204.

79. Robinson, Rowena. "The construction of Goan interculturality: A historical analysis of the inquisitorial edict of 1736 as prohibiting (and permitting) syncretic practices." In *Goa and Portugal: History and Development*. Edited by Charles J. Borges, Óscar G. Pereira and Hannes Stubble. New Delhi: Concept, 2000, pp. 289–318.

80. Brewer, Carolyn. *Shamanism, Catholicism and Gender Relations in Colonial Philippines*. Aldershotand Burlington: Ashgate, 2004.

![religions logo] *religions*

MDPI

Article

Glocalization and Religious Communication in the Roman Empire: Two Case Studies to Reconsider the Local and the Global in Religious Material Culture

David C. D. van Alten

Department of Education, Utrecht University, Heidelberglaan 1, 3584 CS Utrecht, The Netherlands;
D.C.D.vanAlten@uu.nl

Received: 18 July 2017; Accepted: 31 July 2017; Published: 3 August 2017

Abstract: Over the period in which the ancient Roman empire grew to its greatest extent, religion in the provinces underwent change. In this article, the author argues that glocalization as an explicit modern conceptual framework has added value to the analysis of religious material culture. First, the glocalization model is discussed in the context of a wider debate on the biased concept of Romanization. Second, a rationale is presented for interpreting Roman religious change with a glocalization perspective. Third, two concrete bodies of archaeological source material are re-interpreted within the glocalization framework: first the little studied rural sanctuary of Dhronecken near ancient Trier and second a particular form of religious gifts that appeared on an empire-wide scale as a ritual with respect to the *salus*, the well-being of the emperor. Based on the application of the glocalization framework to these sources, the author concludes that religious material culture in these cases can be seen as a process in which new forms of religious communication were created out of an interrelated and ongoing process of local and global cultural expressions.

Keywords: glocalization; globalization; Roman religion; Romanization; religious communication; Dhronecken; salus; material culture

1. Introduction

In the period between ca. 50 BC and AD 300, the Roman Empire gained control over a territory incorporating large parts of modern Europe, North Africa and East Asia. The people who lived in these newly conquered areas faced changes in their lives. The interpretation of how these people experienced religious change, based on material culture and ancient texts, is a difficult task and subject to change. The dominant "grand-narrative" implying that Graeco-Roman religion was in great decline in the first centuries AD has become subject to fierce deconstruction (Rives 2010). In addition, Rives shows that the indigenous traditions of the various peoples who made up the empire, and the way that these developed under Roman rule, has long been a neglected topic in research on religion in the Graeco-Roman world (Rives 2010). Now, Graeco-Roman religious tradition is attributed a more vigorous and creative role, and "the degree of Roman influences, strength of local traditions and the emergence of mixed forms have all been radically re-assessed" (North and Price 2011, pp. 2–3).

In a larger context, the interpretation of Roman cultural change in general is subject to fierce debate, as the ancient material does not speak for itself and historians and archaeologists ask and answer the questions, biased by a preset of conceptions of their own time (Finley 1987; Hingley 2005). In this article, the author investigates if glocalization is a valuable conceptual framework for the interpretation of religious change in the western part of the Roman Empire in the period of ca. 50 BC–AD 300. In short, glocalization involves the adaption of global expressions in local particularities and derives from theorizing ideas about globalization. As glocalization as a concept is increasingly applied across a variety of disciplines and fields—Roudometof (2016a) speaks of a glocal turn—this paper contributes to a wider debate on globalization and Roman archaeology in the first part, and applies the glocalization framework that has been set out in two case studies in the second part. First, glocalization theory is discussed in the context of a wider debate on the concept of Romanization, a deconstructed top-down framework from the late 19th century. The author argues that the glocalization framework is valuable because it uncovers a complex negotiation process behind Roman archeological material, in which seemingly Roman (i.e., global) cultural elements were differently adopted and adapted in various local contexts. Second, the author sets forth how Roman religion in its ancient context can be understood, and how religious change can be interpreted within a glocalization framework. It is argued that religious change on a local scale was a process in which new forms of religious communication were created out of an interrelated and ongoing process of local and global religious expressions. Third, two concrete bodies of archaeological source material are studied as case studies: first the rural sanctuary of Dhronecken near ancient Trier and second a particular form of religious gifts that appeared on an empire-wide scale as a ritual related to the *salus*, the well-being of the emperor. In doing so, this paper adds to the continuing theoretical debate on Romanization, the expanding interdisciplinary research on glocal religions, and provides new insights into the understanding of two religious types of material culture.

2. Beyond the Romanization Paradigm? Glocalization and the Roman World

"The extent to which conquest transformed the lives of the majority of the population is a contentious area of debate" (Hingley 2005, p. 115). This summarization by Hingley touches upon the fundamental problem of scholars studying Roman material culture and cultural interaction. Several scholars successfully demonstrated that an imperialistic top-down perspective became dominant from the late 19th century onwards, until it has been the subject of fierce deconstruction in the late 20th century inspired by postcolonial theories (e.g., Freeman 1997, pp. 27–50; Hingley 2005, pp. 1–48; Mattingly 2011, pp. 203–45). In reaction, several new frameworks have been proposed and discussed, which has led to an increasingly self-reflective, but highly fragmented research field (Pitts and Versluys 2015). While these frameworks often focused on bottom-up processes, some scholars have opposed that these postcolonial perspectives paradoxically maintain the Roman-Native dichotomy (Versluys 2014; Pitts and Versluys 2015; Gardner 2013; Woolf 1997). Another recent approach, that of globalization theory, aims to get beyond the Romanization paradigm (Versluys 2014; Pitts and Versluys 2015; Gardner 2013).

Globalization theory recently developed to describe the awareness of a process of growing interconnectivity, connecting different localities and making them more interdependent. Globalization has numerous meanings in different contexts, and is used to describe processes of a changing, globalizing world, in the spheres of culture, gender, ecology, capitalism, inequality, power, development, identity and population (Nederveen Pieterse 2009). I will focus on the area of cultural globalization, following Pitts who argues that globalization has high potential in the study of cultural change in antiquity (Pitts 2012). I argue it is a misunderstanding to interpret globalization as leading to cultural unity, where local places become increasingly interconnected with each other that one dominant culture will fade out the local cultures eventually (Appadurai 1996; Featherstone 1995). Rather, there is an inherent paradox in globalization, namely that processes of increasing homogenization and the incorporation of objects and ideas from a "global culture" ultimately involve transformations of these objects and ideas that always reassert self-identity at a local level (Hodos 2010). Robertson (1994, 1995) shows that glocalization is a twofold process involving the interpretation of the universalization of particularism and the particularization of universalism, the so-called paradox of globalization or the local-global nexus. Therefore, Robertson (1992, 1994, 1995) argues that the concept of glocalization better expresses the way globalization actually operates, as he explains that local and global culture are not two opposing forces, but they are interdependent and enable each other. In contrast, Roudometof (2016a, 2016b) argues, in his clear illustration of current theoretical interpretations of glocalization, for seeing glocalization as an analytically autonomous concept. It holds that glocalization should be seen as a process in which the agency of the local and the global is respected, leading to a *multitude of glocalities*. Roudometof (2016b, p. 399) defines glocality as "experiencing the global locally or through local lenses." Therefore, I use the term glocalization to point towards the glocal in terms of processes of adopting and adapting globalization though the local.

Critique has been raised to apply globalization to the ancient Roman world, addressing the anachronistic approach (Dench 2005), the argument that the Roman world was not a global empire (Naerebout 2006–2007; Greene 2008), and that this framework offers no new insights or is even a mere fashionable substitute buzz-word for Romanization (Mattingly 2004). Gardner (2013) questions whether globalization might even serves to legitimize current inequalities, as it may be used as a gloss for neo-colonialism.

However, the glocalization framework fits into a general recent trend in archaeology where several justified globalization approaches have been made (e.g., Hodos 2017), as well as in the particular field of Roman archaeology (e.g., Pitts and Versluys 2015; Versluys 2014; Haeussler 2013; Hingley 2005; Hitchner 2008; Pitts 2008). Woolf (1994, 1995, 1997, 2005) already argued that it is not helpful to approach cultural contact in the Roman world by holding up the dichotomy of natives versus Romans. On the question as to why globalization can offer a solution seeking a way forward beyond Romanization, Versluys (2014) makes a strong case by arguing for instance that the Roman world can be seen as one *oikumene* which is all about increased connectivity between localities culturally and socially interacting within the same (global) group. Further perspectives and opportunities, including a coherent rationale for globalization theory in Roman archaeology and history are further set out in Versluys (2015). Gardner (2013) too suggests that it is able to both study empire-wide phenomena and local experiences. In addition, several scholars already successfully used the glocalization framework in their work. For instance, Witcher (2000) shows that both earlier described approaches (top-down 'Romanization' and localized perspectives) made interesting advances, but are working at either end of a continuum. He concludes that "globalization offers the potential to work between these scales and to offer more rounded approaches to the mechanisms of Roman imperialism. Both the modern and ancient worlds involve overlapping scales of identity—global, national, regional, and local. The key is to locate these multiple identities in relation one another" (Witcher 2000, pp. 220–21). Along similar lines, Pitts (2008) argues that this framework adds more sophistication to the understanding of the homogenizing supply of pottery vessels in Roman Britain, as it was shaped by the integration of both local and global cultural elements.

Another justification for applying a glocalization framework to the Roman world is explicitly or implicitly made by scholars who have shown processes of globalization—in the form of increased connectivity—being active in the ancient Roman society (cf. Horden and Purcell 2000; Versluys 2014; Pitts and Versluys 2015; Hodos 2014). For example, Woolf argues that there was a relative short period of rapid cultural change, a formative period as he calls it, that went through the whole empire and coincided with the rule of Augustus (Woolf 1998). This wider process of socio-political and cultural change is not depended on the time of a region being conquered by Romans, but rather that this formative period took off on an empire-wide scale from roughly the transformation period between the 'Roman Republic' and the 'Roman Empire' (Simon and Terrenato 2001; Woolf 1995). It may seem clear to conclude that it was not the matter how long a region was conquered before change was visible, but rather in this specific period of time empire-wide change can be seen (Woolf 1998). In addition, the Roman elite themselves noticed that in this formative period around the time of Augustus there were some significant political and cultural changes occurring in the Roman empire, as can be seen in the writings of Dionysius of Halicarnassus (*de Oratoribus Veteribus* 3) and Strabo (Γεωγραφικά 6.4.3.) as shown by Woolf (2005, pp. 117–18). It seems clear that from this period onwards we can increasingly speak of an imperial structure of a formalized system of rule and government, census, and taxation over conquered territories. As Woolf points out: "the horizons of the Roman world had changed. Within those horizons the provinces were more numerous, were managed with more uniform systems, and were more securely held. With hindsight it seems a watershed had been passed: Rome had moved from greedy and unstable conquest state to tributary empire" (Woolf 2005, p. 117). Besides the fact that the political change brought about an increasing Roman imperial administration, a rapid spread and adaption of objects, practices, monuments characterized as Roman culture is also visible (Noreña 2011). Noreña (2011) argues for not seeing this as the expansion of one dominant culture at the expense of other local cultures, but as the emergence of a new, highly differentiated social formation of culture that was differently constructed on the basis of local and global power relations and hierarchy. This dominant culture was widely recognized as Roman, as it was closely connected to citizenship, and it evolved around shared notions of Roman identity in which habits of dress, speech, manners and conducts became more important than ethnical descent (Woolf 2005). Gardner (2013) argues that glocalization is able to analyze how transformation in the speed and reach of communication, movements of goods and people, information, and identities occurred differently in various places in the Roman empire, creating new forms of local identities.

3. Roman Religion as a Cultural Communication System

Before I can turn to the application of the glocalization framework on two religious archaeological datasets, it is necessary to briefly describe how religion in the ancient Roman world can be understood, and explain how Roman religion and its material culture can be seen as a cultural communication system. In his work on religion in the Roman empire, Rives (2000) explicates that Roman religion was closely tied to issues of culture, identity, and power. "Religion is very closely bound up with the way a person views the world and his or her own place within it; both shapes and reflects the system of values according to which a person lives his or her life" (Rives 2000, p. 245). Rives is inspired by the works of Geertz (Geertz 1993), who makes a case throughout his work for studying the religion of groups of people, societies and communities, rather than individuals, because even individual religious experience is part of a larger group (e.g., family, tribe, nation). For Geertz, culture is a system of meanings embodied in symbols, a communication system that serves as framework for individuals and social groups to understand reality, the world, and as a guidance for their behavior (Geertz 1993). Geertz defines religion fully as "a system of symbols which acts to establish powerful, pervasive and long-lasting moods and motivations in men by formulating conceptions of a general order of existence and clothing these conceptions with such an aura of factuality that the moods and motivations seem uniquely realistic" (Geertz 1993, p. 90). Thus, in his understanding, religion is an instance of culture (Segal 2003). Religious symbols as part of such a cultural system serve a particular function, as they convey a direct connection between our worldview and *ethos*, how we perceive the world and how we live according to that view (Geertz 1993; Segal 2003).

Here we come to the point of explaining why this theory by Geertz is still relevant (cf. Schilbrack 2005), and is particularly useful in the context of Roman religion. Geertz' basic assumption rests upon the notion that sociologists and anthropologists need to study and interpret meanings people express through culture and religion, rather than explaining the cause of cultural and religious expressions (Segal 2003). Thus, it makes the study of religious material possible by interpreting how people used religious material in everyday life in a set of customs, traditions and rituals to shape their understanding of the world, rather than focusing on what people actually believed and questioning their theological views on religious truth.

Thus, in a period of rapid change due to globalization, the way in which people construct religious meanings can show us how their (glocalized) worldview changed (Robertson and Garrett 1991). Roudometof (2005) argues that religion and language in particular are relevant indicators in which local communities faced with global pressures will re-evaluate their support and attachment to local culture. In a society faced with globalization pressures, an increasing awareness of local differences and attitudes toward that difference is increasingly visible (Roudometof 2005).

Now, how are these ideas related to Roman religion? The similarities will be clear if we understand Roman religion in the definition by Rives that I would like to adhere to, as "a conception of, reverence for, and desire to please or live in harmony with some superhuman force, as expressed through specific beliefs, principles and actions" (Rives 2007, p. 4). However, the term Roman religion is a scholarly construct that is itself subject of extensive discussion; it is debated if there even was such a conceptual understanding of religion in the Roman world (Ando 2007, 2008). Therefore, it is necessary to briefly look at how Romans themselves perceived religion.

Turning to the ancient Roman works by Cicero (*De Deorum Natura* 2.28) (Cicero 1933), it is helpful to understand the difference between the concepts *pietas* and *religio*. "It is our duty to revere and worship these gods under the names which custom has bestowed upon them. But the best and also the purest, highest and most pious (*pietas*) way of worshipping the gods (*cultus deorum*) is ever to venerate them with purity, sincerity and innocence both of thought and of speech. For religion (*religio*) has been distinguished from superstition (*superstitio*) not only by philosophers but by our ancestors" (Cicero 1933). *Pietas* wrongly carries the Christian notion of piety, but in the Roman world it meant something like loyalty to the gods in behavior (Belayche 2007). The Latin concept of *religio* does not equal our concept of religion as a religious system, but rather, *religio* as Roman concept means a conviction that there is an asymmetrical reciprocal-relationship between the gods and humans (Ando 2003). Cicero also contrasts *religio* with *superstitio*, the persuasion of the contractual relationship between gods and humans (*religio*) versus the belief in mystical power beyond the gods, not simply a mere superstition but more a dread of the supernatural and anxious credulity (*superstitio*). In this classification of the right religious attitude, Cicero uses the concept of *cultus deorum*, which is closer to our sense of religion, as a system to "have the proper regard to the gods" (Ando 2003). As Rives shows, the term *cultus* derives from *colere*, which means to tend to, to look after, and in this context to make the object of religious devotion (Rives 2007). Therefore, though I will continue to speak of Roman religion as this is common practice, we need not only keep in mind the considerations from above about ancient terminology, but also continue to realize that Roman religion was not a static concept, but was rather constantly developing and dynamically changing over time (Beard et al. 1998).

In another fragment of a speech written by Cicero (*On the Response of the Haruspices* 19), he claims that the Romans outdo all other people in their *pietas* and *religio* and taking care of the gods, who govern and manage all things (Cicero 1891). Furthermore, in the first half of the quote he states that the Roman empire was only achieved and preserved by the divine authority. Therefore, he sees taking the proper care of the gods as a main reason for the military and political success of all the Romans. To some extent, this part of Cicero's speech shows that there was at least some consensus in how Roman religion was perceived by Cicero and the late Republican Roman elite (Beard et al. 1998). Namely, this fragment shows that cultivating the gods to maintain the *pax deorum* (peace of the gods) is one of the fundaments of Roman religion. In addition, as these religious statements were done in the context of a strong political speech against Clodius, a political rival of Cicero, it makes clear that the political and religious spheres were inextricably connected in the ancient Roman world. All in all, it is often regarded that everything in the Roman world was dependent on the reciprocal relationship with the gods. In fact, the nature of Roman religion was founded upon an empiricist epistemology, as Ando (2003) argues, which means that religious cults addressed problems in the here and now; the effectiveness of rituals, in short success or failure, determined whether they were repeated, modified, or abandoned.

It is here that Roman religion shows a close resemblance with Geertz's conception of religion seen as a cultural communication system. Other scholars argued along similar lines, as for example Van Andringa (2011) views ancient religious systems as human and historical constructs, continuously changing as ancient societies who produced them continuously evolved according to changing circumstances. In particular, at the time when the Roman world became increasingly interconnected as illustrated above, cult and religion played a particular role in processes of redefining ones place in a changing world order, and one's own place in this new order (Stek 2009; cf. Roudometof 2005). As Derks (1995, p. 111) also put it: "One of the most suitable fields of study for examining the integration of native societies in the wider context of the Roman state is their religion. Nowhere is the self-definition of a group or of an individual more clearly perceptible than in their rituals."

Now, I would like to connect the previous points about interpreting religion as cultural communication system and the nature of Roman religion. Rüpke (2009, 2011), in parallel with Rives and Geertz, argues that if we interpret religion as communicative system, it offers a framework to analyze religious material expressions as inscriptions, images and architecture. He explains that Roman religion functioned through vows and dedications to maintain good relations with the gods. These vows and dedications are real performative deeds, first and foremost expressed in language (i.e., reality), just like saying thank you is not just a token of gratitude, but also a real performative deed (Rüpke 2009). In making vows, normally one asked a certain help or gift from a god and promised something in return. When human deeds had a positive outcome, the recipient gave the particular fulfillment promised to a god in the vow, that forms the final action part of the vow (Rüpke 2009; cf. Derks 1995). This fulfillment could be a votive of all kinds of material, but for example temples were usually vowed in this manner too. Vows could also be accompanied by an inscription as witness of this transaction (usually we only find these written records), and sometimes the written record became the actual dedication itself (Bodel 2009). As Rüpke shows, this form of ritual communication with the gods was not always accompanied with material, but in time this process of constructing a religious infrastructure of communication became more materialized and an internal part of Graeco-Roman religion (Rüpke 2009).

Therefore, religious material culture like dedicatory inscriptions, statuettes of various material, temples and other votive objects can be interpreted as materialized and monumentalized forms of communicating with the gods. These are the material remainders of what Rüpke defines as the 'media' of symbolic religious communication, but we have to realize that these objects were once part of acts and rituals of religious communication, loaded with intentions and meanings (Bodel 2009; Rüpke 2011). In a sense, the focus on religious material culture and in particular its agency and various contexts presented here is in line with the point made by Versluys (2014, p. 17) of seeing "material culture as an active agent in its relationship with people, rather than simply a representation of (cultural) meaning (alone)."

Religious communication took place at different times, places and occasions. As the primary goal of religious communication was to maintain a healthy and beneficial relationship with the gods, primary recipients were the gods. In addition, religious communication also began to play a role at the level of social competition, by showing other humans how (well) one was able to communicate with the gods, and one's capacity to afford expensive votive gifts (Bodel 2009). Recording these offers, often accompanied with the names of the dedicants, not only served the goal that the gods would recognize the gifts, but also that other peers could recognize them, as they served a second communicative purpose of social competition and status demarcation. All in all, Rüpke (2010, p. 204) reasonably summarize that "by its use of inscriptions, images, and architecture, religion became one of the most important media of public communication."

Before turning to the case studies, there is one more problem to touch upon. If an archaeologist finds a religious (and seemingly Roman) object, it is hard to signify the adoption of Roman religious attitudes therewith. Furthermore, there is little that scholars can say with certainly about indigenous pre-Roman religions. Still, the artefacts of religious material culture (votives, inscriptions, altars, temples and other monuments for instance) that frequently began to appear in the Roman provinces after conquest could be used to reconstruct religious glocalization. A discussion of the ancient concept of *interpretatio Romana* can be illustrative here. It is a concept that is used in studies of ancient religion to refer to the identification of foreign gods with Roman gods. In Latin literature, it is used only once by Tacitus (*Germania* 43.4), commenting on the Naharvali tribe that, according to *interpretatio Romana*, commemorated Castor and Pollux in a prehistoric ritual grove with pre-existing non-Roman rituals (Ando 2008, p. 44). Ando (2008) points to the unreflective use of this fragment by scholars in their studies on Roman provincial practice, where the material culture for syncretism between 'Roman and Native' gods is more abundant. He rightly argues that this passage, in its Roman context, shows that *interpretatio Romana* was much more an ongoing, dynamic process of translation and cross-cultural understanding; not in time and place, but from time to time and place to place (Ando 2008).

In the same way, interpreting votive inscriptions to gods with double names, one local and one Roman such as for instance Lenus-Mars, remains problematic. Derks (1998) argues that this label of native-Roman will "hold the Roman authorities responsible for the associations, whether or not intentionally", and rather argues for seeing these associations in essence as products of local interpretations. Webster (1995), in contrast, points to the problem that *interpretatio Romana* was not simply a mutual recognition of similar gods, as the unequal power relation in this syncretizing process should not be under-emphasized. This implies that the Roman conquerors somehow implicitly or explicitly forced their religious communicational framework upon locals in a top-down way, because of the unequal power discourse. Webster further argues that "foreign gods were not simply viewed in terms of the Roman pantheon—they were converted to it by force" (Webster 1995, p. 160).

However, the combination of local and Roman gods as native-Roman religion (or as Gallo-Roman for the province of Gaul) does not work to enhance our conceptual understanding of religion in the Roman Empire. Van Andringa (2011, p. 133) illustrates this point by concluding that "Lenus-Mars is not a Gallic god, nor is he an indigenous god, any more he is Roman or Gallo-Roman." Versluys (2015) similarly states that thinking about Isis as 'Egyptian' goddess in 'Greek' and 'Roman' contexts makes no sense, as this is an example of a Hellenistic, Mediterranean innovation in which all 'players' were involved in creating something new. Here is where the glocalization model offers perspective, since it is able to study the described religious material not just as solely bottom-up or top-down processes. The material culture shares characteristics of a global/Roman context, which makes it trans-locally recognizable, but it is locally different.

Van Andringa (2002, 2007) argues that during the socio-political transformation in the western provinces of the Roman empire, the processes of incorporating local communities into a larger territorial empire, alongside urbanization, led to a religious transformation. A crucial point in this religious transformation was that these new local communities now had a twin-fold interest in the well-being of their own community and their gods, and the empire as a whole and their gods, of which they now formed a part. Van Andringa (2007, 2011) sees this religious change as the creation of a whole new religious language. He argues against visions of Roman and native religion as coexisting, borrowing from each other, fusing or undergoing hybridization, because this implies that both religious cultures were static non-changing entities before Roman conquest, and because they are based on syncretized images isolated from their archaeological and historical context. Rather, these new local civic communities were established in a new global order within the power of Rome and its empire, and therefore the future of provincial communicates was closely connected to that of the state of Rome (Van Andringa 2002). Religious communication served the goal of enabling local communities to express their understanding of their place in a global context and in relation with other local communities (Van Andringa 2007).

The processes Van Andringa describes are in perfect harmony with the implications of the glocalization framework. Local communities were faced with global (i.e., Roman) power and culture. To come to terms with this changing world and their own place in it, new communities were created, which established new religious expressions in which both local and global interests were combined. I agree with Van Andringa in that this caused a new and common (i.e., global) religious language. These developments were both influenced by an interconnected process of top-down and bottom-up negotiation; firstly locally by local communities creating a new religious system of gods and cults that reflected their new status. Secondly in a top-down manner, as, for example, Roman soldiers and governors present in the provinces preferred to worship local gods, but did this in a Roman manner, thereby thinking globally but acting locally and influencing local communities too (cf. Derks 2002).

4. Case Study 1: Rural Sanctuary at Dhronecken

Now, as the theoretical framework of glocalization is explicitly discussed in the context of Roman religious change, I will apply it to the religious archaeological material of two case studies. In line with Versluys (2014), it seems important to me to study the material culture in its own right and various contexts to discover the various functions these objects had. New insights on these archaeological data can be provided by incorporating both the local and the global context of the material culture. The first case study deals with the understudied material of a rural sanctuary of Dhronecken in modern Germany, while the second case study involves the material used in a religious ritual performed in the whole Roman empire.

The rural sanctuary of Dhronecken belonged to the *civitas Treverorum*, a region that was populated by the tribe of the Treveri with an urban center that became known as *Augusta Treverorum* (modern Trier).[1] In its historical context, the *civitas Treverorum* became steadily under Roman control from the conquests of Julius Caesar (*Bellum Gallicum* 3.11; 4.3; 4.10; 4.6; 6.32) onwards (Caesar 1869). After the Treverans played various roles during the Gallic wars, the Treveran region ultimately became part of the Roman province *Belgica* around the late first century BC and early first century AD, and from this period onwards the significance of the region and *Augusta Treverorum* grew, as it became the capital at this point. According to Woolf (1998), the Treveri were one of the local tribes that readily adapted Roman cultural influences, as he argues they underwent a significant cultural change after the Roman conquest. This is based on the large amount of archaeological material that has been found and can be dated to this period, and this rural sanctuary is just one of many examples.

4.1. Archaeological and Spatial Context

During road constructions in 1899, the precinct of 65×60 m^2 and its directly adjacent buildings were discovered and excavated by archaeologist Hettner (1901) as can be seen in Figure 1. According to Hettner, cremation graves 1 and 2 in the northern corner outside and against the precinct wall can be dated to the first half of the first century AD, based on bone material, coal and votive gifts. Hettner thinks it is likely that the other two adjacent graves belong to approximately the same period. Although it is not clear whether Dhronecken was a newly created sanctuary in this time or built upon a pre-Roman cult place, it is certain that from the first century AD onwards Roman religious materials were used in this cult place.

There are four main find places of votive material, as Hettner categorized them (Figure 1). First, there is finding place Aab in the eastern corner just below the entrance of the temple (building A), which lies in the center of the precinct. Unfortunately, due to a lack of manpower, only a small fragment of temple A was excavated. In addition, because Hettner could not distinguish different stratigraphical sections, we do not know anything about the development of the temple and the possibility of several building phases. In finding place Aab, mostly weapons, *fibulae*, mirrors, lead discs (*bleischeiben*), bronze fragments, shards and glass objects and coins were found (Hettner 1901, pp. 43–44, 75–81).

Second, finding place AB is a closed secondary votive deposit, found between the buildings A and B. With only a few exceptions, the largest part of the terracotta votive gifts was found in this context, numbering less than 300 in total (Hettner 1901, pp. 43–44, 75–81). Most of the bronze statuettes were found here (cf. De Beenhouwer 1979, pp. 1278–79). Coins from this closed context from Tiberius (AD 14–37) until (Valens (AD 364–378) indicate that somewhere in the late fourth century a certain cleansing of one of the temples had taken place. The uniformity of the context layer, the position of late coins in the lower part of the context, and the damaged and fragmented state of the votives are also indicators that instigated Hettner to argue for the interpretation of a cleansing of displayed votives from all or one of the temples (Hettner 1901; De Beenhouwer 1979; Cüppers 1983).

---

[1] The sanctuary is also known as Dhronecken-Thalfang-Bäsch, in the Hunsrück mountain area in the modern district Bernkastel-Wittlich, province Rheinland-Pfalz, Germany.

The third and fourth find contexts are those of the minor buildings B and C. In finding place B mostly weapons, fibulae, mirrors, lead washers, bronze fragments, shards and glass objects and coins have been found. In finding context C, however, a number of stone dedicator figures and gods (not more than twenty in total) were found at the eastern part of the building (Hettner 1901). Hettner argues that these votives were on display in this building, and therefore he suggests this was a minor temple (Hettner 1901). Other scholars, however, do not exclude the possibility that buildings B and C were annex buildings of temple A, in which only votives were on display (Cüppers 1990).

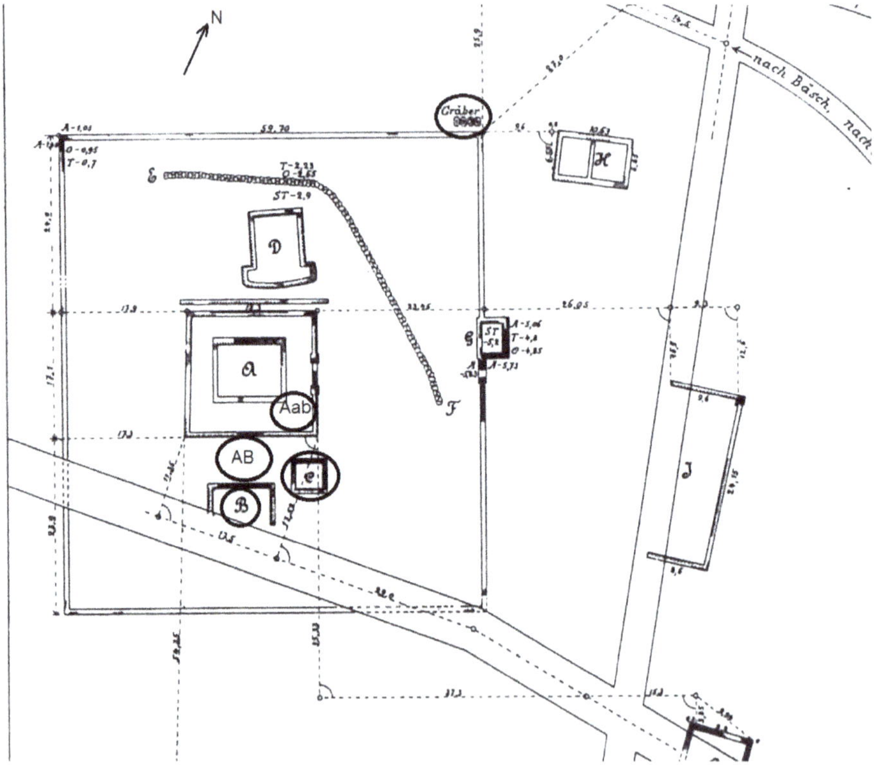

Figure 1. Details of the excavation map of Dhronecken, by Hettner (1901, p. XXII, 3a). Highlights and finding place indicators added by the author.

In addition, material was found in the four graves dating from the first century AD, against the northern precinct wall. In the first two burial places, fragments of terracotta statuettes, a gladius, two iron knives, two bronze *fibulae*, and shards have been found, as well as a fragment of a naked terracotta boy in grave 1, and a *fibula*, terracotta lion, an iron lance point in grave 2 (Hettner 1901).

4.2. Interpreting Religious Communicative Objects

How should we interpret the material objects that have been found in this sanctuary? Since no inscription has been found to provide an answer, it is not clear to which god(s) the sanctuary was dedicated. So far, only a few scholars have made suggestions. Based on the six bronze statuettes of Mars and the different kinds of weaponry found at different find contexts, Roymans argues the sanctuary was dedicated to local Mars deities (Roymans 1996). In contrast, the overwhelming majority of mother goddesses and fertility-type goddesses in the terracotta votives has led Wightman (1970) and Green (1986, 1992) to argue that the precinct in Dhronecken was exclusively connected with Mother goddesses.

However, I believe it is not possible nor desirable to pinpoint a specific god or goddess to this sanctuary based on the limited and fragmented evidence available. It is more likely that the rural sanctuary of Dhronecken was never dedicated to one god in particular, for it was in the nature of Roman religion that the housing of gods could be flexible. Even if a temple was dedicated to a particular god, one could worship other gods there as well. An analysis of all the votive material that has been characterized as gods by Hettner (1901) and Kyll (1966) provides quite a diverse picture of votive gods (Table 1).

Table 1. Analysis of the votive material characterized as gods by Hettner (1901) and Kyll (1966).

Votive Identification	Quantity [1]	Represented by
Amor and Psyche	10 (T)	
Apollo	1 (T)	
Cybele	4 (T)	
Fortuna	9 (T)	
Genius cucullatos (hooded gods)	7 (T)	
Jupiter	1 (B)	
Mars	6 (B)	
Mercurius	2 (T)	
Minerva	1 (B) + 8 (T)	
Serapis	1 (T)	
Sucellis Silvanus	1 (T)	
Venus	20 (T)	
Mothergoddesses	89 (T)	Fruits, bowls 12 (T)
		Mural crown 32 (T)
		Dog on lap 32 (T)
		Seated, with child 13 (T)

[1] (T) = Terracotta material; (B) = Bronze material.

So far, scholars have only regarded the local context of this sanctuary. I will argue that the glocalization framework offers a richer and reconsidered understanding of this particular dataset by including the global context and changing the focus to the specialization of this sanctuary. Derks already put forward (Derks 2006a, 2006b, 2009) a similar argument for a closely related and nearby sanctuary in Trier, that of Lenus Mars. Derks argues that this sanctuary should be seen as functioning as a site for the coming of age rite of passage (Van Gennep 1960). This was the ritual of Roman boys reaching manhood and their donning of the toga, a ritual that was adopted and adapted in the empire in different ways by local elites and non-elites (Derks 2010). I argue that in virtually all of the votive material that has been found in Dhronecken, both the deity statuettes and other votive representations, can be associated with the same ritual of coming of age too. Below, I will illustrate how glocalization can be understood as interconnected processes of the universalization of the particular (i.e., how the ritual became detached from its original context and plays a different role in the global context) and the particularization of the universal (i.e., how this globally understood ritual was shaped in the local context of Dhronecken) (cf. Witcher 2000; Versluys 2015).

The most important evidence is demonstrated by the several representations of naked children that have been found in Dhronecken, usually accompanied with representations of birds and additional fruits. The same votives have been found in larger amounts at a closely related temple for Lenus Mars near Trier. The representation of boys and girls with birds and toys became an increasingly dominant cultural element of Greaco-Roman sculpture (Derks 2006b, 2009). Derks (2006a, 2006b, 2009) summarizes that up until recently, scholars interpreted these images as direct representations of the dedicants, for example when parents gave these representations of their children as thanksgiving to the gods for the care of their children. In contrast, Derks (2009) convincingly argues that these votives should not be seen as direct representations that have been offered. Material objects were in fact often used in transitional rites of passage from one social status to another (Derks 2006b, 2009, 2010; cf. Van Gennep 1960). Thus, this material should rather be interpreted as symbolic representations of a non-elite rite of coming of age (Derks 2009).

This is a good example of where the glocalization framework provides new insights into the understanding of archaeological material. A local community sought to redefine their position within the new political context, and locally adapted the Roman (i.e., global) ritual of coming of age.

Boys or their parents used this religious votive material as fulfillment in the vows that were made for the well-being of the children associated with the rite of passage of coming of age. Unfortunately there are no inscriptions found at Dhronecken to further strengthen this point, but at the Lenus Mars sanctuary nearby some votives are epigraphically attested to be concerned with the welfare of the children as new adults, which were sometimes explicitly vowed for by their parents (Derks 2006b, 2009).

This argument can be further enhanced by investigating a possible difference between boys and girls (Derks 2006b). The focal variation of these sanctuaries may not reflect the change of votive material being discovered, but rather, as Derks (2006b) mentions, reflect the reality of different life cycles of men and woman and the different roles they played in Roman society. According to the discovered votive material, it seems that votives of boys are overrepresented in the Lenus Mars sanctuary at nearby Trier, while female votive gifts are overly present at Dhronecken (Derks 2006b). This does not insist that boys could not make offerings to the gods in rituals associated with becoming adult in Dhronecken, as approximately 10 votives of naked boys with birds were found, similar to the votives that were discovered in greater numbers at the Lenus Mars sanctuary.

As the majority of the votives catalogued as deities are mother goddesses, or at least goddesses related with fertility such as Venus, Cybele and Fortuna, some scholars so far associated the sanctuary of Dhronecken mainly with the ritual function of fertility. Wightman (1970) argues that the approximately 90 mother goddess votives indicate a fertility function, and that busts of children, sometimes accompanied with the mother goddesses themselves, served as a kind of protective function. Green (1992) argues that the nursing mother goddesses, *Deae Nutrices*, were very common in Gaul and German, as well as the mother goddess with a dog on her laps in the Treveran region, and argue they originated in the Celtic religion and are all concerned with fertility, life and regeneration, with a symbolic aspect of rebirth and regeneration. However, I already argued that looking at these votives in terms of continuation of native tradition versus what is Roman is an outdated and unfruitful approach. That local pre-Roman traditions played a role is not to be excluded, but it goes too far to argue, as Green (1992) does, that the images of the votives represent a true continuation of pre-Roman religion. Rather, the global (i.e., Roman) appearance of these votives should be interpreted in the context of glocalization, as the creation of new religious rituals out of global culturally dominant elements in a locally adapted context. This is visible in the ca. 90 votives representing some kind of a mother goddess. Only four votives are clearly indicated as Cybele (i.e., Magna Mater), but it is clear that the ca. 90 mother goddess votives share features that are common in the representation of Cybele too, such as mural crowns, the company of lions and being seated on a throne. Therefore, even in a remote rural sanctuary such as Dhronecken, in the outer region of the Roman empire, global religious elements (e.g., Cybele) appeared to be used in this context.

In addition, as Schwertheim (1974) has already shown with his ichnographically analysis, it is clear that the representations of Cybele found in the Treverian region have a clear local regional appearance. The votives found in Dhronecken and other sanctuaries in this region are based on one representation of Cybele sitting on a throne, her feet on a footstool, alongside the throne accompanied with lions. Her regionally local appearance in Dhronecken and its near area, shows to me on the one hand how Cybele as global religious element by means of glocalization processes is locally adapted (i.e., particularization of the universal). On the other hand, it further strengths the point that Dhronecken could be associated with the coming of age ritual for girls.

Regarding the found figurines of mother goddesses, Beck (2009) suggests that they could have been some kind of amulets. They were small and girls could easily carry them around, perhaps symbolizing protection in everyday life, or in particular during pregnancy (Beck 2009). The fact that they have been found in houses and in sepulchral contexts suggests that they perhaps could also have been used when girls or women died and the votives were buried alongside them (Beck 2009). Again, it illustrates the idea that a large amount of the votives found in Dhronecken associated with childhood, motherhood and fertility, could be associated with the rite of passage of coming of age of a woman. We can only speculate on the underlying reasons, but the amulets might have had a similar function to the toga ritual of boys coming of age, as they could have been offered when women successfully raised their children who then passed towards adulthood.

Other votive objects found that are used in daily life point in a similar direction. First, Kyll (1966) argues that some busts of boys that have been found at Dhronecken contain rattling stones in their head, making them likely to be personal toys of the children offered them. If this interpretation is valid, it is another example of objects that played a role in the coming of age rite of passage, in which children entering adulthood offered their toys. If we look at the primary literary sources, we may find a fragile but relevant fragment to back up this interpretation. For the ritual of the toga and the dedication of the *bulla* amulet from their youth, Derks (2009, p. 206) put together all historical references to this ritual in *fasti* inscriptions or texts. It is striking that in a fourth to fifth century AD work *Docrina* by Nonius Marcellus, a small fragment by Varro (1903) dating to ca. 116–127 BC (*Saturarum Menippearum* 150.463), was preserved in which he describes a ritual in which a girl before her marriage would dedicate her dolls and toys in the shrine of the *Lares* (cf. Warrior 2006, p. 32). While this is a piece of evidence on a ritual in Rome at an earlier stage, it is not possible to directly relate it to the sanctuary at Dhronecken, and we have to remain careful. It shows, nevertheless, that rituals in which girls dedicated toys and dolls before her marriage did exist in the Roman world. The interpretation of the figurines and toys thus might be enhanced by involving global contexts as the ritual described above.

Lastly, as Woolf (2003) points out, *Matronae* cults in general were quite popular and common in the provinces of the north-western part of the Roman empire. The *Matronae* cults in this particular region shared common iconographical appearance, but were locally addressed in a different way (Woolf 2003). The several *Matronae* cults are sometimes interpreted as ancestral worshipping that represented a continuation of pre-Roman religion, expressing a strong local identity and resistance to Roman religion and power (Woolf 2003). However, as Woolf (2003) makes clear, the *Matronae* cults do not refer to local kin/groups and tribes, but rather symbolically represent adult women and similar concepts. The fact that this type of cult was popular around this region is significant, because it was an increasingly competitive and global (Woolf uses the term cosmopolitan) environment in which a relatively high amount of religious choice was involved (Woolf 2003). Similarly, Beard et al. (1998) characterize the early Imperial period as a 'marketplace of religions'. In this context Woolf (2003) explicitly assesses the value of the application of globalization theory, as Roman imperialism caused an increasing emphasis on the local, but the local could only make sense in a global context. As illustrated with the *Matronae* cults, they were all monumentalized in a common religious language style practices were conducted according to the precise rules of Roman ritual across the whole empire, and epigraphically attested in the same style. However, apart from this common Roman style, locally the cults were different in their meaning, focus, naming and sometimes in their images (Woolf 2003). Thus, the *Matronae* cults too are an example of glocalization processes in the Roman religious sphere, as they possess both local and global factors. The cults did not make any sense in the local or the global context alone, but rather this dynamic and complex interplay between local and global shaped these cults.

5. Case Study 2: Pro Salute Imperatoris

In the second case study, a particular kind of votive material that emerged on an a global (i.e., empire-wide) scale is discussed. It is a common epigraphically attested *pro salute imperatoris* ritual, a vow for the well-being of the emperor and sometimes also imperial family members, dedicated to a wide variety of gods. As I will argue, this ritual is both publicly and privately expressed and is developed out of a clear glocalization process, containing both local and global interests. It involves the universalization of the particular (i.e., originally a Republican ritual now globally associated with the emperor and Rome) and the particularization of the universal (i.e., the various local adaptions of this global form of religious communication).

To start with, and perhaps most significantly, this ritual in the Imperial era was actually a transformed ritual that already existed in the Republican era. *Salus* was a prominent virtue and a public cult of *Salus* seems to be dated back to Rome to the late fourth century BC, when a temple was vowed in 307–306 BC during the Samnite war, and dedicated on the Quirinal in 303–302 BC, according to Livius (*Ab Urbe Condita* 9.43.25; 10.1.9) *Salus* can be related both to personal well-being and safety, including physical health (Livius 1926; cf. Winkler 1995, pp. 16–19), and also to communal security (Noreña 2011). This last point is attested in the public rituals (*vota publica*) in the Roman republic, namely the *pro salute rei republica* at five- and ten- year intervals, and annually on the first of January at the event when new magistrates took office (*sollemnis votorum nuncupatio*) (Daly 1950, p. 164). In the Roman empire, these vows were transformed into public vows for the emperor. Cassius Dio (ca. 155–235 AD) reports (*Historia Romana* 44.6; 51.19) (Dio 1914–1927) that vows were annually taken on behalf of Caesar, and that an *annual votum pro salute imperatoris* was established in the time of Augustus. There is abundant epigraphical evidence to prove that this ritual was performed throughout the empire and in the same style as in Rome (Hahn 2007). The ritual could also be performed on special occasions, for example on the birthday of an emperor or on his return to the city (Noreña 2011, p. 142). These examples illustrate that a particular ritual became universalized and received different functions and meanings.

This ritual is sometimes discussed from a merely political viewpoint, as Ando (2000) for example argues that these annual *vota* were mainly oaths of loyalty, re-assuring the prime position of one individual, the emperor, upon whom the well-being of the commonwealth depended. However, we only have to take into account the records of the fulfillments of the rituals by the Arval Brethren to see that the vows are foremost invoked to (the supreme) gods, and the religious conviction that everything was dependent on the will of these gods (Hahn 2007, p. 240). This example, and the fact that the ritual form is identical throughout the empire in both public and private *pro salute imperatoris* votives shows to me that, in contrast with Ando, these *pro salute* rituals were not just mere acts of loyalty to the emperor, but certainly contained a reflection of an important religious conviction that conveys the coming together of local and global interests.

In addition, the ritual is examined from different perspectives within studies on the so-called Imperial cult. I agree with Gradel (2002) line of reasoning that emperor worship was neither exclusively a religious nor political practice, which expressed the supreme power of the emperor, just like worship of gods acknowledge their supreme powers. The Imperial cult was not a cohesive system, and Gradel (2002) shows how a variety of complex cults and rituals differ in their approach towards seeing the emperor as god. Asking to what extent Romans regarded emperors as gods is a modern question to ask; in the ancient world divine honors were established and could appear in different contexts and formulas (Gradel 2002). In addition, Fishwick (2012) explicitly excludes the *vota pro salute* from his discussion on the divinity of the emperor, because they are virtually all on behalf of the emperor voted towards the gods, not towards the person of the emperor itself. While we may conclude that the *vota pro salute imperatoris* are not a pure religious practice towards the emperor, it is striking that an emperor received such a prominent place in the religious lives of people in the whole empire, who participated in the religious rituals and dedicated private votives on behalf of the emperor as well (Liertz 1998).

The cult for the *salus* of the emperor fits into a broader pattern of cults that were established for "divine qualities that were closely connected with the person of the emperor. To this group belonged the cult of the imperial peace (*pax Augusta*) or the fortunate destiny of the emperor (*fortuna Augusta*). In this case divinities that before the empire had been the property of the whole Roman state were redirected to the emperor and privatized" (Herz 2007, p. 307). This is the essential element of the votives that I would like to highlight, as it is here that glocalization is able to enhance our understanding of the material culture. We see a universalized way of communication that was globally understood and shared representational elements. The ritual is recorded in inscriptions throughout the empire in nearly the same style and model and became associated with the well-being of the emperor. This might imply a certain top-down regulation of the ritual if only the global context is regarded, or a Romanization framework is applied. It certainly seems plausible that, as Noreña (2011) argues, *salus* was one suitable virtue in the representation on coins too, as it was used to actively promote the ideological benefits of the Roman empire and the person of the emperor to a broad audience. Noreña (2011) argues that with coins with the Roman emperor and *salus*, Roman imperial members could ideologically transmit that the *salus* of the state, the emperor, and also the local communities were in principle interdependent, as everyone was dependent on it. In addition, Várhelyi (2010) argues that Roman senators who dedicated these votives in other parts of the empire expressed power relations in the empire, with the emperor on top. These very public votives made on behalf of the emperor were ascribed with their own names, enhancing their status in the province and defining their power position as well. In this way, religious communication was, besides being religious in the first place, on a second level a process of continuously negotiating and establishing power relations (Várhelyi 2010).

However, I will argue that besides a clear global importance, considering the local interest in this global ritual further enhances our understanding. The *pro salute* votives are in fact locally different, as they were vowed to a broad variety of gods (Beard et al. 1998, p. 360). Liertz (1998), studied the discovered 11 *pro salute* inscriptions in the western provinces of *Belgica*, 32 in *Germania Inferior* and 64 in *Germania Superior*, showing that all kinds of variable and combinations of ascribed gods could be made. It seems to me that, in line with Laurence and Trifilò (2015), it was the connection with the global institution—here the imperial family—that spread the concept of this *pro salute imperatoris* ritual, not its geographical connectivity. For example, it also occurred that senatorial administrators in the empire dedicated the votives to local divinities Várhelyi (2010). As I argued earlier, it might not be helpful to regard the combination gods in one *pro salute* votive in terms of native and Roman gods and possible cyncretisms (cf. Fishwick 2004), but rather see them in their newly created context in which local and global interests played a complex role. Thus, it seems clear that processes of particularization of the universally understood ritual took place in each local context and were shaped in different ways.

In addition, Plinius (*Epistulae* 10.35–36; 10.52) reports that he, as responsible provincial governor, conducted the annual *pro salute imperatoris* ritual with the help of the local community (Plinius 1906). Presented with a clear model, local communities both publicly and privately took up this ritual and gave the emperor a prominent place in their religious communication (Liertz 1998). The content of the vow is the perfect illustration of a type of religious communication that before Roman conquest did not exist in the provinces, and, more importantly, now clearly constituted both local and global interests converging in one ritual on behalf of the *salus* for the emperor. I agree with Hahn (2007, p. 247), the *pro salute* inscriptions "are clearly modifications of republican prayers offered annually for the safety and prosperity of the state. Now, however, the state's welfare is represented as dependent on that of the emperor. The new prayers served to communicate this novel state of affairs but also, through the power of ritual, to establish it as convention."

Local elites could manipulate and enhance their social positions by, for example, performing these *pro salute imperatoris vota* (Rizakis 2007). From the reign of Augustus onwards, local elites began to use global cultural expressions in general, but the *pro salute* ritual exemplifies that at this point the religions of other communities were becoming systematically oriented towards Rome (Woolf 2012). In addition, they could clearly give shape to the changed world and their own position in a global empire. As Herz (2007) concludes, the personal security and well-being of the emperor (*securitas imperatoris*) was identified with the security and well-being of the whole empire (*securitas imperii*). In the eyes of local communities who vowed *pro salute imperatoris*, they had to contribute their share in safeguarding the well-being of the emperor, the empire and their own, by turning directly to their local gods (Herz 2007). The religious material culture here described is just one instance of how local communities accomplished this, as Herz (2007) further illustrates other (collective) actions in which regular prayers and sacrifices were made, including publicly offered vows in which the assembled population took a solemn vow.

Thus, while Cicero in the late Republic (*Oratio pro Rabirio Posthumo* 20) could express that the *salus* of every man of every order lay in the *salus* of the *res publica* (Cicero 1909), in the Imperial period one's own *salus* was symbolically attached to the *salus* of the emperor. Although it became a common and widely attested ritual, I argue that it was not solely a top-down global ritual to spread power and global religious communication, nor was it a solely bottom-up local ritual to religiously honor the welfare of the emperor. It can best be understood as a glocalized phenomenon in which both local and global interests played a part in the complex creation of a new form of religious communication; a vow for the well-being of the emperor, representing the global empire, of which all local communities now were part, invoking not Roman nor indigenous gods, but gods that at that time and that moment globally made sense in each local situation.

6. Conclusions

This article began by engaging in theoretical discussions on Romanization, globalization theory and Roman religious change. Arguments were provided to show that glocalization can be applied to the Roman world for substantive reasons. By connecting the analytical framework of glocalization with the idea of Van Andringa for seeing religious change as the creation of a whole new and common (i.e., global) religious communication language, I proposed using the framework of glocalization as an explicitly modern interpretative model to study the material culture presented in the two subsequent case studies. Furthermore, I argued that glocalization should not be seen as a process leading to cultural homogeneity, but as a complex negotiation process in which new forms of Roman (i.e., global) cultural elements were developed on a global and local scale, both in top-down and bottom-up directions. The material culture was differently adopted and adapted in various local contexts, but at the same time globally defined as Roman.

Application of the glocalization framework led to richer understandings of two types of religious material culture, which showed that religious change on a local scale was a complex process in which new forms of religious communication were created out of an interrelated and ongoing process of local and global religious expressions, in which local communities could express their understanding of their place in a global context. First, the religious material found in Dhronecken consisted of objects that show a relationship between the local community and the global Roman empire. A universalized ritual of coming of age became particularized in this region, adopting the dominant common religious language. The votives, shaped in a globally recognizable forms, should be interpreted as a symbolical representation of the coming of age ritual, locally adopted and adapted. The votive material represent an instance of a small part of the Treveran community in terms of how they constructed their own version of what they thought was Roman religion (which become their religion as well) reflecting their place in the new global Roman empire. Second, with the *pro salute Imperatoris* ritual, a glocalization perspective illustrated that both imperial administrators and local communities had their reasons for participating in the rituals. Both groups shared the conviction that their own safety and well-being was closely connected to the safety and well-being of the emperor. This global ritual was therefore differently applied in each local context, also as a reflection of local understanding of their position in a global context.

Although the conclusions of this paper remain limited, as only two small case studies are provided, both case studies showed that analysis of material culture becomes enriched if the local and global contexts are taken together and are not studied in isolation. Further research should be conducted to investigate the viability of glocalization for other types of material culture. In addition, it might also be interesting to statistically analyze distribution patterns of the *pro salute imperatoris* votives discussed in case study 2 (see for instance Laurence and Trifilò 2015), and further analyze local particularizations.

As a last remark, I would like to make clear that I do not regard glocalization as the framework that can provide all the answers that previous frameworks could not, nor that it is free from limitations. However, I believe it to be the ultimate task of every generation of historians and archaeologists to reconstruct and explain the past to their own generation, using conceptual frameworks that are relevant and understandable in their own time. I view that the growing body of studies taking a glocalization approach shows that using glocalization as a heuristic and explicitly modern tool to reinterpret material culture is a worthwhile endeavor.

Acknowledgments: I gratefully acknowledge Saskia Stevens and Leonard Rutgers for their critical yet constructive comments on my Research Master thesis (which this paper is based on), from which I learned a lot. I would also like to thank the Royal Netherlands Institute in Rome (KNIR) for the scholarship I received to work on the present study. In addition, I would like to express my gratitude to the editors and the anonymous reviewer for their help in improving this paper.

Conflicts of Interest: The author declares no conflict of interest.

References

Ando, Clifford. 2000. *Imperial Ideology and Provincial Loyalty in the Roman Empire*. California: University of California Press.

Clifford Ando, ed. 2003. *Roman Religion*. Edinburgh: Edinburgh University Press.

Ando, Clifford. 2007. Exporting Roman Religion. In *A Companion to Roman Religion*. Edited by Jorg Rüpke. Oxford: Wiley-Blackwell, pp. 429–45.

Ando, Clifford. 2008. *The Matter of the Gods: Religion and the Roman Empire*. Berkeley: University of California Press.

Appadurai, Arjun. 1996. *Modernity At Large: Cultural Dimensions of Globalization*. Minneapolis: University of Minnesota Press.

Beard, Mary, John North, and Simon Price. 1998. *Religions of Rome*. 2 vols. Cambridge: Cambridge University Press.

Beck, Noémie. 2009. *Goddesses in Celtic Religion*. Lyon: Université Lumière.

Belayche, Nicole. 2007. Religious Actors in Daily Life: Practices and Related Beliefs. In *A Companion to Roman Religion*. Edited by Jorg Rüpke. Oxford: Wiley-Blackwell, pp. 275–91.

Bodel, John. 2009. "Sacred dedications": A problem of definitions. In *Dediche Sara nel Mondo Greco-Romano: Diffusione, Funzioni, Tipologie (Religious Dedications in the Greco-Roman World: Distribution, Typology, Use)*. *Acta Instituti Romani Finlandiae 35*. Edited by John Bodel and Mika Kajava. Rome: Institutum Romanum Findlandiae and American Academy in Rome, pp. 17–30.

Caesar, Caius Julius. 1869. *Bellum Gallicum*. Translated by William Alexander McDevitte, and W. S. Bohn. New York: Harper & Brothers.

Cicero, Marcus Tullius. 1891. *Oratio de Haruspicum Responso*. Translated by Charles Duke Yonge. London: George Bell & Sons.

Cicero, Marcus Tullius. 1909. *Oratio pro Rabirio Posthumo*. Translated by Charles Duke Yonge. London: George Bell & Sons.

Cicero, Marcus Tullius. 1933. *De Deorum Natura*. Translated by Harris Rackham. Harvard: Loeb.

Heinz Cüppers, ed. 1983. *Römer an Mosel und Saar; Zeugnisse der Römerzeit in Lothringen, in Luxemburg, in Raum Trier und im Saarland*. Mainz: Verlag Philipp von Zabern.

Cüppers, Heinz. 1990. *Die Römer in Rheinland-Pfalz*. Stuttgart: Theiss.

Daly, Lioyd W. 1950. Vota publica pro salute alicuius. *Transactions of the American Philological Association* 81: 164–68. [CrossRef]

De Beenhouwer, Jan. 1979. *De Gallo-Romeinse Terracottastatuetten van Belgische Vindplaatsen in Het Ruimer Kader van de Noordwest-Europese Terracotta-Industrie*. Leuven: Katholieke Universiteit Leuven.

Dench, Emma. 2005. *'Romulus' Asylum: Roman Identities from the Age of Alexander to the Age of Hadrian*. Oxford: Oxford University Press.

Derks, Ton. 1995. The Ritual of the Vow in Gallo-Roman Religion. In *Integration in the Early Roman West: The role of Culture and Ideology*. Edited by Jeannot Metzler. Luxembourg: Musée National D'histoire et D'art, pp. 111–28.

Derks, Ton. 1998. *Gods, Temples and Ritual Practices. The Transformation of Religious Ideas and Values in Roman Gaul.* Amsterdam: Amsterdam University Press.

Derks, Ton. 2002. Roman imperialism and the sanctuaries of Roman Gaul. Review. Archéologie des Sanctuaires en Gaule Romaine. Textes reunis et presentes par William van Andringa. *Journal of Roman Archaeology* 15: 541–45. [CrossRef]

Derks, Ton. 2006a. Le grand sanctuaire de Lenus Mars á Tréves et ses dédicaces privées: Une Reinterpretation. In *Sanctuaires, Pratiques Cultuelles et Territiores Civiques Dans l'Occident Romain.* Edited by Monique Dondon-Payre and Marie-Thérèse Raepsaet-Charlier. Brussels: Le Livre Timperman, pp. 240–70.

Derks, Ton. 2006b. Les rites de passage et leur manifestation matérielle dans les sanctuaires des Trévires. *Antiqua* 43: 191–204.

Derks, Ton. 2009. Van toga tot terracotta: Het veelkleurige palet van volwassenwordingsrituelen in het Romeinse Rijk. *Lampas* 42: 204–28.

Derks, Ton. 2010. Les Rites de Passage Dans L'Empire Romain: Esquisse d'une Approche Antropologique. In *L'antiquité et L'anthropologie: Bilans et Perspectives. Actes du Colloque Toulouse 18–19 Mars 2010.* Edited by Pascal Payen and Évelyne Scheid-Tissinier. Turnhout: Collection Antiquité et Sciences Humaines, vol. 1, pp. 43–80.

Dio, Cassius. 1914–1927. Ρωμαϊκὴ Ἱστορία, *Historia Romana.* Translated by Earnest Cary. Harvard: Loeb.

Featherstone, Mike. 1995. *Undoing Culture: Globalization, Postmodernism and Identity.* London: Sage Publications.

Finley, Moses I. 1987. *Ancient History: Evidence and Models.* London: Chatto & Windus.

Fishwick, Duncan. 2004. The Imperial Cult in the Latin West. Studies in the Ruler Cult of the Western Provinces of the Roman Empire. Volume III: Provincial Cult. Part 3: The Provincial Centre: Provincial Cult. In *Religions in the Graeco-Roman World* 147. Leiden and Boston: Brill.

Fishwick, Duncan. 2012. *Cult, Ritual, Divinity and Belief in the Roman World.* Farnham: Ashgate Publishing.

Freeman, Philip W. M. 1997. Mommsen to Haverfield. The origins of studies of Romanization in late 19th-c. Britain. In *Dialogues in Roman Imperialism: Power, Discourse, and Discrepant Experience in the Roman Empire, Supplement.* Edited by Susan E. Alcockand and David J. Mattingly. *Journal of Roman Archaeology* 23: 27–50.

Gardner, Andrew. 2013. Thinking about Roman Imperialism: Postcolonialism, Globalization and Beyond? *Britannia* 44: 1–25. [CrossRef]

Geertz, Clifford. 1993. Religion as a Cultural System. In *The Interpretation of Cultures: Selected Essays.* Edited by Clifford Geertz. London: Fontana Press, pp. 87–125. First published 1973.

Gradel, Ittai. 2002. *Emperor Worship and Roman Religion.* Oxford: Oxford University Press.

Green, Miranda. 1986. *The Gods of the Celts.* Gloucester: Barnes & Noble.

Green, Miranda. 1992. *Symbol and Image in Celtic Religious Art.* London and New York: Routledge.

Greene, Kevin. 2008. Learning to consume: Consumption and consumerism in the Roman Empire. *Journal of Roman Archaeology* 21: 64–82. [CrossRef]

Haeussler, Ralph. 2013. *Becoming Roman? Diverging Identities and Experiences in Ancient Northwest Italy.* Walnut Creek: Left Coast Press.

Hahn, Frances Hickson. 2007. Performing the Sacred: Prayers and Hymns. In *A Companion to Roman Religion.* Edited by Jorg Rüpke. Oxford: Wiley-Blackwell, pp. 235–49.

Herz, Peter. 2007. Emperors: Caring for the Empire and Their Successors. In *A Companion to Roman Religion.* Edited by Jorg Rüpke. Oxford: Wiley-Blackwell, pp. 304–16.

Hettner, Felix. 1901. Drei Tempelbezirke im Trevererlande. In *Festschrift des Hundertjährigen Bestehens der Gesellschaft für Nützliche Forschungen im Trier.* Trier: Kommissionsverlag der Fr. Lintz'schen Buchhandlung.

Hingley, Richard. 2005. *Globalizing Roman Culture: Unity, Diversity and Empire.* New York and London: Routledge.

Hitchner, R. Bruce. 2008. Globalization Avant la Lettre: Globalization and the History of the Roman Empire. *New Global Studies* 2: 1–12. [CrossRef]

Hodos, Tamar. 2010. Local and Global Perspectives in the Study of Social and Cultural Identities. In *Material Culture and Social Identities in the Ancient World.* Edited by Shelley Hales and Tamar Hodos. Cambridge: Cambridge University Press, pp. 3–31.

Hodos, Tamar. 2014. Stage settings for a connected scene. Globalization and material-culture studies in the early first-millennium B.C.E. Mediterranean. *Archaeological Dialogues* 21: 30–40. [CrossRef]

Tamar Hodos, ed. 2017. *The Routledge Handbook of Archaeology and Globalization.* London and New York: Taylor & Francis.

Horden, Peregrine, and Nicholas Purcell. 2000. *The Corrupting Sea: A Study of Mediterranean History.* Oxford: Blackwell.

Keay Simon, and Nicola Terrenato, eds. 2001. *Italy and the West: Comparative Issues in Romanization.* Oxford: Oxbow Books.

Kyll, Nikolaus. 1966. Heidnische Weihe- und Votivgaben aus der Römerzeit des Trierer Landes. *Trierer Zeitschrift für Geschichte und Kunst des Trierer Landes und Seiner Nachbargebiete* 29: 5–114.

Laurence, Ray, and Francesco Trifilò. 2015. The global and the local in the Roman empire: Connectivity and mobility from an urban perspective. In *Globalisation and the Roman World: World History, Connectivity and Material Culture.* Edited by Martin Pitts and Miguel John Versluys. Cambridge: Cambridge University Press, pp. 99–122.

Liertz, Uta-Maria. 1998. Kult und Kaiser. Studien zu Kaiserkult und Kaiserverehrung in den germanischen Provinzen und in Gallia Belgica zur Römischen Kaiserzeit. In *Acta Instituti Romani Finlandiae 40.* Rome: Institutum Romanum Findlandiae.

Livius, Titus. 1926. *Ab Urbe Condita.* Translated by Benjamin Oliver Foster. London: Loeb.

Mattingly, David J. 2004. Being Roman: Expressing identity in a provincial setting. *Journal of Roman Archaeology* 17: 5–25. [CrossRef]

Mattingly, David J. 2011. *Imperialism, Power, and Identity: Experiencing the Roman Empire.* Oxford: Princeton University Press.

Naerebout, Frederick G. 2006–2007. Global Romans? Is globalization a concept that is going to help us understand the Roman Empire? *Talanta* 38–39: 149–70.

Nederveen Pieterse, Jan. 2009. Globalization: Consensus and controversies. In *Globalization and Culture: Global Mélange.* Edited by Jan Nederveen Pieterse. Plymouth, New York and Toronto: Rowman & Littlefield, pp. 7–24.

Noreña, Carlos F. 2011. *Imperial Ideals in the Roman West: Representation, Circulation, Power.* Cambridge: Cambridge University Press.

North, John, and Simon. R. F. Price. 2011. *The Religious History of the Roman Empire: Pagans, Jews, and Christians.* New York: Oxford University Press.

Pitts, Martin. 2008. Globalizing the local in Roman Britain: An anthropological approach to social change. *Journal of Anthropological Archaeology* 27: 493–506. [CrossRef]

Pitts, Martin. 2012. Globalization. In *The Encyclopedia of Ancient History.* Hoboken: Wiley, Available online: http://onlinelibrary.wiley.com (accessed on 20 March 2017).

Pitts, Martin, and Miguel John Versluys. 2015. Globalisation and the Roman World: Perspectives and Opportunities. In *Globalisation and the Roman World: World History, Connectivity and Material Culture.* Edited by Martin Pitts and Miguel John Versluys. Cambridge: Cambridge University Press, pp. 3–31.

Plinius, Caius Caecilius Secundus (minor). 1906. *Epistulae.* Translated by Karl Friedrich Theodor Mayhoff. Leipzig: Teubner.

Rives, James B. 2000. Religion in the Roman Empire. In *Experiencing Rome: Culture, Identity and Power in the Roman Empire.* Edited by Janet Huskinson. London: Psychology Press, pp. 245–76.

Rives, James B. 2007. *Religion in the Roman Empire.* Malden: Blackwell Publishing.

Rives, James B. 2010. Graeco-Roman Religion in the Roman Empire: Old Assumptions and New Approaches. *Currents in Biblical Research* 8: 240–99. [CrossRef]

Rizakis, Athanasios. 2007. Urban Elites in the Roman East: Enhancing Regional Positions and Social Superiority. In *A Companion to Roman Religion.* Edited by Jorg Rüpke. Oxford: Wiley-Blackwell, pp. 317–30.

Robertson, Roland. 1992. *Globalization: Social Theory and Global Culture.* London: Sage Publications.

Robertson, Roland. 1994. Globalization or Glocalisation? *The Journal of International Communication* 1: 33–52. [CrossRef]

Robertson, Roland. 1995. Glocalization: Time-Space and Homogeneity-Heterogeneity. In *Global Modernities.* Edited by Mike Featherstone, Scott Lash and Roland Robertson. London: Sage Publications, pp. 25–44.

Roland Robertson, and William R. Garrett, eds. 1991. *Religion and Global Order.* New York: Paragon House.

Roudometof, Victor. 2005. Transnationalism, Cosmopolitanism and Glocalization. *Current Sociology* 53: 113–35. [CrossRef]

Roudometof, Victor. 2016a. *Glocalization: A Critical Introduction.* London and New York: Routledge.

Roudometof, Victor. 2016b. Theorizing Glocalization: Three Interpretations. *European Journal of Social Theory* 19: 391–408. [CrossRef]

Nico Roymans, ed. 1996. *From the Sword to the Plough: Three Studies on the Earliest Romanisation of Northern Gaul.* Amsterdam: Amsterdam University Press.

Rüpke, Jorg. 2009. Dedications accompanied by inscriptions in the Roman Empire: Functions, intentions, modes of communication. In *Dediche Sara nel Mondo Greco-Romano: Diffusione, Funzioni, Tipologie (Religious Dedications in the Greco-Roman World: Distribution, Typology, Use). Acta Instituti Romani Finlandiae* 35. Edited by John Bodel and Mika Kajava. Rome: Institutum Romanum Findlandiae and American Academy in Rome, pp. 31–42.

Rüpke, Jorg. 2010. Hellenistic and Roman religion. *Journal of Religion in Europe* 3: 197–214. [CrossRef]

Rüpke, Jorg. 2011. Roman Religion and the Religion of Empire: Some Reflections on Method. In *The Religious History of the Roman Empire: Pagans, Jews, and Christians.* New York: Oxford University Press, pp. 9–36.

Schilbrack, Kevin. 2005. Religion, Models of, and Reality: Are We Through with Geertz? *Journal of the American Academy of Religion* 73: 429–52. [CrossRef]

Schwertheim, Elmar. 1974. *Die Denkmäler Orientalischer Gottheiten im Römischen Deutschland.* Leiden: Brill.

Segal, Robert A. 2003. Clifford Geertz's Interpretive Approach to Religion. In *Selected Readings in the Anthropology of Religion: Theoretical and Methodological Essays.* Edited by Stephen D. Glazier and Charles A. Flowerday. Westport: Praeger, pp. 17–34.

Stek, Tesse Dieder. 2009. *Cult Places and Cultural Change in Republican Italy: A Contextual Approach to Religious Aspects of Rural Society after the Roman Conquest.* Series Amsterdam Archaeological Studies 14; Amsterdam: Amsterdam University Press.

Van Andringa, Willian. 2002. *La Religion en Gaule Romaine: Piété et Politique (Ier-IIIe Siècle apr. J.-C.).* Paris: Errance.

Van Andringa, Willian. 2007. Religion and the integration of cities in the Empire in the second century AD: The creation of a common religious language. In *A Companion to Roman Religion.* Edited by Jorg Rüpke. Oxford: Wiley-Blackwell, pp. 83–95.

Van Andringa, Willian. 2011. New combinations and New Statuses: The Indigenous Gods in the Pantheons of the Cities of Roman Gaul. In *The Religious History of the Roman Empire: Pagans, Jews, and Christians.* New York: Oxford University Press, pp. 103–35.

Van Gennep, Arnold. 1960. *Rites of Passage.* Chicago: University of Chicago Press.

Várhelyi, Zsuzsanna. 2010. *The Religion of Senators in the Roman Empire: Power and the Beyond.* Cambridge: Cambridge University Press.

Varro, Marcus Terentius. 1903. Saturarum Menippearum. In *Nonius Marcellus. De Compendiosa Doctrina.* Translated by Wallace M. Lindsay. Leipzig: Teubner.

Versluys, Miguel John. 2014. Understanding objects in motion. An *archaeological* dialogue on Romanization. *Archaeological Dialogues* 21: 1–20. [CrossRef]

Versluys, Miguel John. 2015. Roman Visual Material Culture as Globalising *Koine.* In *Globalisation and the Roman World: World History, Connectivity and Material Culture.* Edited by Martin Pitts and Miguel John Versluys. Cambridge: Cambridge University Press, pp. 141–74.

Warrior, Valerie M. 2006. *Roman Religion.* Cambridge: Cambridge University Press.

Webster, Jane. 1995. *Interpretatio*: Roman world power and the Celtic gods. *Britannia* 26: 153–61. [CrossRef]

Wightman, Edith Mary. 1970. *Roman Trier and the Treveri.* London: Rupert Hart-Davis.

Winkler, Lorenz. 1995. *Salus. Vom Staatskult zur Politischen Idee.* Heidelberg: Archäologie und Geschichte 4.

Witcher, Robert E. 2000. Globalization and Roman imperialism: Perspectives on identities in roman Italy. In *The Emergence of State Identities in Italy in the First Millennium BC.* Edited by Edward Herring and Kathryn Lomas. London: Accordia Research Institute, pp. 213–25.

Woolf, Greg. 1994. Becoming Roman, staying Greek. Culture, identity and the civilizing process in the Roman East. *Proceedings of the Cambridge Philological Society* 40: 116–43. [CrossRef]

Woolf, Greg. 1995. The formation of Roman provincial cultures. In *Integration in the Early Roman West. The Role of Culture and Ideology (= Dossiers D'archéologie du Musée National d'Histoire et d'Art 4).* Edited by Metzler Jeannot. Luxembourg: Musee National de Luxembourg, pp. 9–18.

Woolf, Greg. 1997. Beyond Romans and natives. *World Archaeology* 28: 339–50. [CrossRef]

Woolf, Greg. 1998. *Becoming Roman: The Origins of Provincial Civilization in Gaul.* Cambridge: Cambridge University Press.

Religions **2017**, *8*, 140

Woolf, Greg. 2003. Local Cult in Imperial Context: The Matronae Revisted. In *Romanization und Resistenz in Plastik, Architektur und Inschriften der Provinzen des Imperium Romanum Neue Funde und Forschungen: Akten des VII Internationalen Colloquiums über Probleme des Provinzialrömischen Kunstschaffen*. Edited by Peter Noelke, Beate Schneider and Friedericke Naumann-Steckner. Mainz: Verlag Philipp von Zabern, pp. 131–38.

Woolf, Greg. 2005. Provincial Perspectives. In *Cambridge Companion to the Age of Augustus*. Edited by Karl Galinsky. Cambridge: Cambridge University Press, pp. 106–29.

Woolf, Greg. 2012. *An Empire's Story*. Oxford: Oxford University Press.

religions

MDPI

Article

"This Is Our Jerusalem": Early American Evangelical Localizations of the Hebraic Republic

Steele Brand

Politics, Philosophy, and Economics Program, The King's College, 56 Broadway, New York, NY 10004, USA; sbrand@tkc.edu; Tel.: +1-212-659-7200

Academic Editors: Victor Roudometof and Peter Iver Kaufman
Received: 16 October 2015; Accepted: 20 December 2015; Published: 28 December 2015

Abstract: This paper examines how evangelical pastors applied Protestant notions of a Hebraic Republic for their parishioners as America transitioned from a colonial frontier to a new republic. As the American constitutions took shape during and after the Revolution, many evangelical pastors argued that America emulated or was inspired by the Israelite polity as described by the Old Testament. America and its institutions thus became a reincarnated Hebraic Republic, a new "city on a hill", and a new Jerusalem. Originally these pastors drew on a broader, global movement that was shaping republican attempts at reform in Europe, but as they localized the biblical model to their own particular experiences, they brought new meaning to it and exported the transformed model back out to the world.

Keywords: hebraic republic; evangelical; preaching; sermon; constitutionalism

---

On 5 October 2015, contractors used the cover of darkness and an increased presence of state police to separate a granite monument of the 10 Commandments from its base and remove it from the premises of the Oklahoma capitol. So ended the long drama stirred by objections that the monument violated the constitutional separation of church and state, objections upheld by the Oklahoma Supreme Court earlier that year. The situation in Oklahoma was another episode in an ongoing American saga. Attempts to remove a similar monument at the Texas capitol a decade ago were unsuccessful. The 10 Commandments controversy has also been acted out recently in other states, including Kentucky, Arkansas, and Alabama, and the constitutional question is far from settled. With Moses and his famous body of laws present in many civic buildings throughout the country—including the architecture of the U.S. Capitol and the Supreme Court—it is unlikely that Americans have seen the end of attempts to remove them or defend them.

America's peculiar history regarding the 10 Commandments stretches back to its origins, and this paper will explain the role that early American evangelical pastors played in this history. Throughout the 17th and 18th centuries, American ministers formulated a distinctive political theology derived from the broader movements of Protestantism and republicanism in Europe. These two movements were localized in particular ways as pulpit-orators attempted to weigh in on the structure and institutions of the new governments coming into existence in America. The first task here, then, is to define early American evangelicals in their glocal context, after which this study will describe the history of how they applied the Hebraic Republic in the colonial, revolutionary, and constitutional periods.

1. The Glocal Nature of American Evangelicalism

So what is American evangelicalism? The terms "evangelicalism" and "evangelical" are difficult to define precisely according to two prominent scholars of American evangelicalism, George Marsden and Barry Hankins. Evangelicalism is a broader movement with unique and diverse strains that have shifted over time. Nonetheless, it is possible to provide parameters. Evangelicalism's origins can be traced to the Reformation inaugurated by Martin Luther in 1517. As the name implies, evangelicals emphasized the "gospel" and grew out of earlier movements such as Pietism and Puritanism. The spiritual awakenings of the 18th century carved out evangelicalism as a distinct movement within the English-speaking, Protestant world. Evangelicals came to be associated with revivalism, biblical preaching, dramatic conversions, and a personal relationship with Christ, whose death on the cross afforded salvation ([1], pp. 3–4). Evangelicalism predominated in American religious life and influenced "virtually all American denominations...such as the Methodists, Baptists, Presbyterians, Congregationalists, Disciples of Christ, and others" ([2], pp. 1–2). Given their overwhelming influence in American religious life, understanding how evangelicals originally conceived the Hebraic Republic as a model will help demystify why symbols such as the 10 Commandments still cause strife.

Scholars of evangelicalism such as Marsden, Hankins, Mark Noll, and Ellis Sandoz have discussed the biblical applications that evangelical pastors used to influence American citizens, institutions, and constitutions. At the same time political theorists such as Eric Nelson have recently described the growing intellectual appeal of the "Hebraic Republic" in the wake of the Protestant Reformation. This study brings together these two fields and examines how American evangelical pastors localized the Hebraic Republic to the unique circumstances of America during its inception.

This article's chronological approach—the early colonial period, the pre-revolutionary and revolutionary period, and then the constitutional phase—illustrates that glocalization often happens "through multiple currents or waves" rather than a purely binary global or local framework ([3], p. 1392). American evangelicals and their manner of applying the Hebraic Republic was shaped by international events—first colonization and mercantilism, then wars with European powers like the French, and then the colonists' rebellion against Great Britain, and finally the American desire to create a new constitutional order that would serve as a republican beacon to the world. The entire process was shaped by this interactive nature. For evangelicals, the globalization of the 17th and 18th centuries initially decreased the tension between global and local forms of religion. It presented opportunities to apply new concepts in different ways. However, Americans then re-territorialized their hybridization of concepts like the Hebraic Republic ([4], pp. 1018–19). America had begun as an experiment in religious liberty, which served as a release valve for European religious dissenters, but as Americans increasingly saw their states and nation as republics on the Hebraic model, they were willing to take up arms to create their own, independent state, complete with its own civil religion.

On the one hand American evangelicals were part of a global Protestant project that was interpreting and applying the Old Testament in new republican political orders. Colonists syncretized Protestantism and early modern republicanism with their evangelical worship services. On the other hand, Americans localized the Hebraic Republic. As a part of the *Mundus Novus*, Protestant republicans were given a freer hand to advocate more comprehensive political reforms. Indeed, they were not merely reforming Old World political systems, but creating new ones in a new world. Europe was exporting its evangelicals, and America was a natural destination. Political and religious thought was thus reborn, giving it a longer lifespan than pietistic Protestant republicanism in Europe.

In some cases, Jews and Catholics participated in the project of defining America's messianic mission. For the Jews America provided opportunities to experiment with the tradition of federal covenantalism [5,6]. Nonetheless, early American Protestants clearly saw Jews—regardless of their willingness to envision America as a new messiah in the covenantal tradition—as subordinate to the evangelical cause. Former President of the Continental Congress and U.S. Congressman, Elias Boudinot, for example, participated in a scheme to incorporate Jews into America's new world order, with the clear intention of converting them in the process. Jews could make America their new Zion, but they did so under the influence of evangelical Zionism ([7], pp. 101–3). Catholics were less amenable to evangelical visions of America. Evangelicals were as anti-Catholic as most Protestants, and although Catholics such as Charles Carroll signed the Declaration of Independence and served as U.S. Senator, he was the exception. The Catholic establishment was still opposed to republicanism and evangelicalism, meaning that Catholics were forced to establish a separate identity and a separate civil religion [8]. It was the evangelical conception of the Hebraic Republic, and not the Jewish or Catholic interpretation, that would be applied in the 18th century. And when evangelicalism in the United States began to fade in later centuries, so would the Hebraic Republic ([9], pp. 107–9).

As Ugo Dessi recently pointed out in his study of Hawaiian Shin Buddhism, glocalization can catalyze an alteration in the substance and style of religion [10]. In the American colonies, individual pastors were using the most important part of evangelical worship—the preaching of the word—to exhort their parishioners to think of their sacred text as an incitement to rebellion and a model for republican governance. Local evangelical church services were thus being transformed into democratic political movements of national importance. Evangelicalism was itself being democratized in a distinctly American way. As these sermons spread more broadly in pamphlet form throughout the colonies, other faiths in the Americas—most notably Jews and Catholics—were encouraged to syncretize or assimilate into the nascent American civil religion.

This evangelical application of biblical concepts, being both global and local, has left a lingering legacy on American political life. Modern evangelicals still routinely apply Old Testament passages to modern political issues from homosexual marriage to foreign policy [11,12]. Some activists want to restore a particular brand of evangelical political thought that would make America a "Christian nation" [13]. And past presidents from Bill Clinton to George W. Bush to Barack Obama have felt the necessity to defend their evangelical credentials (or, at the very least, their Christ-appreciating, Protestant credentials) because large proportions of the voting population clamor for it.

During Oklahoma's 10 Commandments controversy, one evangelical pastor even led a horse troop on a 109-mile ride to the Capitol to protest its removal. He believes American institutions and freedoms are inextricably linked to the Ten Commandments, and he and his parishioners, the "Glory Riders", were taken seriously. When this saintly cavalry arrived at the Capitol in late October of 2015, they were greeted by a supportive crowd and then granted an audience with the governor to make their case [14]. American evangelicals have not always taken to such dramatic, equestrian displays of piety, but impassioned pleas for the Bible's application in politics have been in America from the moment that evangelicalism began.

2. Europe's "Hebraic Republic" Reaches the American Colonies

As a model for Western governments, Old Testament Israel first gained political traction between the emperors Constantine and Theodosius in the 4th century. The acceptance and incorporation of Christianity into the Roman political structure created Christendom. The political, religious, and moral behaviors of Israel were filtered through the Old Testament into Christendom, and from there into the pulpits, political treatises, and constitutions of Europe and the Americas. Whether Christendom was good for the European church or state, it made Israel an important historical source for lawmaking and war-making. European Christians were eager to apply the Bible to the Christian states that emerged in the early medieval period. The famous early British king, Alfred the Great of Wessex, for example, appended the 10 Commandments to his codification of Anglo-Saxon laws.

Old Testament laws and political ideals carried over into the medieval world, but it was not until the early modern period that Israel's "Hebraic Republic" became popular like it had never been before. In the 16th century, mass printing and the Protestant Reformation combined to spread theological and political republicanism, and the Bible was becoming the most important source for political theory. The 17th century became so inundated with biblical political thought that it is often called the "Biblical Century". Protestants eagerly interpreted ancient Israel as a constitutional order that should be applied to their own circumstances, and the spread of rabbinic exegesis on the Old Testament polity accelerated Protestant scholarship on the Hebraic Republic. In the 16th and 17th centuries, political thinkers like Bonaventure Cornelius Bertram, Carlo Sigonio, Franciscus Junius, Wilhelm Zepper, Joachim Stephani, Hugo Grotius, Petrus Cunaeus, and Wilhelm Schickard composed treatises on the continent. The nascent Dutch Republic was a crucial hub for Hebraic political thought at this time because it provided presses for publication and afforded protection to authors ([15], pp. 17–22).

Scholars on the British Isles began completing their own treatments of the Hebraic Republic by the 17th century. Thomas Godwyn authored *Moses and Aaron: Civil and Ecclesiastical Rites Used by the Ancient Hebrews*, and John Selden followed with similar works in Latin. The republicans John Milton and Algernon Sidney relied on the biblical texts in Deuteronomy 17 and 1 Samuel 8 to argue for republican exclusivism (that only republics are the proper sort of government). England's most important treatments came from James Harrington and Thomas Hobbes, who used the ancient Israelite Commonwealth as a model for their writings when Puritans were establishing their commonwealth in England in the events surrounding the English Civil War ([15], pp. 20–22, 37–56). Harrington and Hobbes used the example of the ancient Israelite Commonwealth in combination with other examples from history to support their own very different visions of the ideal state. For Harrington, the best and most stable form of government would be an aristocracy of limited, balanced powers inspired by the Hebraic example [16]. Hobbes reacted against this model amidst the turbulence of the English Civil War. He argued that absolute monarchy was the best form of commonwealth and the one most able to provide peace and security as a model [17].

By the time that Hobbes and Harrington were writing, the Hebraic Republic had already gained traction in the American colonies. In 1611, for example, Anglican minister Alexander Whitaker wrote to the Virginia Company with ancient Israel in mind. Whitaker had arrived in Jamestown and then taken part in the founding of Henrico. In reassuring the Virginia Company that its economic prospects were sound, he shrewdly applied the Israelites wandering in the desert for 40 years. Just as Israel had been selected and guided to enjoy the fruits of the Promised Land by God himself, so would the colonies of the Virginia Company eventually. In their case, he encouraged, they should "look for a shorter time of reward" ([18], pp. 26, 35–36).

The founding of the Massachusetts Bay Colony by Pilgrims and Puritans laid a stronger evangelical foundation in New England than in Virginia, and the scriptural applications were proportionally heavier. In the Mayflower Compact from 1620, the Pilgrims pledged to "covenant and combine ourselves together into a civil body politic". In 1638 the Portsmouth Compact used similar language and even appended Old Testament passages from Exodus, Chronicles, and Kings in the margin. The language used here was simultaneously biblical and republican. To "covenant together" is an Old Testament pledge involving Yahweh as the divine witness to a sacred agreement. In the case of the Israelites, Yahweh was both a divine witness and a party to the act of ancient Israel's formation as a people group bound together by a religious and political constitution, the Torah.

The "civil body politic" was a legal term derived from English political thinkers who emphasized the shepherding leadership of their king and the consent of his citizens. But the idea was also biblical. In its ancient context, Israel's covenantal political ideology was a unique contribution to Near Eastern political thought. Biblical writers adopted Hittite or Assyrian suzerain-vassal treaties for the covenants found in Exodus-Numbers and Deuteronomy, and then they created a via media between imperial monarchies like Egypt, petty warlords like the Canaanites, and the patriarchal tribalism common to nomads. The covenants thus used existing treaty structures to unify the Israelites as a vassal citizenry under their suzerain Yahweh. The Pentateuch and the historical books went beyond the treaty structure, however, by establishing an early breed of constitutionalism, which included ancient parallels to the rule of law, consent of the governed, mixed government, and civic virtue. This was a novel system in its own day, and even though it was hardly a republic by modern standards, biblical exegetes from the 16th to the 18th centuries were eager to see it as a republican form of government that they should emulate (on the ancient covenant see ([19–22]; [23], pp. 283–307); for modern takes, see ([5,24,25]; [26], pp. 16–27).

This polity of the Hebraic Republic inspired 17th-century English Puritans in various ways. Some would participate in the Parliamentary struggles that led up to the English Civil War of the 1640s and the Commonwealth of the 1650s. In America, however, the Puritans had already established their own commonwealths. John Winthrop, for example, famously described the Massachusetts Bay Colony he and his fellow colonists were erecting as a "city upon a hill" [27]. A lawyer and future governor of the colony, Winthrop used biblical metaphors in his 1630 speech to inspire colonists as they crossed the Atlantic. The "city on a hill" metaphor, which is a commonplace in America's self-image today, was a reference to Matthew 5:14 [28]. This passage follows the Beatitudes, and Christ himself applied the "city on a hill", "salt", "light", and "candlestick" metaphors to describe the nature of the Kingdom of God. Christ referred to a spiritual community, but Winthrop applied the passage to a temporal, political community in America. And this is the interpretation that Americans latched on to. John F. Kennedy later applied Winthrop's political use of the metaphor to the American nation [29], and Ronald Reagan ensured its permanence as an American metaphor by invoking it in his campaign and presidency [30].

Ironically, Winthrop would probably have been surprised that this one phrase has become so popular today given that there were so many to choose from. His speech invoked numerous scriptural passages, and the "city on a hill" phrase is sandwiched between Old Testament invocations to justice and piety. In fact, he charismatically closes his sermon with Moses' farewell speech in Deuteronomy, and the parallels between Moses' Hebraic Republic and Winthrop's New World commonwealth would have been powerful in the colonists' minds. Like ancient Israel emerging from the Exodus and the Wilderness, the Puritans were seeking religious freedom and a new political community in their own promised land.

By the 1650s, however, it was clear that Winthrop's biblical commonwealths were not about to inaugurate a new republican utopia in the Hebraic mold. Puritans in England were watching their own republican experiment decay at the same time that American colonists saw the judgment of God in a series of "crop failures, Indian wars, droughts, and epidemics" ([18], p. 27). In *God's Controversy with New England*, published in 1662, Michael Wigglesworth applied events in biblical Israel's history to Puritan New England. Wigglesworth saw Yahweh's judgment of Israel now applied to the colonists. Like Israel, they had broken their "Covenant", and like the generations that followed Joshua and the elders in the book of Judges, the colonists incurred the wrath and judgment of God "for growing like the cursed Canaanites" ([18], pp. 44, 47, 49). It seemed as though the dream of a new promised land in the American colonies would dissolve before it had ever truly begun.

The Great Awakening that began in 1741, however, reanimated Old Testament applications to the American colonies, especially in New England. Pulpit and pamphlet were popular places for biblical analogies. From 1740 to 1800 "over 1800 sermons were published in Massachusetts and Connecticut alone" ([31], p. x). Average colonists caught up in the escalating series of events from the mid-18th century to the end of the Revolution were not reading the sophisticated treatises of Blackstone, Montesquieu, and Locke. Instead, they were influenced by those everyday orators, their pastors. And when many American pastors weighed in on political topics, they were prone to use the historical example of Israel and its body of laws.

The two most famous orators of the Great Awakening were Jonathan Edwards and George Whitfield, and both invoked Israel as a model for the colonies. Edwards claimed that it was no coincidence that America was discovered at the same time as the Reformation was about to begin. He saw America—and especially New England—as the new light of the church, born out of the wilderness like Israel had been ([18], pp. 55–57).

George Whitfield's 1746 sermon *Britain's Mercies and Britain's Duty* was preached in Philadelphia and printed in Boston. Throughout the sermon he jumped back and forth between classical and biblical references, but he cited "the scriptures" as more valuable than the summation of all the classical. The "Jewish polity" in particular was "too applicable" ([32], p. 128). By employing the language of European Protestant republicanism, Whitfield was making one of the first direct parallels of the Old Testament's Hebraic Republic to America. His application was both politically and militarily appropriate given that he preached in light of the ongoing King George's War. Whitfield closed his sermon with the admonition to think of the perils that confronted Israel throughout its history. Colonial Americans should keep in mind Samuel's admonition to the Israelites to "Only fear the Lord and serve Him" ([32], p. 135).

The polity of the Israelites provided ministers with an abundant resource of sound laws, just institutions, and virtuous statesmen. It also presented political villains: tyrants such as the pharaoh, Rehoboam, and Ahab and foreign enemies such as the Egyptians, Canaanites, and Babylonians. Boston Congregationalist Charles Chauncy, for example, cited a favorite biblical hero of American pastors, Moses' father-in-law Jethro. Jethro's federalism and the Pentateuchal law that followed his counsel to Moses were useful examples for colonial magistrates ([32], pp. 152–53, 164). In the midst of the French and Indian War, the ardently Calvinist Samuel Dunbar preached an election sermon on another hero, King Asa; Dunbar compared his righteousness at one point to that of King George ([32], p. 223).

The Hebraic Republic was starting to inspire institutional structures as well. By the middle of the 18th century, Americans were already characterizing colonial governments as mixed polities. Their muse however, was not Montesquieu, who had not yet reached the English-speaking world. Montesquieu's *The Spirit of the Laws* would play a predominant role in the constitutional debates later in the century, but republicanism for evangelicals began with scripture. They were thinking of Jethro, Moses, Pentateuchal laws, and early Protestant applications of the Old Testament's mixed government in places like the Dutch Republic. As the colonies began formulating their own governments free of their British overlords, the Hebraic Republic would be drawn on again as pastors counseled citizens and statesmen alike.

3. The "Exodus" of the American Revolution

Six years after Dunbar preached his election sermon praising King George, American pastors began trading biblical heroes for villains in their comparisons. In the midst of the Stamp Act controversy Unitarian Jonathan Mayhew likened the colonists and "the flight of our forefathers into the desarts [sic] of America" to Joseph's betrayal and plight in Egypt ([32], p. 260). Mayhew was also thinking about the political misdeeds of Britain against the colonists. He referenced ancient and modern philosophers from Plato and Cicero to Sidney and Locke in his defense of liberty, but he claimed that he first learned about liberty from scripture. God punished the ancient Israelites with an "absolute monarchy", and they lost their "free commonwealth". For Mayhew Americans should heed this lesson from the collapse of the ancient Jewish Republic and remember that God alone was king.

When the Stamp Act was repealed in 1766, Charles Chauncy described the Americans as having survived an ordeal not unlike the Hebrew bondage in Egypt ([33], pp. 127–29). In 1773 the Baptist minister John Allen drew out the subtleties of the Old Testament model as referenced by Mayhew and Chauncy. Allen explained that the British monarchy was not inherently evil. After all, the Israelites still functioned as a commonwealth under David and Solomon, who behaved as "kings...made for the people". But when British monarchs behaved like Rehoboam or Ahab, they set themselves up as tyrants that scorned the people and placed their own majesty before God's ([32], pp. 316–17, 321, 323).

By the mid-1770s the Hebraic Republic was a powerful example in the American colonies, and not simply for evangelical pastors. Even that impassioned opponent of organized religion, Thomas Paine, used the political thought of the Old Testament. In his famous pamphlet, *Common Sense*, Paine extensively employed themes from 1 Samuel to challenge the institution of monarchy and argue for a new American republic. Yet Paine was only one of hundreds who were regularly advocating how the Bible should apply to America at the moment of its birth. New Jersey Presbyterian Abraham Keteltas, for example, referenced 1 Samuel's litany of kingly abuses in a similar but original manner in 1777 ([32], p. 589). Every Sunday pastors like Keteltas ascended into the pulpit and inveighed against this or inspired their parishioners to do that. They addressed a spectrum of ethical and theological topics, but politics was one of their favorites—especially in their routine elections sermons before political decision-making at the local or regional level. Donald Lutz found that 80% of political writings during the 1770s were published sermons ([34], pp. 140, 142). Like the Portsmouth Compact and Paine, these sermons prioritized the Pentateuch and historical books—especially Exodus, Deuteronomy, and the books of Samuel [31,33].

American evangelicals were interested in how the Hebraic Republic could apply to the United States, but to varying degrees and with different conclusions. Whereas descendants of the Pilgrims and Puritans endeavored to use the Bible as a legal guide for developing specific institutions and laws, Baptists like John Leland viewed these tendencies with trepidation. They could easily lead to political and religious tyranny. In their thinking, the Bible emphasized the freedom of the church, not political templates ([35], pp. 25–36). Baptist pastor Isaac Backus found the Hebraic Republic a remarkable ancient model, but he was uncomfortable making parallels because of the discontinuity between Old Testament laws and modern states. In his *An Appeal to the Public for Religious Liberty* in 1773, he criticized Massachusetts for attempting to apply "Moses's laws...to frame a Christian commonwealth here." In doing so, Backus feared that the church would be ensnared by the state ([32], pp. 338, 342–47). Backus and Leland's critiques represented a view of the Hebraic Republic that would become more prominent over time in the American colonies. It may have much to offer in terms of checks and balances and rule by the people, but the Old Testament model should not be used to recommend a fusion of church and state. Instead, the church should be freed from the state, and the state should afford religious liberty to its citizens.

Most ardent evangelical advocates of the Revolution were not wary of such parallels, however. As the American colonies moved closer to war with Britain, pastors needed to draw on their most dramatic and compelling arguments, and the ancient Israelite polity was the best possible choice. Connecticut minister Samuel Sherwood's 1774 sermon, for example, discussed the British constitution. He found it helpful in the impending crisis to describe David's rule in terms of a constitutional monarchy, and enjoined modern rulers to rule according to his standards of righteousness (he graciously ignored the decidedly unrighteous incident where David raped Bathsheeba and murdered her husband Uriah) ([32], pp. 384–85).

When the revolution erupted, Moses Mather's 1775 sermon title proclaimed the partisan opinion of patriotic pastors: *America's Appeal to the Impartial World*. Mather exhorted his listeners to endure the present conflagration by recalling that only the strong made it through the Exodus from Egypt to the promised land ([32], p. 476). Britain was like the mighty tyrant Egypt, but God would guide the Americans through their contest just as he had miraculously guided the Israelites ([32], p. 489). Jacob Cushing's fiery sermon commemorating Lexington and Concord argued that as Yahweh promised to smite the enemies of Moses' new republic, he would do the same for the enemies of America's new republic ([32], pp. 611–13). Philadelphia Presbyterian George Duffield, and Connecticut Congregationalists Samuel Wales and Joseph Lathrop also trumpeted the American analogy to Israel of the Exodus ([32], pp. 776, 839, 869). Congressman Elias Boudinot even made the same parallel ten years after he served as President of the Continental Congress ([36], p. xxx). Samuel Cooper used another biblical analogy and compared British tyranny to the Babylonian tyranny over the Jews ([32], p. 631).

Another significant parallel for ministers during the lead-up to and war of the Revolution was Rehoboam, who oppressed the Israelites with corvee labor and taxes against their consent, prompting a rebellion that was sanctioned by Yahweh's prophet (1 Kgs 12:1–24). It was an appropriate comparison for American preachers, with King George playing Rehoboam and the Americans playing the justified, breakaway northern tribes. Baptist radical John Allen preached the analogy with the fervor of Patrick Henry ([32], pp. 317, 321, 323). Keteltas and New York's A Moderate Whig also employed it ([32], pp. 589–90, 722–24). In 1781 Massachusetts Congregationalist Henry Cumings used the Joseph, Exodus, and Rehoboam analogies, and then he added the Esther story to the mix ([32], pp. 663–71). Massachusetts minister Oliver Noble had used the Esther model in 1775, casting Lord North as the conspiratorial and bloodthirsty Haman ([37], p. 127).

Samuel Sherwood's 1776 sermon, *The Church's Flight into the Wilderness* used the same analogy of the Exodus, but identified the emergent Israel as the American church. Sherwood's message was primarily based on Revelation 12 and was one of the best representatives of American millennialism ([32], pp. 494, 507–8). Not only was America the new Israel, but its church would inaugurate the new millennium.

Back in Britain, those ministers who opposed the Revolution argued the Bible from the other direction. Methodist John Fletcher, for example, preached against the revolution in 1776 in *The Bible and the Sword*. He described the colonists as the Benjamite "sons of Belial" that raped and murdered the Levite's concubine in Judges 19. The British were as justified in stamping out the American rebellion as were the Israelites in crushing the Benjamites ([32], p. 570).

American ministers also inveighed against Britain's professional armies from the pulpit. At the same time they realized that to defend themselves against Great Britain, the colonial militias would have to unify against Britain's proficient, professional soldiers. Questions regarding professional armies *vs.* militias had emerged centuries before. The English scholar John Colet (1467–1519) used the Bible to argue against the militarism of professional soldiering, and he was followed by Thomas More (1478–1535) ([38], p. 16). James Harrington (1611–1677) later addressed the question from his perspective as a republican theorist, citing the examples of both the Israelite and Roman militias as models in his *Oceana* ([16], pp. 213–17). His military mentality was then applied to 18th-century concerns by others, such as John Trenchard (1662–1695) and Thomas Gordon (1691–1750), who used these models to articulate the "radical Whig" sentiment against standing armies ([16], pp. xix–xx). By the early 18th century, their works had begun to define the American preference for militias over professional armies ([38], p. 196).

One biblical reference used by American pastors to exhort colonial citizen-soldiers to unite in defense of the patriot cause was the obscure phrase "curse of Meroz". The phrase is from Judges 5:22 and describes those Israelite tribes that did not come to the aid of their oppressed brethren. The Song of Deborah inveighs, "Curse Meroz...Utterly curse its inhabitants; Because they did not come to the help of the Lord, to the help of the Lord against the warriors." A Moderate Whig enjoined the colonists to defend their joint liberties and come to each other's rescue, lest they suffer the curse. His lengthy *Defensive Arms Vindicated* focuses on the unity Israel needed to maintain in the anarchic world of the ancient Near East. Colonists should take heed to the military lessons of ancient Israel in the midst of their own geopolitical crisis ([32], pp. 715–70).

George Duffield had personally experienced the wrath of British armies early in his career as minister at Pine Street Church in Philadelphia. His church was locked against him when he came to preach, so he forced the doors and held service anyway, prompting the arrival of a British magistrate, who was physically ejected. A riot ensued and Duffield was jailed. When the Continental Congress was in Philadelphia, he served as its chaplain ([32], p. 772). Duffield's 1783 sermon celebrated the peace after America's victory, but it was nonetheless filled with injunctions for military readiness and American unity. Israel's citizen-soldiers had conquered Canaan as America had conquered Britain. The curse of Meroz applied to those who had not participated in America's righteous cause ([32], pp. 779–86).

The comparison to the Hebraic Republic's military institutions was appropriate. Like most pastoral societies of the ancient world, once Israel had settled in Palestine, its economy was primarily agricultural. However, its covenant placed sovereignty in the hands of these farmers, and not pharaohs, military aristocracies, or other hierarchical schemes. The covenant relied on the idealized virtue of the average, smallholding farmer-citizen to hold the ancient republic together. They participated in the popular assemblies, but more important was their participation as part-time soldiers. Israel relied on its subsistence-farming militias until midway through the United Monarchy with the rise of the royal, professional army, known in scripture as the "mighty men" (2 Sm 23:8–39; 1 Chr 11:10–47). American pastors reveled in the parallel and were eager to continue its application for the new American constitutions. As these examples illustrate, the American cause was nearing a victorious conclusion, so pastors had begun shifting their focus to how the Old Testament should inform the new republic.

4. America's Hebraic Constitution

The Hebraic Republic was just as valuable in the creation of the American order after the revolution. Pastors were already eager to use the Hebraic Republic when state constitutions were formulated during the war. As the debates regarding Massachusetts' new form of government were concluding in 1780, Simeon Howard preached an election sermon before the Council and House of Representatives. He counseled the people and their representatives to remember the frame of government established by Jethro, Moses, and the divine legislator. He opened his sermon by appealing to the genius of the Jewish "constitution" and its "code of laws" before elaborating with his own counsels ([33], pp. 360–61).

Later that year Samuel Cooper preached before John Hancock and the Massachusetts House of Representatives on the commencement of the Massachusetts Constitution. Cooper went into great detail regarding the Hebraic Republic, explaining:

> The form of government originally established in the Hebrew nation by a charter from heaven, was that of a free republic, over which God himself, in peculiar favour to that people, was pleased to preside. It consisted of three parts; a chief magistrate who was called judge or leader, such as Joshua and others, a council of seventy chosen men, and the general assemblies of the people. ([18], p. 634).

Cooper continued with a history of Israel—from its triumphs under Moses and Joshua to the loss of its republican "civil constitution" under the kings ([32], p. 636). His purpose was to remind his audience how Israel lost this perfect balance of the three pure forms of government. They should not allow the same fate to befall them.

Cooper's message before the governor and representatives of the people on the day of their own constitution's commencement was remarkable proof that evangelical applications of the Bible to current events and politics had wide appeal. The people of Massachusetts, heirs of Winthrop and the Pilgrims, were now writing a new page within the larger tale of Protestant republicanism. They had applied the Hebraic Republic's lessons to their own particular constitution as a model for the world to see. This would indeed be the case because Cooper's sermon was so popular that it was translated into Dutch ([32], p. 628).

Connecticut pastor and president of Yale, Ezra Stiles, offered a similar election sermon, *The United States Elevated to Glory and Honour*, in 1783 before Governor Trumbull. His epic, 100-page sermon opened with a passage from Deuteronomy and an appeal to Moses' political and historical genius. He briefly traced the rise and fall of the Hebrew commonwealth before reminding his audience that even when the Israelite polity had been destroyed, a remnant was preserved. In millennial ecstasy he then proclaimed that America was itself descended from this remnant, and he would provide "a discourse upon the political welfare of God's American Israel" ([18], pp. 82–83). America's chief accomplishment for all men to behold was that it had conquered monarchy and purified republicanism ([18], p. 63). The winding sermon continued to opine about America's new chosen glory, both in the world and for the world. Through America God would not only provide another light to the nations on par with Israel, but ultimately perhaps bring about the conversion of the entire world ([18], p. 92).

Five years later Elizur Goodrich preached before the Connecticut General Assembly on the eve of the Philadelphia Convention in 1787. Goodrich inclined toward millennialism as well but was theoretically less critical of monarchy than Stiles, for there could be no greater inspiration for the American governments than Israel's ancient constitutional monarchy. The "Hebrew Empire" was made strong by a king seated in Jerusalem who was subordinate to the people. He describes the Jewish polity as "all the tribes of Israel...a holy nation and commonwealth, under Jehovah their king and their God" ([32], p. 913). Drawing on this description, he saw America's future as bright as the enthroned constitutional monarchy of ancient Jerusalem, saying:

We have also a Jerusalem, adorned with brighter glories of divine grace, and with greater beauties of holiness than were ever displayed, in the most august solemnities of the Hebrew-temple-worship, and presents, to our devout admiration, gratitude and praise, more excellent means of religion and virtue, peace and happiness, than ever called the attention of the assembled tribes of Israel. We enjoy all the privileges of a free government, the blessings of the gospel of peace, and the honours of the church of God. This is our Jerusalem. ([32], pp. 913–14).

As Americans looked to the possibility of a new federal constitution, ministers were equally enthusiastic in applying the Hebraic Republic. This should be no surprise given their references in constitutional literature from the time. Lutz categorized political literature from 1760 to 1805, finding that the Bible predominated at 34%, with Enlightenment (22%), Whig (18%), common law (11%), classical (9%), and other (6%) references following ([34], pp. 140–41).

Presbyterian minister John Witherspoon was a President of Princeton University and Signer of the Declaration. He used the biblical covenant model to advocate federalism over incorporation in the new national system. He believed local communities, and not individuals, were the fundamental building blocks of society. Witherspoon represented the American Whig view that "thought preserving local communities more important than having a legislature that reflected the community in detail and was supreme" ([34], p. 130). This notion, which is increasingly obsolete among modern republicans, was historically grounded in the federal covenant seen in Israel's pastoral republic.

Congregationalist Samuel Langdon was a President of Harvard during the Revolution, where he staunchly advocated for the Revolution. He was a political Whig and a close friend of Samuel Adams. In 1788 he played a key role in New Hampshire's ratification of the constitution. His election sermon, *The Republic of the Israelites an Example to the United States*, was preached before the General Court at Concord. Like Stiles, Langdon opened with a passage from Deuteronomy and a description of the "civil polity" and "constitution" of ancient Israel. With its checks and balances, rule of law, and sovereignty in the people, the Israelite government, he exclaimed, "was a proper republic". Like A Moderate Whig and Duffield, he saw a close link between Israel's republicanism and citizen armies. And like Witherspoon, he argued that the Hebraic Republic should guide considerations of America's own constitution, as his sermon title implies. Israel's ancient federalism, republicanism, and militia system were proof that America's constitutional similarities in these matters were just and righteous. Unlike the Israelites, he exhorted, the United States must not depart from these principles and fall prey to corruption, unrightcousness, tyranny, and foreign captivity ([32], pp. 942–67).

Universalist clergyman Elhanan Winchester made an even more elaborate comparison to the Exodus on the anniversary of the Spanish Armada, the Glorious Revolution, and the new American constitution in 1788. All were fitting Anglo-American parallels to Israel's freedom from Egyptian tyranny ([32], pp. 973–1000). The fact that sermons such as these spoke to broader global events and were published widely outside the colonies demonstrated the maturation of American conceptions of the Hebraic Republic. The travails of American evangelicals during the Revolution and the birth of a new American republic allowed pastors the opportunity to provide their own models to sympathetic adherents in the Netherlands and Britain.

By 1789 Americans had transformed the manner in which the Western world was using the Hebraic Republic. They had inherited the model from Protestantism, especially republican authors publishing in the Dutch Republic and Britain, but over the course of the two centuries from Jamestown to the Federal Constitution the model had been applied and elaborated on in unanticipated ways. Pilgrims and Puritans saw America as a new wilderness that could be transformed into a new promised land. Evangelicals following the Great Awakening used the Israelite polity as an example of communal piety and the judgment that would follow if Americans strayed from God's righteous laws like the Israelites had. Evangelicals during the Revolutionary period were inspired by Israel's Egyptian bondage and Exodus. They saw the millennial possibilities that lay on the horizon if America could unshackle themselves from the British pharaoh and accept the grace and power of a republican God that believed in their liberty as he believed in the liberty of the Israelites. The Americans that emerged victorious then once again appealed to the Hebraic Republic. As it had inspired, chastised, and consoled, it would now provide a model for glorious new governments that would bring about a new age for the world.

Despite its early prevalence Americans, including many evangelicals, would eventually abandon the Hebraic Republic as a model in the 19th and 20th centuries. The recent legal battles regarding that memorable aspect of the ancient republic—the 10 Commandments—occasionally reference this tradition, but most have forgotten the power of the Decalogue and the polity that surrounded it had over the minds of early Americans. Recalling this legacy is unlikely to solve the debate. For some, it will only remind them of a peculiar theology applied in particular ways that should be abandoned. For others, it will inspire efforts to reanimate the Hebraic Republic anew so that the global millennial age can finally begin.

Conflicts of Interest: The author declares no conflict of interest.

References

1. Barry Hankins. *American Evangelicals: A Contemporary History of a Mainstream Religious Movement*. New York: Rowman & Littlefield Publishers, 2009.
2. George Marsden. *Understanding Fundamentalism and Evangelicalism*. Grand Rapids: William B. Eerdmans Publishing Company, 1991.
3. Myung-Sahm Suh. "Glocalization of 'Christian Social Responsibility': The Contested Legacy of the Lausanne Movement among Neo-Evangelicals in South Korea." *Religions* 6 (2015): 1391–410. [CrossRef]
4. Victor Roudometof. "Forms of Religious Glocalization: Orthodox Christianity in the Longue Duree." *Religions* 5 (2014): 1017–36. [CrossRef]
5. Daniel Judah Elazar. *Covenant & Polity in Biblical Israel: Biblical Foundations & Jewish Expressions*. New Brunswick: Transaction Publishers, 1995.
6. Daniel Judah Elazar, and Stuart A. Cohen. *The Jewish Polity: Jewish Political Organization from Biblical Times to the Present*. Bloomington: Indiana University Press, 1985.
7. Shalom Goldman. *God's Sacred Tongue: Hebrew and the American Imagination*. Chapel Hill: The University of North Carolina Press, 2004.
8. Philip Hamburger. *Separation of Church and State*. Cambridge: Harvard University Press, 2009.
9. Robert N. Bellah. *The Broken Covenant: American Civil Religion in Time of Trial*. Chicago: The University of Chicago Press, 1992.
10. Ugo Dessi. "Religious Change as Glocalization: The Case of Shin Buddhism in Honolulu." In *Buddhist Responses to Globalization*. Edited by Kalmanson Leah, and Shields James Mark. Lanham: Lexington, 2014; pp. 33–50.
11. Wayne Grudem. "The Bible and Homosexuality." 6 April 2013. Available online: http://www.worldmag.com/2013/04/the_bible_and_homosexuality/page4 (accessed on 16 December 2015).
12. Andree Seu Peterson, and John Piper. "Point-Counterpoint: Father Abraham's Children." 18 October 2014. Available online: http://www.worldmag.com/2014/10/point_counterpoint_father_abraham_s_children (accessed on 16 December 2015).
13. Wallbuilders. Available online: http://www.wallbuilders.com/default.asp (accessed on 16 December 2015).
14. Lacie Lowry. "Texas Pastor, Others Saddle Up to Fight for the Ten Commandments." 23 October 2015. Available online: http://www.news9.com/story/30338216/texas-pastor-others-saddle-up-to-fight-for-the-ten-commandments (accessed on 16 December 2015).
15. Eric Nelson. *The Hebrew Republic: Jewish Sources and the Transformation of European Political Thought*. Cambridge: Harvard University Press, 2010.
16. James Harrington. *The Commonwealth of Oceana and a System of Politics*. Cambridge: Cambridge University Press, 2006.
17. Thomas Hobbes. *Leviathan*. Cambridge: Cambridge University Press, 1996.
18. Conrad Cherry. *God's New Israel: Religious Interpretations of American Destiny*. Chapel Hill: The University of North Carolina Press, 1998.

19. Viktor Korosec. *Hethitische Staasvertrage*. Leipzig: J.C. Hinrichs'sche, 1931.
20. George E. Mendenhall. "Covenant Forms in Israelite Tradition." *The Biblical Archaeologist* 17 (1954): 49–76. [CrossRef]
21. Meredith G. Kline. *The Structure of Biblical Authority*. Grand Rapids: Eerdmans, 1972; p. 183.
22. John Arthur Thompson. *The Ancient Near Eastern Treaties and the Old Testament*. London: Tyndale Press, 1964; p. 39.
23. Kenneth A. Kitchen. *On the Reliability of the Old Testament*. Grand Rapids: William B. Eerdmans Publishing Company, 2003.
24. Joshua A. Berman. *Created Equal: How the Bible Broke with Ancient Political Thought*. Oxford: Oxford University Press, 2008.
25. S. Dean McBride, John T. Strong, and Shawn Tuell Steven. *Constituting the Community: Studies on the Polity of Ancient Israel in Honor of S. Dean McBride, Jr.* Winona Lake: Eisenbrauns, 2005.
26. William R. Everdell. *The End of Kings: A History of Republics and Republicans*. Chicago: The University of Chicago Press, 2000.
27. John Winthrop. *A Modell of Christian Charity*. Boston: Collections of the Massachusetts Historical Society, 1838; vol. 7, pp. 31–48.
28. Richard M. Gamble. *Search of the City on a Hill*. New York: Continuum, 2012.
29. John F. Kennedy. "'City upon a Hill' Speech." 9 January 1961. Available online: http://millercenter.org/president/speeches/speech-3364 (accessed on 10 November 2014).
30. Ronald Reagan. "Farewell Speech." 11 January 1989. Available online: http://www.pbs.org/wgbh/americanexperience/features/primary-resources/reagan-farewell/ (accessed on 10 November 2014).
31. David R. Williams. *Revolutionary War Sermons*. Delmar: Scholars' Facsimiles & Reprints, 1984.
32. Ellis Sandoz. *Political Sermons of the Founding Era*. Indianapolis: Liberty Fund, 1998.
33. John Wingate Thornton. *Pulpit of the American Revolution*. New York: Burt Franklin, 1860.
34. Donald S. Lutz. *The Origins of American Constitutionalism*. Baton Rouge: Louisiana State University Press, 1988.
35. John Witte Jr. *Religion and the American Constitutional Experiment: Essential Rights and Liberties*. Boulder: Westview Press, 2000.
36. Verna M. Hall. *The Christian History of the American Revolution*. San Francisco: The Foundation for American Christian Education, 1976.
37. Bernard Bailyn. *The Ideological Origins of the American Revolution*. Cambridge: Harvard University Press, 1967.
38. Lois G. Schwoerer. *"No Standing Armies!" The Antiarmy Ideology in Seventeenth-Century England*. Baltimore: The Johns Hopkins University Press, 1974.

religions

MDPI

Article

Glocalization of "Christian Social Responsibility": The Contested Legacy of the Lausanne Movement among Neo-Evangelicals in South Korea[1]

Myung-Sahm Suh

Divinity School, The University of Chicago, 1025 East 58th Street, Chicago, IL 60637, USA; mssuh@uchicago.edu

Academic Editors: Victor Roudometof and Peter Iver Kaufman
Received: 16 October 2015; Accepted: 2 December 2015; Published: 9 December 2015

Abstract: This paper examines the contested legacy of the First Lausanne Congress in South Korean neo-evangelical communities. In response to growing political and social conflicts in the Global South during the 1960s and 1970s, thousands of evangelical leaders from more than 150 countries gathered at Lausanne, Switzerland, in 1974 to discuss the proper relationship between evangelism and social action. The meeting culminated with the proclamation of the Lausanne Covenant, which affirmed both evangelism and public involvement as essential elements of the Christian faith. However, the absence of practical guidelines in the Covenant opened the door for all sorts of evangelical social activism, whether from the Evangelical Right or the Evangelical Left, for years to come. In light of such diverse ramifications of the Congress at both the global and local level, this paper explores the various ways in which the idea of "Christian social responsibility" has been interpreted and implemented by two distinct generations of neo-evangelical social activists in contemporary South Korea in relation to their respective socio-historical experiences of the Cold War and the 1980s democratic movement.

Keywords: glocalization; generation; Lausanne movement; neo-evangelicalism; Christian Right; Evangelical Left; South Korea

---

1. Introduction

Since the early 2000s, among socially-concerned neo-evangelicals in South Korea, a debate has proliferated concerning Christian public engagement with reference to the Lausanne Congress resolution on "Christian social responsibility" [1,2]. On the one side is a group of right-leaning neo-evangelical leaders of the older Korean War generation [3], who introduced the Lausanne movement into South Korea in the 1970s and 1980s and who, from then on, championed the gradual reform-oriented civic movement in competition with both reactionary conservatives and radical progressives. In 2004, they launched a new right-leaning civil organization, *Kidokkyo sahoe ch'aegim* (Christian social responsibility (CSR)) and more or less aligned themselves with conservative forces to suppress the ascendance of the liberal-left force in the public sphere [4,5]. On the other side is a group of neo-evangelical activists of the younger 1980s democratic movement generation [6]. In the mid-1980s, they were introduced to the Lausanne movement through some of the key founders of the CSR, and yet, even though they identify themselves as "the Lausanne generation", this group generally takes a liberal-left position on many socio-political issues [7]. Thus, when the CSR was launched in 2004, most of the younger evangelical activists not only refused to join the organization, but also levelled criticism against their former mentors for allegedly deviating from the original spirit of the Lausanne movement [8]. In other words, although the senior Evangelical Right and the junior Evangelical Left drank from the same well of the Lausanne movement, they developed quite different understandings of its implications without being aware of their mutual divergences for almost two decades.

This paper uses this generational divergence of the Lausanne-inspired neo-evangelical circle in South Korea as a case study to explore how a religious idea, stemming from particular locales, has been projected onto the global field and differently adapted in other spatio-temporal localities. Thus, the overarching theme is the concept of "glocalization", the idea that the global and the local are mutually constitutive and that globalization does not efface, but rather heightens and reconstructs, local particularities [9]. However, it must be pointed out that the glocalizing process has often been conceived within a societal framework implicitly based on binary terms, as in interactive relations between the universal and the particular or between the global and the local. Certainly, this model may work well at certain abstract-systemic levels, such as in cases of the glocalizing processes of the ideas and practices of modern nationalism or capitalism [10,11]. However, glocalization often takes place through multiple currents or waves, each of which simultaneously moves in interaction with, and in disjunction from, one another [12]. In other words, there is a range of different socio-cultural "flows" or "-scapes" that move side-by-side with political and economic currents: e.g., the movements of people, media, technology, finance, ideology, sound, religion, and so on, along the global-local continuum [12–14]. It is therefore important to take into account possible variables that might condition and influence such pluralistic and multi-directional glocalization processes. After all, factors such as temporality, power dynamics and human agency, can effectively accelerate, impede, modify or even reverse the transmission of various political, economic and cultural waves [15–17].

To demonstrate this point, this study focuses on the ways in which the notion of "Christian social responsibility" has been variously appropriated by diverse evangelical actors with different interpretive lenses and practical concerns. Through the medium of ideology-carrying individuals or groups, this particular evangelical discourse has travelled from the mission fields, *ipso facto* a site of the global-local nexus, of 1960s and 1970s Latin America to the global evangelical event of the 1974 Lausanne Congress in Switzerland and from thence to various evangelical communities around the world, including those in the United States and South Korea. However, at every juncture of its journey, the transmission of this idea was often blocked, interrupted and delayed by those who were uncomfortable with its left-leaning implications. Even after it became one of the key defining terminologies of the post-Lausanne global evangelicalism, the notion of "Christian social responsibility" has been variously re-interpreted and transformed according to given historical and socio-political circumstances.

This study is part of the author's larger research project on the emergence and development of the Christian Right in contemporary South Korea. The data were primarily collected during fieldwork through a combination of semi-structured interviews and oral history, which intermittently took place in the Republic of Korea and the United States from 2010 to 2012. For this specific subject on the generational split of Korean evangelicalism, the author, from the perspective of an "outsider" to the evangelical tradition, interviewed a total of 22 evangelical pastors or lay leaders, who had been directly or indirectly involved in faith-based socio-political activism, as well as the controversy on the formation of the CSR in 2004 and 2005. To corroborate and crosscheck interviewees' personal accounts, a range of historical research was also conducted on the development of the global Lausanne movement, as well as the process of its introduction to South Korean evangelical communities. The materials used for the related text-oriented research include documents of the Lausanne movement, articles in evangelical journals and magazines and secondary literature on Korean and global evangelicalism.

The following discussion starts with a survey of the contested legacy of the First Lausanne Congress, which has arguably become the authoritative reference point for all sorts of evangelicals' socio-political engagement. Building upon this, the second section explicates why the Lausanne movement initially had limited influence upon Korean evangelicals in the 1970s, but was subsequently rediscovered by an emerging, neo-evangelical movement amid the revolutionary social environment of the 1980s. The final part explores how a generational rift was created within Korean evangelicalism and how that affected the evangelical socio-political orientations of different generations.

2. Evangelism and Social Concern: The Contested Legacy of the Lausanne Congress

In July 1974, more than 2700 evangelical leaders from 150 countries gathered to take part in the International Congress on World Evangelization in Lausanne, Switzerland. Seemingly, this global evangelical event was poised to repeat what Christians with evangelizing fervor had done for a long time: to take stock of diverse mission fields and discuss the particular tasks or challenges therein. A significant portion of its sessions were actually devoted to the conventional agendas of the traditional centers of Christian missions located in the Global North [18,19].

However, this year's gathering was especially significant. Both the planners of the meeting and a fair number of delegates from the Two-Thirds World were well aware that one of the main points would be a discussion of the dispute concerning "the question of the proper place of social action in the overall program of the Church" ([18], p. 29). Seeking an answer to this question was the urgent reason many evangelicals of the Global South, as well as the new generation of evangelicals of the Global North made a trip to Lausanne, as they were finding it increasingly difficult to separate evangelism from the great many political, economic and racial problems that swept across the world throughout the 1960s and 1970s [20,21]. It was against such a historical backdrop that the Lausanne Committee for World Evangelization assembled an unprecedentedly large number of evangelical leaders from all over the world to discuss, and possibly determine, a consensus on a proper relationship between evangelism and socio-political concerns from the evangelical perspective.

Some liberal critics denigrate the Lausanne movement as an evangelical attempt to "pay lip service to the social and political changes underway in the Third World" ([22], p. 213). Nevertheless, as Tizon points out, there was a significant minority voice of the so-called "radical evangelicals" present at the First Lausanne Congress, who strived to redefine the traditional notion of evangelism as integrally related to social concern and political engagement [21]. During the Congress, those who took such a stance tried to insert their broader understanding of evangelism in the Lausanne Covenant. As a result, their voice was partly reflected in Article Five of the Covenant:

> ... We express penitence both for our neglect and for having sometimes regarded evangelism and social concern as mutually exclusive. *Although reconciliation with other people is not reconciliation with God, nor is social action evangelism, nor is political liberation salvation, nevertheless we affirm that evangelism and socio-political involvement are both part of our Christian duty.* For both are necessary expressions of our doctrines of God and man [sic], our love for our neighbor and our obedience to Jesus Christ ...

> ([2], emphasis added)

As it stands, this statement was a half-compromise between the two competing schools of thought among evangelical leaders in the 1970s. On the one hand, mainstream evangelicals strove to draw a clear line between "evangelism" and "social action" and affirm the primacy of evangelism over other missionary activities. Thus they managed to insert their view in Article Six of the Lausanne Covenant, which stipulates: "In the church's mission of sacrificial service, evangelism is primary" [2]. On the other hand, radical evangelicals opposed the whole idea of separating evangelism from public engagement, let alone giving priority to one over the other. To a certain extent, they achieved a desired result in making the Covenant acknowledge the point that these two practices are both an essential part of "Christian duty". Nonetheless, the Covenant not only made a distinction between "evangelism" and "social action", but also failed to specify any concrete principle of action, on which evangelicals could determine "what is included in 'social responsibility', whose responsibility it is, and how it relates to evangelism" ([23], p. 171). This was partly the reason why, during the Congress, the radical evangelicals formed a special sub-group to issue a response to the drafts of the Lausanne Covenant. In a document, entitled "Theological Implications of Radical Discipleship," they not only repudiated "as demonic the attempt to drive a wedge between evangelism and social action," but also clearly articulated their positions on such socio-political issues as racism, class struggle, political freedom and economic justice [18]. In other words, the mainstream and the radical evangelicals reached an uneasy consensus, which opened the door for much confusion on the relationship between evangelism and socio-political involvement.

Then, it should come as no surprise that such a built-in ambiguity in the Lausanne Covenant allowed the proponents of each side to proclaim victory over the other. For instance, in his personal account of the first Lausanne Congress, as published in *Christianity Today* in 1975, C. Peter Wagner, then the professor of church growth at Fuller Theological Seminary in California and a strong advocate of a traditional and narrower definition of evangelism, expressed his general satisfaction with the final outcome of the Lausanne Covenant. Throughout the Congress, Wagner reckoned, "evangelism had emerged intact" from "torpedoes" fired by those who tried to "divert the emphasis from world evangelization to other ... aspects of the total mission of the Church" ([19], p. 7). In contrast, in 1985, an Ecuadorian radical evangelical leader, Carlos René Padilla, published an article with an overview history of the debate on the relationship between evangelism and social responsibility in the global evangelical movement. Therein, Padilla described the first Lausanne Congress as having made a decisive step in affirming evangelical socio-political engagement and opined that the Covenant brought "a death blow to every attempt to reduce the mission of the Church to the multiplication of Christians and churches through evangelism" ([24], p. 29). Although they were present at the same global evangelical event during the same period of time, Wagner and Padilla obviously drew very different implications from the Lausanne Congress.

For years to come after the First Lausanne Congress, the debate on the relationship between evangelism and socio-political concern continued in various working groups, conferences and *ad hoc* consultation meetings. First, the radical evangelicals continued pushing to expand the notion of Christian mission to include public engagement and elaborated their positions on such socio-political issues as human rights, political freedom and social justice. To be sure, they were numerically outnumbered by the likes of Peter Wagner, who wanted to keep evangelism separate from any social concern. Nevertheless, the voices of the radical evangelicals were more or less well represented in a few consultation meetings, such as those on "Simple Lifestyle" (Hoddesdon, England, 1980) and "The Church in Response to Human Need" (Wheaton, USA, 1983) [23]. Especially, the 1983 Wheaton consultation gathering produced a statement on "Transformation: the Church in Response to Human Need" [25], which, according to Padilla, articulated "the integral view of the church and its [socio-political] mission" more clearly than any other evangelical texts on the subject ([26], p. 15). This document explicitly condemned the tendency among conservative evangelicals to maintain political neutrality or quietist withdrawal from the world as being ultimately in the service of the *status quo* and unequivocallycalled for taking a side with the poor and the oppressed, even if this socio-political choice might lead evangelicals into direct conflict with worldly powers [25].

On the other hand, mainstream evangelicals persisted in giving priority to evangelism over social concern, while tangentially accepting the idea of "Christian social responsibility" as an important, although not an essential, concern in Christian missions. In consultations on "World Evangelization" (Pattaya, Thailand, 1980) and "the Relationship between Evangelism and Social Responsibility" (Grand Rapids, USA, 1982) [23,27], as well as in the Second International Congress on World Evangelization, otherwise known as Lausanne II (Manila, Philippines, 1989) [28], the dominant mood was to affirm the primacy of evangelism based on the conviction that the root of all social problems lay in the sinful nature of humanity and that any attempts at social change would be futile without a regeneration of human souls [23,27]. Moreover, the rapid socio-political change taking place in the last decades of the 20th century added fuel to the rekindling of evangelizing impulses in evangelical missionary circles around the world. A combination of multiple historical factors, e.g., the intensification of millennialist expectations among Christians toward the end of the century, the signs of the disintegration of communist countries and the phenomenal church growth in the Two-Thirds World, inspired many evangelical Christians "to shift into high gear to fulfill the Great Commission ... [and] the task of world evangelization by the year 2000 and beyond" ([28], p. 346). The official catchphrase of the 1989 Lausanne II Congress, "Proclaim Christ Until He Comes", clearly reflected the voice of traditional evangelicals who were more concerned about bringing the Gospel to the yet "unreached" population than promoting evangelicals' socio-political involvement [28].

Nevertheless, it is hard to deny that many of those who previously insisted on keeping evangelism and socio-political concerns separate also underwent a paradigm shift from the 1980s onward. In the United States, for instance, a number of fundamentalist Christians, represented by Jerry Falwell and his Moral Majority movement, renounced their isolationist attitude toward the public sphere and made a strategic alliance with the conservative-evangelical wing of the Lausanne movement, which was growing increasingly anxious about the ascendance of young, radical evangelicals after the First Lausanne Congress. Together, this evangelical-fundamentalist alliance declared that "it is time we denied the 'lunatic fringe' of our movements and worked for a great conservative crusade to turn America back to God" ([29], p. 222). This alliance gave rise to the so-called Christian Right in the 1980s, and a number of neo-evangelical leaders who advocated public Christian engagement in the First Lausanne Congress, especially, Carl F. H. Henry and Francis Schaeffer, played an important role in their joint cultural war to fight against the so-called secular humanism in the USA [30].

Meanwhile, from the 1980s and onward, evangelicals of a Pentecostal-Charismatic bent also developed a greater interest in engaging in "spiritual warfare" against "the principalities and powers of evil" in the secular realm [31]. In dialogue with such new trends in the conservative evangelical circle, Peter Wagner, who used to be a champion of the narrower definition of evangelism, gave up his previous conviction about pre-millennial eschatology and recanted his earlier objection to radical evangelical attempts to link evangelism with social concern [32]. Using terms, such as "Dominion" and "Kingdom theology", Wagner now strongly advocates evangelical commitment to "social transformation" and asserts that "it is the duty of God's people to identify and change those ungodly aspects of culture so that God's Kingdom comes on earth as it is in heaven" ([32], p. 44). Granted, Wagner's particular method of transforming society might not resonate well with radical evangelicals who are no less critical of market-oriented capitalism than centrally-planned economies of socialism ([33], pp. 27–28); for the premise of Wagner's version of evangelical public engagement is an explicit promotion of capitalism in which wealthy "providers" or "anointed [fund] managers" mobilize material wealth for "the advance of the Kingdom of God" ([32], pp. 181–200). In any case, it is clear that there is now a growing consensus among a wide spectrum of evangelicals on the legitimacy and necessity of Christians' active socio-political engagement with reference to the Lausanne Covenant's discourse of "Christian social responsibility".

In sum, the 1974 Lausanne Congress marked a landmark shift in the evangelical attitude toward the public realm, as it officially reinstated what had been thought to be a foregone conclusion of evangelicalism's socio-political involvement before the so-called "Great Reversal": namely, evangelical Christian withdrawal from the public sphere as a reaction against theological modernism and the Social Gospel at the turn of the twentieth century [34]. By retrieving and reaffirming the publicly-engaged tradition of Evangelicalism in the 1970s, the Lausanne Covenant has virtually earned a canonical status, to which socially-concerned evangelicals of all types repeatedly return to justify their social and political participation. Still, there seems to be no agreement among the global evangelical communities on what kinds of social, economic and political visions they should collectively espouse or how they would translate those visions into actions in specific local contexts [23].

3. The Older Evangelicals' General Disregard for Christian Social Responsibility

Given that the Lausanne movement made such a great impact on evangelicals' mode of public engagement around the world, when and how was it introduced into South Korea? In pursuing this question, special attention will be given to the ways in which the neo-evangelicals of the older and the younger generations differently encountered the discourse of "Christian social responsibility" and selectively digested its implications in relation to their specific experiences at a given period of time. Just as there were multiple ways to interpret the Lausanne Covenant among the participants of the first Lausanne Congress, the different generations of Korean evangelicals also exercised a hermeneutic agency in digesting and reading into the imported text of the Lausanne Covenant, the agency that was a product of their distinctive historical experiences *vis-à-vis* contemporaneous socio-political situations.

A good way to explore the history of the reception of the Lausanne movement in South Korea is to ask why there was a ten-year gap between the 1974 Congress and the formation of the so-called Evangelical Social Concern Group in the mid-1980s; for the discourse of "Christian social responsibility" had limited influence on Korean (neo)-evangelicals of the older generation, although their temporal location was closer to the 1974 Lausanne Congress than that of the younger generation neo-evangelicals. How do we account for such a temporal lag in Korean neo-evangelicals' reception of the Lausanne movement?

Granted, a fair number of evangelicals of the older Korean War generation had direct contact with the Lausanne movement in the 1970s. Wesleyan theologian and head of the Korean delegate, Cho Chong-nam, reports that there were some 65 Korean delegates present at the first Lausanne Congress [35]. Among them, more than half a dozen leaders were deeply involved in the proceedings of the Congress as they presided over sub-committee sessions or presented papers therein [18]. In addition, the Lausanne theme of tying evangelism to social concern was almost immediately introduced to Korean churches by a handful of neo-evangelical scholars of the older generation in the 1970s, who acted, in a sense, as "forerunners" of the younger radical neo-evangelicals of the 1980s democratic movement generation ([3], p. 308). Through the efforts of these "forerunners", the Lausanne Covenant, as well as its related documents were introduced to the Korean church as early as the mid-1970s. For instance, in his 1974 article "*Sŏn'gyo wa sahoe chŏngŭi* (Evangelism and Social Justice)", Calvinistic moral philosopher, Son Pong-ho, translated the entire Section Five of the Lausanne Covenant into Korean, and opined that "if the Gospel of Christ involves liberation of the weak, the poor, and the wretched . . . , social structures must be transformed to make [liberation] take place in the society where the Gospel is preached" ([36], p. 70). In a similar vein, upon returning from the First Lausanne Congress, Cho Chong-nam published a report on this global evangelical gathering, in which he explicitly refers to the section on "Christian social responsibility" as one of the most prominent and memorable aspects of this meeting [35].

Therefore, it might not do full justice to say, as many evangelical activists of the 1980s democratic movement generation often claim, that Korean evangelicals of the pre-1980s were completely unaware of, or unaffected by, the Lausanne Covenant's teaching on "Christian social responsibility" [37]. There were indeed some (relatively unknown) cases in which a handful of neo-evangelical leaders of the older generation spoke up, if not openly acted out, against political oppression and economic injustice under the right-wing authoritarian government during the 1970s. As Son Pong-ho reflects upon the history of Korean evangelicalism, "[Evangelicals] might not have stormed into the street or been on hunger strikes but made efforts to speak out as the voice of conscience in accordance with the teachings of the Bible" ([38], p. 3). Certainly, his apologetic remark does not fully provide an answer to the criticism that, to borrow words from the American radical neo-evangelical, Ron Sider, "South Korean evangelicals seem hesitant to speak out for justice and freedom" ([39], p. 28). Overall, this is indeed an accurate description of the general Korean evangelical attitude towards socio-political matters during the 1970s and early 1980s. Nevertheless, the point is that the evangelical church in South Korea has constantly readjusted and revised its mode of engagement with the public realm, and the introduction of the Lausanne movement into Korea marked a crucial turning point in its relationships with state or civil society. In this sense, Kim Myŏng-hyŏk is mostly correct, when he points out that, from the mid-1970s and onward, "the Korean evangelical church *began* to examine itself . . . and gradually became concerned about its socio-political responsibilities" ([39], emphasis added). In one way or another, the 1974 Lausanne Congress served as an important "encouragement" for the Korean evangelical church to make the first small, but irreversible, step of taking a critical stance against the incumbent authoritarian state, which had often been thought to represent divine authority in this world [39].

That being said, a qualification must be added to the impact of the Lausanne movement on the evangelicals of the older Korean War generation. When all is said and done, in the 1970s socio-political atmosphere in South Korea, the evangelical Christians who showed a mere appearance of civil disobedience were minority voices and could not form a standing group or sustained faith-based social movement. Meanwhile, the majority of fundamentalist-evangelical Christians were generally preoccupied with individual salvation and numerical church growth. The point is that it was mostly this latter kind of evangelical leader who represented the Korean church at the first Lausanne Congress in 1974.

The 1960s and 1970s was the time when the evangelical church in Korea experienced exponential growth and underwent a transition from receiving foreign missionaries to sending out their own as a rising hub of the Christian mission in the Asian region. Inspired by the record-breaking success of the Billy Graham Crusade in 1973 and anticipating the Campus Crusade for Christ's EXPLO (evangelistic conference) in August 1974 [40], the main concern of the Korean delegates at the Lausanne Congress was, first and foremost, to continue "the unfinished task" of carrying the Gospel to the yet unreached population, while turning deaf ears to mounting criticism against the traditional form of Christian mission as ideologically and politically intertwined with colonial enterprise in the era of decolonization. Therefore, they were generally uninterested in the proposition of the radical evangelicals to critically revise the inherited notion of evangelism and associate it with public engagement in responding to the contemporaneous social and political upheavals across the world. Their complete preoccupation with worldwide evangelization is clearly articulated in No Pong-nin (Bong Rin Ro)'s personal recollection of the first Lausanne Congress:

> Although I met numerous people and heard many lectures [at the Congress], nothing has really stuck in my mind. Yet there was one thing that I have never forgotten. In the hallway ... was an electrical population clock. It showed the world population growth rate-adding two persons ... per second, and indicated that six hundred thousand people were newly added to the world during the week-long session of the Congress. Thereby, it encouraged me take up the grave responsibility of delivering the gospel to the fast-growing world population.

([41], p. 55)

In parallel with the Korean delegates' great preoccupation with church growth and worldwide evangelization, it is important to note that they were politically aligned with the incumbent right-wing authoritarian regime and therefore sought to favorably represent the governmental manhandling of political dissidents before evangelical leaders from all over the world. Earlier in 1974, the general-turned-president Park Chung-hee not only issued several "Emergency Decrees" to silence those who criticized his regime, but also concocted trumped-up charges against thousands of political dissidents and student protesters for allegedly making plots to overthrow the government. By the time the Lausanne Congress took place in July 1974, stories about the Korean government's repression of political dissidents and religious leaders had spread throughout the world via transnational church networks and the international media [42,43]. In the midst of such growing tension between the government and the anti-authoritarian movement, the Korean evangelical delegates at the Lausanne Congress acted as a sort of spiritual guardian of the authoritarian regime and reported to their fellow global evangelical leaders that the recent media coverage concerning "religious or political oppressions and persecutions" in South Korea was mostly "distorted" and "false" ([18], pp. 1398–99). Given the Korean delegates' pro-government stance toward the oppressive, authoritarian state, it must have been far from their intention to share the radical evangelicals' confession that: "We have frequently denied the rights and neglected the cries of the underprivileged and those struggling for freedom and justice" ([18], p. 1295).

In hindsight, the older evangelical leaders had more than enough chance to learn firsthand of the Lausanne's central theme of the relationship between evangelism and social concern. Nevertheless, except for a few forerunners, most of the evangelicals of the Korean War generation did not pay attention to the practical implications of evangelical social responsibility as articulated in the Covenant or seriously considered applying it to the South Korean situation. Carried away by explosive church growth, on the one hand, and closely aligned with the authoritarian *status quo* on the other, the Korean evangelical church of the pre-1980s was generally out of tune with the Lausanne movement's key agenda of relating evangelism with socio-political participation.

4. Generational Rift within the Evangelical Social Concern Group

If the Covenant's precept of "Christian social responsibility" was mostly neglected by older evangelicals in the 1970s, it started to receive renewed attention in the revolutionary crucible of the 1980s. As discussed earlier, the Lausanne movement and its principle of tying evangelism with social concern were introduced into the Korean evangelical church as early as the mid-1970s by a handful of older neo-evangelical leaders. At that time, however, there were no "ears to hear," so to speak, who would seriously pay attention to its messages and translate them into practices.

It was not until the 1980s that what may be called the Evangelical Social Concern Group emerged, which belatedly (re-)discovered, enthusiastically absorbed and self-consciously practiced the Lausanne Covenant principle of "Christian social responsibility" in view of the tumultuous contemporaneous socio-political atmosphere. The credit of re-introducing the Lausanne movement into South Korea in the mid-1980s is generally given to two neo-evangelical leaders of the older generation, namely Yi Sŭng-jang (1942~) of the Evangelical Student Fellowship (ESF) and Ko Chik-han (1952~) of the Korean Intervarsity Christian Fellowship (IVF). Through his global connections in the ESF, Yi had a chance to come across the radical evangelical tradition of the Lausanne movement sometime in the 1970s, but simply shrugged off its existence and let it slip from his mind for almost a decade [44]. Only later, during his graduate study at the London School of Theology in the U.K., did he begin to re-appreciate its significance. After returning home, Yi published a full translation of the Lausanne Covenant in the ESF's magazine, *Sori* (Voice), in 1985 [45]. Likewise, Mr. Ko first encountered the Lausanne movement when he was studying the history of the world mission in Australia from late 1982 to early 1986 [46]. Upon returning to Korea and re-assuming a leadership role in the Korean IVF in 1986, one of the first things he did was to create the Social Concern Group and disseminate the writings of radical evangelicals among his younger evangelical students.

When compared to the aborted reception of the Lausanne movement in the 1970s, its successful re-introduction in the mid-1980s was largely due to the importers' social location as leaders of campus ministry organizations where they had direct contact with a number of young evangelical college students of the 1980s democratic movement generation. This later group was already searching for theological justifications for socio-political activism, even before they learned about the existence and content of the Lausanne Covenant [47]. Therefore, the emergence of the evangelical social concern group in the 1980s was only possible through a convergence of the older and younger neo-evangelicals who flocked under the banner of the Lausanne movement.

In light of the eventual split of this group into two competing camps in the 2000s, it is significant to note that there were signs of such a politico-generational division right from the start. It is true that those who belonged to the Evangelical Social Concern Group were generally in agreement on many points, including the approval of Christians' public engagement, the necessity of democratization and political freedom and Christian advocacy for the poor and the underprivileged ([48], pp. 10–13). If it were not for such agreements, the formation of this group would not have been possible in the first place. Nonetheless, evangelicals of the different generations had varying reasons and motivations to take part in faith-based social activism, which from the outset contained a seed of intergenerational conflict. To illustrate this point, one needs to compare the ways in which the evangelicals of these two generational groups came to join the Evangelical Social Concern Group in the mid-1980s.

4.1. The Younger Evangelicals of the 1980s' Democratic Movement Generation

Hwang Pyŏng-gu's personal history exemplifies a case of the younger neo-evangelicals whose socio-political stance was dramatically transformed through the influence of the contemporaneous anti-government student movement. Born in the predominantly conservative Taegu-Kyŏngbuk province in 1967, Hwang grew up in an evangelical family. His father was a Korean War veteran and his mother a college alumna of then-president Park Chung-hee. Expectedly, in his childhood, Hwang naturally imbibed a right-leaning political worldview under the influence of his parents and the right-leaning social milieu.

However, an intergenerational tension wormed its way into his family, when his elder brother and two sisters entered Seoul National University in the late 1970s and early 1980s. As college students, his siblings were, one-by-one, swept up by the students' opposition to General Chun Doo-hwan's coup in 1979 and his bloody suppression of political resistance in Kwangju in 1980 [49,50]. Living through one of the most troubled moments in modern South Korean history, Hwang's brother and sisters were compelled to change their intended life trajectories due to either government sanctions or acute psychological breakdown induced by the horrible news from Kwangju. Like his siblings, Hwang also underwent a dramatic shift in his worldview, when he entered the college in 1986 and witnessed a cacophony of conflicting events on 20 May:

> Hwang: [The events] took place during the campus festival. On the one side, the Campus Crusade for Christ was holding a student revival meeting, called the Jesus Great March. On the opposite side, student activists gathered for a mass political rally, where [*Minjung* theologian][2] Rev. Mun Ik-hwan was a keynote speaker. The two mega-rallies collided at the main square . . . .On the CCC's side, [evangelical students] were praying and singing hymns, who must have appeared to be religious fanatics to many [non-evangelical] students. On the opposite side, Rev. Mun was giving a fiery speech [on the subject of "the significance of the Kwangju Resistance in national history"]. At some point, a student named [Yi Tong-su] set fire to his body and threw himself from the rooftop of the Students' Hall [in protest against American imperialism and Chun Doo-hwan's fascist regime]. These three events happened in the same place at the same time . . . .
>
> Q. Where were you at the moment? Which group did you belong to?
>
> Hwang: I was not part of any of these events. I was in the Students' Hall, watching over these events. It was a chaotic situation. I am sure many students were very confused as well . . . From then on, my identity as a Christian was thrown into question, as I witnessed self-immolation or radical protests of my colleagues in college, and began to reflect upon my faith in relation to these events throughout that year. Should I pray? The Bible seemed to teach me nothing about this kind of situation [37].

Note here the ambiguous position of Hwang Pyŏng-gu. He was not part of the conservative evangelical group represented by the CCC or the anti-fascist, anti-imperialist activist student group represented by the *Minjung* theologian Mun Ik-hwan. Strictly speaking, Hwang was a third-party bystander. Even so, he was by no means blithe or uninterested in what was happening around him. In agony and distress, Mr. Hwang was there to witness these events, wondering how he could deal with the contrast of the two radically different modes of Christian life in such a conflict-ridden situation and what he should do about it.

---

[2] *Minjung* theology is a Korean version of liberation theology. This progressive Protestant movement grew out of liberal ecumenical Christians' struggle for democracy and social justice during the authoritarian years of the 1970s and 1980s. The term, *Minjung*, comes from the Greek biblical word χλοσ (ochlos), which basically means a crowd or a mass of people. However, when used in the theological context, *Minjung* refers to those who suffer from oppression and injustice.

From then on, Hwang Pyŏng-gu began to lead a "double life," participating in anti-government, democratization student rallies with campus colleagues and continuing his faith life with Christian brethren and sisters [37]. Obviously, it was difficult to hold together these two conflicting social relations, modes of life and worldviews together, marked as they were by the political consciousness of the 1980s' democratic movement generation on one side and on the other by a conservative evangelical identity. At that time, evangelical campus ministry organizations (Hwang was a member of the JOY Mission)[3] did not offer an environment in which evangelical students could openly talk about socio-political issues. On the other hand, students participating in the anti-government movement generally considered evangelical students as political quietists or other-worldly, "conformist ascetics" solely "engrossed in individualistic piety toward God" [51]. In the first half the 1980s, the young evangelicals were constantly pressured to choose between the quietist church life and the radical student movement, since there were few evangelical student groups that embodied and practiced the Lausanne movement's principle of "Christian social responsibility". Nevertheless, Hwang refused to choose one over the other. While his evangelical faith was something that he grew up with and could not be easily divorced from his personal identity, Hwang also felt a strong tie to his generation. When asked why he was not content with his pre-existing worldview and had to lead a "double life", Hwang replied: "The arguments of the students were more credible than those of the government. And it was undeniable that the government was wrong on many points. Although I did not seriously study social sciences or Marxist ideologies, I think the [contemporary political] circumstance led all students to develop a similar moral sense of distinguishing between right and wrong" [37]. In other words, Hwang's politico-moral sensibility underwent a trans-valuation process, which tied him to the generational consciousness of the 1980s' student activism regardless of his conservative, regional, religious or family backgrounds.

Significantly, in the 1980s, Hwang was not the only one leading such a "double life" of compartmentalized evangelical faith and socio-political activism. To his surprise, it turned out that there were a fair number of young evangelical students who more or less sympathized with the anti-government movement of the 1980s [7]. Although constantly pressured to stay out of "rebellious activities" by their "senior church leaders" [52], the students nevertheless sought out and collaborated with other like-minded evangelical students through several newly-established para-church venues like the "fair election campaign" of the Evangelical Youth and Students Council and the Christian student group within the Citizens' Coalition for Economic Justice in the late 1980s. By participating in these evangelical student organizations, the young evangelical activists tried to compensate for their feelings of "indebtedness" towards anti-government student activists fully devoted to resisting the authoritarian *status quo*. Such a transition from evangelical students' frustration with their inaction to a call for socio-political engagement is clearly displayed in the following public testimony, which Hwang Pyŏng-jun, then a twenty-one-year-old college student, narrated in front of thousands of evangelical students on 29 October 1989:

> The God whom I believe in should be the King and Lord of the entire universe . . . But when I came to the campus, I realized that it is not really the case . . . .While our friends are dying and the world is rife with violence and injustice, we have stubbornly insisted within our closet, our church, that God, who is apparently not a King, should be the King no matter what. In the campus, our friends are hit by tear grenades and fall down, while the police are hit by stones and pass out. Even so, we pray to God to grant us His peace. [In this situation], praising God is not a joyful experience for me anymore. It is rather a pain. It only gives me a burden, a feeling of indebtedness . . . Nevertheless, I am sure that God is alive. . . . I need to find proof that Yahweh God, our Lord, cannot be less powerful

---

3 The JOY Mission is a non-denominational, evangelical campus organization based in South Korea. The name, JOY, is an abbreviation of "Jesus first, Others second, You third."

than political protests organized by mere humans. If there is no such proof, I feel that I should make one up. In order to demonstrate His Lordship over the world, we should go through an ordeal. If humbling ourselves might lead people to take note of His Lordship, we should be poor both in spirit and body and endure hardships. In the world where injustice is rampant, we should fight against injustice, [social] contradictions, and evils, both visible and invisible, to proclaim His love and justice [51].

Seen in this light, it is fair to say that the radical student movement of the 1980s stirred up in the minds of the younger evangelicals an urge to develop social concerns. Granted, they hesitated to get fully involved with the student movement because they saw a sharp discrepancy between their belief in God and the progressive ideologies that pervaded among the radical students, ideologies that were materialistic, humanistic and anti-imperialistic [52]. However, it is undeniably true that the radical evangelical students of the 1980s democratic movement generation resolved to take part in socio-political actions because they were stimulated by and in step with the contemporaneous student movement. As Mannheim puts it, "history is surely shaped, among other things, by social relations in which [people] confront each other, by groups within which they find mutual stimulus, where concrete struggle produces entelechies and thereby also influences, and to a large extent shapes . . . , religion" ([3], p. 285).

4.2. The Older Evangelicals of the Korean War Generation

Shifting attention to the older evangelicals, some of them had been in contact with the Lausanne movement since 1974, and although confined within their denominational boundaries or academic training at different places of the world during the 1970s, they individually practiced its principle of "Christian social responsibility" by making critical remarks against the authoritarian military regime ([53], pp. 194–95). Even so, it was not until the late 1970s and early 1980s when some theologians and church leaders, after returning home and starting their ministerial or academic careers in earnest, began to raise their voices and consciously present themselves as "(neo-)evangelicals", keeping a distance from both ecumenical liberals and evangelicals of the politically quietist bent. Thus, in the early 1980s, the neo-evangelicals of the older Korean War generation launched several inter-denominational, inter-ecclesiastical organizations, such as the Korean Evangelical Fellowship, the Korean Evangelical Theological Society and the *Kangnam yŏnhap sinang kangjwa* (Kangnam consortium for lectures on faith). While insisting that "Christianity should be at once a supernatural . . . and intra-historical . . . religion" ([48], pp. 10–11), these newly-established neo-evangelical groups served as important conduits to propagate the Lausanne movement's social teachings in the Korean church [53]. When the young neo-evangelical students sought guidance in dealing with the revolutionary atmosphere of the mid-1980s, it was through these venues that, to borrow Ku Kyo-hyŏng's words, they came to the "revolutionary awakening" that "it is not a sin to take sides with alienated neighbors or to participate in the democratization movement" [52]. Unlike conservative evangelicals who preferred social stability within an authoritarian political structure to any disorderly social upheaval, the neo-evangelicals of the Korean War generation brought to the young evangelicals a new message that explicitly supported political democratization, legal equality, freedom of speech, respect for human rights and advocacy of workers' rights [48].

This notwithstanding, it must be noted that there was an important obverse to the older neo-evangelicals' affirmation of the Lausanne movement's teaching on "Christian social responsibility". While they generally disapproved of "authoritarianism and corruption," the older neo-evangelicals were also "second to none when it came to censuring progressive theology and communism" [38]. In fact, one of the very first acts the Korean Evangelical Theological Society performed was to unleash a barrage of criticism against liberation and *Minjung* theology that advocated "*hyŏnsil ch'amyo* (praxis in reality)" based on a Marxist analysis of the contemporary socio-political situation ([54], p. 10). From the perspective of neo-evangelicals of the older Korean generation, such radical progressive theologies tended to put more weight on the significance of structural evil over individual sin, thereby downplaying the fallenness of the human condition and reducing salvation to political liberation [55–57]. True, they advocated that Christians should be concerned not only with individual salvation, but also with political, economic and cultural problems of the time in light of the Lausanne Covenant. Nonetheless, their wariness toward communism and North Korea continuously prevented them from being sympathetic to or at least tolerant toward all progressive ideologies and practices, including the radical forms of the student or labor movements. The following public statement of the Korean Evangelical Fellowship, issued on 12 May 1986, well demonstrates such wariness toward the 1980s generation's radical political orientations:

> We [that is, the older echelon of the Evangelical Social Concern Group] admit that students have performed an important role in awakening the older generation from moral numbness by crying for political democratization and social justice out of a pure heart, and they should continue to fulfill this role. However, it must not be ignored that the student movement could be swayed by impure motivations like personal aspiration, heroism, or political ambition, and, thus, easily manipulated by impure ideology. Especially, the revolutionary slogans and destructive violence of radical students in recent days run counter to the students' goal of reaching a just society, and would not be welcomed by the general people. Therefore, there should not be another social change caused by violence and revolution. Without peaceful measures and moral appeal, an equal and just society will never emerge. Above all, in the time of such a chaotic situation, we, evangelical Christians, firmly stand against an infiltration of atheistic communism, and urge all legitimate social movements which hope to achieve social justice, to not be manipulated by such an attempt.

([48], p. 12)

When actually carried out, their anticommunist and anti-revolutionary stance largely took two forms: one characterized by preventing "impure," revolutionary passions from flaring up among the younger neo-evangelicals and the other characterized by channeling the students' simmering grievances against the authoritarian *status quo* into "pure" forms of moderate, law-abiding and reformist social movements. Thus, Ko Chik-han of the IVF adopted a two-pronged approach to the young radical evangelical students. On the one hand, he played the role of "an understanding senior leader who empathized with younger students" with regard to their resentment towards the existing socio-political establishment [46]. On the other hand, he discreetly pressured, if not explicitly purged, from the IVF students tinged with Marxism or North Korean *Juch'e* ideology. As long as the leaders of the IVF could persuade the students to follow "the [Lausanne Covenant's] teaching of coalescing evangelism and social responsibility", Ko was confident that "[the younger neo-evangelical students] would not be swayed by ideologies based on class analysis or *Juche* Ideology" [46].

Moreover, the same concern for channeling the grievances of younger evangelicals turned into the older neo-evangelicals' enthusiastic support for the nascent "*simin* (civil or NGO)" movement at the end of the 1980s. The socially-concerned neo-evangelicals of the Korean War generation more or less acknowledged that Christians should not shrink from publicly opposing social injustice. At the same time, they were severely critical of progressive groups resorting to law-breaking or violent measures to achieve their goals. However, the particular problem the evangelical activists faced was that, "although they talked about social participation," they did not have a "well-defined methodology" of social movement [46]. Without clearly articulated principles and guidelines for evangelical social action, there was a concern that many evangelical youth and students might be easily swayed by the radical progressive ideologies and practices predominant within the 1980s' student movement. It was at this juncture that the Christian activist, Sŏ Kyŏng-sŏk, reached out to the neo-evangelical communities to ask for endorsement, volunteer workers and sponsorship for the soon-to-be launched Citizens' Coalition for Economic Justice (CCEJ) in 1989. By launching a social movement of, by and for all "*simindŭl* (citizens)," Sŏ and his colleagues at the CCEJ aimed to replace the class-based Minjung movement with a civil movement in the post-democratization context [58]. For many older neo-evangelical leaders, the CCEJ's moderate, reformist social movement seemed like an effective safety valve that could satisfy younger neo-evangelicals' thirst for social participation while simultaneously steering them away from the radical progressive student movement.

In short, while navigating the same socio-political situation, the neo-evangelical activists of the Korean War generation and those of the 1980s' Democratic Movement generation reacted differently to the radicalized student movement of the 1980s. Certainly, they all agreed upon the necessity of democratization and social justice and collectively endeavored to organize faith-based social activism from the late 1980s and onward. Nevertheless, while the younger neo-evangelical activists were generally in step with the 1980s' student-based democratization movement, their senior neo-evangelical leaders firmly opposed all radical social movements, deeming them to advocate a violent and radical social change. Seen in this light, these two groups of neo-evangelicals, one shaped by Cold War anticommunist sentiments, the other by experiences of the 1980s' democratic movement, could not help but have different ideological and political horizons; and these differences, in turn, disposed them to different degrees of tolerance toward left-wing politics.

5. Conclusions

In light of the different motivations of the neo-evangelicals of the different generations in joining the Evangelical Social Concern Group in the 1980s, one can better explain why this group eventually split into the senior Evangelical Right and the junior Evangelical Left along generational lines. Although they agreed upon the necessity of evangelical socio-political engagement with reference to the Lausanne movement, they followed different paths guided by their distinct political and historical experiences.

For many younger evangelicals, their initial venture into evangelical social activism under the guidance of their senior leaders was only a stepping stone to further their social concerns. As they grew older, a number of them became pastors, academics and full-time organizers and activists in their own right, and more or less brought their social concerns further to the left in conversation with a wide range of theological traditions, as well as other liberal-left actors having similar public concerns. Born after the Korean War and relatively free from the Red Complex of the Cold War, socially concerned radical neo-evangelicals of the younger generation tend to appreciate and acknowledge the validity of left-wing positions.

Among the senior neo-evangelical leaders, their involvement in evangelical social activism has consistently operated from a motive to oppose and suppress radical left-wing politics. The socio-political developments of the late 1980s and throughout the 1990s (for instance, the 1987 democratization, the Fall of the Berlin Wall, the growth of the middle-class, the prevalence of neoliberalism and the subsequent weakening of the progressive political force) almost made it unnecessary for the older neo-evangelical activists to deliberately pick a fight against their already wobbling opponent on the left, except to offer patronizing advice to give up a class-based social movement and let the reformist civil movement take the lead in moderate social reforms [59]. Nevertheless, when they faced an ascendance of the left-wing force of the 1980s democratic movement generation at the turn of the 21st century, their resentment drove them to organize anew a right-leaning evangelical movement organization that explicitly took its name from the discourse of the "Christian social responsibility" of the Lausanne movement.

By tracing the trajectories of "Christian social responsibility" discourse that circulated in global evangelical communities around the world, this paper has shown that the glocalization of religious ideas never takes place in a political or historical vacuum. Rather, they are always transmitted through the minds and speech-acts of individuals or groups of individuals, who are concretely embedded in specific relations of power and rooted in particular historical contexts. In one way or another, such politico-historical contingencies significantly affect the ways in which people engage with and absorb the religious discourses circulating in multiple glocal sites. Historical actors tend to encounter those ideas through certain interpretive "lenses" or "prisms", which grow out of, and are modulated in accordance with, particular spatio-temporal circumstances [15]. It is through these "lenses" that ideology-carrying messengers as well as the recipients of that message selectively filter and variously refract what they communicate in order to suit their respective areas of interest and concern. Thus, the end result is always an open-ended possibility for selective assimilation, delayed acceptance, creative distortion, and the co-presence of hybrid interpretations. In the present case study, glocalization of "Christian Social Responsibility" discourse has actually resulted in a world-wide proliferation of evangelical-based socio-political activism, the varieties of which defy any easy classification of evangelical politics into either conservative or progressive camps.

Conflicts of Interest: The author declares no conflict of interest.

Abbreviations

CSR	Christian social responsibility
ESF	Evangelical Student Fellowship
IVF	Intervarsity Christian Fellowship
CCC	Campus Crusade for Christ
CCEJ	The Citizens' Coalition for Economic Justice

References

1. Historically, the neo-evangelical tradition refers to the socially-concerned movement within the conservative wing of American Protestantism. Those who belonged to this group tried to move beyond the fundamentalist-modernist controversy of the 1920s by reconciling the traditional confessions of the Christian faith with the social teachings of the Bible from the 1940s onward. On the rise and development of neo-evangelicalism in the United States, see Arthur H. Matthews. *Standing up, Standing Together: The Emergence of the National Association of Evangelicals.* Carol Stream: National Association of Evangelicals, 1992. Such a (neo-)evangelical tradition began to emerge in the Korean church in the mid-1970s after the Billy Graham Crusade in 1973 and the First Lausanne Congress in 1974.
2. Lausanne Movement. "The Lausanne Covenant." 1974. Available online: http://www.lausanne.org/content/covenant/lausanne-covenant (accessed on 9 October 2015).
3. The term "generation" here is based on Mannheim's discussion of social generation. It basically means a cohort of people who share the zeitgeist of a given period of time, usually demarcated by significant socio-historical events such as war, revolution, and economic depression. See Karl Mannheim. "The Problem of Generations." In *Essays on the Sociology of Knowledge.* Edited by Paul Kecskemeti. London: Routledge & K. Paul, 1952, pp. 276–322. The Korean War generation then refers to those who are old enough to have directly experienced the effects of the Korean War in the 1950s and who generally hold strong anti-communist and pro-American sentiments.
4. Anthony Faiola. "Korean liberals seize the day; South's young voters back impeached president's allies, want accord with North." *SFGate.* 16 April 2004. Available online: http://www.sfgate.com/politics/article/Korean-liberals-seize-the-day-South-s-young-2766980.php (accessed on 14 October 2015).
5. Kyuhoon Cho. "Another Christian Right? The Politicization of Korean Protestantism in Contemporary Global Society." *Social Compass* 61 (2014): 310–27. [CrossRef]
6. The 80s' democratic movement generation generally includes those who were born in the 1960s, after the Korean War, and who had varying degrees of close contact with the left-leaning spirit of the anti-government movement in the 1980s. It is often assumed that this generation played a crucial role in South Korea's historic transition from authoritarian to (formal) democratic governance in 1987. See Namhee Lee. *The Making of Minjung: Democracy and the Politics of Representation in South Korea.* Ithaca: Cornell University Press, 2007.
7. Chulho Han. "A Case Study: The Influence of the Lausanne Movement on Korean Younger Christian Leaders." In *The Lausanne Movement: A Range of Perspectives.* Edited by Larse Dahle, Margunn S. Dahle and Knud Jørgensen. Eugene: Wipf & Stock, 2014, pp. 195–206.
8. Hwan-Chŏl Yun (executive director, Mirae Nanum Chaedan), in discussion with the author, 5 July 2011.
9. Roland Robertson. *Globalization: Social Theory and Global Culture.* London: Sage, 1992.
10. Liah Greenfeld. *Nationalism: Five Roads to Modernity.* Cambridge: Harvard University Press, 1992.

11. Liah Greenfeld. *The Spirit of Capitalism: Nationalism and Economic Growth*. Cambridge: Harvard University Press, 2001.

12. Arjun Appadurai. *Modernity at Large: Cultural Dimensions of Globalization.* Minneapolis: University of Minnesota Press, 1996.

13. Thomas A. Tweed. *Crossing and Dwelling: A Theory of Religion.* Cambridge and London: Harvard University Press, 2008.

14. Charles Hirschkind. *The Ethical Soundscape: Cassette Sermons and Islamic Counterpublics.* New York: Columbia University Press, 2006.

15. Victor Roudometof. "Theorizing Glocalization: Three Interpretations." *European Journal of Social Theory*, 2015, 1–18. [CrossRef]

16. Peter Beyer. *Religion in the Context of Globalization: Essays on Concept, Form, and Political Implication.* London and New York: Routledge, 2013.

17. Manuel A. Vásquez. *More than Belief: A Materialist Theory of Religion.* Oxford and New York: Oxford University Press, 2011.

18. James D. Douglas, ed. *Let the Earth Hear His Voice: International Congress on World Evangelization Lausanne, Switzerland.* Minneapolis: World Wide Publications, 1975.

19. C. Peter Wagner. "Lausanne Twelve Months Later." *Christianity Today* 19 (1975): 7–9.

20. David R. Swartz. "Embodying the Global Soul: Internationalism and the American Evangelical Left." *Religions* 3 (2012): 887–901. [CrossRef]

21. Al Tizon. *Transformation after Lausanne: Radical Evangelical Mission in Global-Local Perspective.* Eugene: Wipf & Stock Publishers, 2008.

22. Sara Diamond. *Spiritual Warfare: The Politics of the Christian Right.* Boston: South End Press, 1989.

23. John R. W. Stott, ed. *Making Christ Known: Historic Mission Documents from the Lausanne Movement, 1974–1989.* Grand Rapids: W.B. Eerdmans Pub, 1997.

24. C. René Padilla. "Evangelism and Social Responsibility: From Wheaton '66 to Wheaton '83." *Transformation* 2 (1985): 27–33.

25. Lausanne Movement. "Transformation: The Church in Response to Human Need." 1982. Available online: http://www.lausanne.org/content/statement/transformation-the-church-in-response-to-human-need (accessed on 11 October 2015).

26. C. René Padilla. *Mission between the Times*, rev. 2nd ed. Carlisle: Langham Monographs, 2010.

27. Bruce Nicholls, ed. *In Word and Deed: Evangelism and Social Responsibility.* Grand Rapids: W.B. Eerdmans Pub. Co., 1986.

28. James D. Douglas, ed. *Proclaim Christ Until He Comes: Calling the Whole Church to Take the Whole Gospel to the Whole World.* Minneapolis: World Wide Publications, 1990.

29. Ed Dobson, Jerry Falwell, and Edward E. Hindson, eds. *The Fundamentalist Phenomenon: The Resurgence of Conservative Christianity.* Garden City: Doubleday, 1981.

30. Susan Friend Harding. *The Book of Jerry Falwell: Fundamentalist Language and Politics.* Princeton: Princeton University Press, 2000.

31. Lausanne Movement. "Statement on Spiritual Warfare." 1993. Available online: http://www.lausanne.org/content/statement/statement-on-spiritual-warfare-1993 (accessed on 11 October 2015).

32. C. Peter Wagner. *Dominion!: How Kingdom Action Can Change the World.* Grand Rapids: Chosen Books, 2008.

33. Herbert Schlossberg, Vinay Samuel, and Ronald J. Sider, eds. *Christianity and Economics in the Post-Cold War Era: The Oxford Declaration and Beyond.* Grand Rapids: W.B. Eerdmans, 1994.

34. David O. Moberg. *The Great Reversal: Evangelism versus Social Concern.* Philadelphia: Lippincott, 1972.

35. Chong-Nam Cho. "Segye pogŭmhwa kukche taehoe wa lojan ŏnyak (The International Congress on World Evangelization and the Lausanne Covenant)." *Sinhak kwa Sŏn'gyo* 2 (1974): 243–59.

36. Pong-Ho Son. "Sŏn'gyo wa sahoe chŏngŭi (Evangelism and social concern)." *Sinhak Chinam* 167 (1974): 67–71.

37. In the author's interview with a number of the younger evangelicals of the 1980s democratization movement generation, all of them downplayed the role of the senior evangelicals leaders in introducing the Lausanne movement to Korean evangelical church, and this is why they self-consciously assume the label of "the Lausanne generation." Chae-Sŏk Sŏ (director, Young 2080), in discussion with the author, 6 July 2011.

38. Pong-Ho Son. "Ch'uch'ŏnsŏ (Recommendation)." In *Han'guk Pogŭmjuŭi Hyŏbŭihoe Sŏngmyŏngsŏ Moŭmjip (Anthology of Public Statements of Korean Evangelical Fellowship)*. Edited by Myŏng-Hyŏk Kim. Seoul: Kidokkyo Munsŏ Sŏn'gyohoe, 1998, p. 3.

39. Myung Hyuk Kim. "Human Right in Korea: Introduction." *Transformation: An International Journal of Holistic Mission Studies* 3 (1986): 28. [CrossRef]

40. Timothy S. Lee. *Born Again: Evangelicalism in Korea*. Honolulu: University of Hawaii Press, 2010.

41. Pong-Nin No. "Lojan taehoe ihu ŭi pogŭmjuŭi sŏn'gyo undong (The evangelical mission movement after the Lausanne Congress)." *Sŏn'gyo wa Sinhak* 5 (2005): 51–85.

42. George E. Ogle. *How Long, O Lord: Stories of Twentieth Century Korea*. Philadelphia: Xlibris Corp., 2002.

43. Jim Stentzel, ed. *More than Witnesses: How a Small Group of Missionaries Aided Korea's Democratic Revolution*. Seoul: Korea Democracy Foundation, 2006.

44. Sŭng-Jang Yi (former pastor, Yesu maŭl Church), in conversation with Ch'ong Pak. "Pogŭm kwa Sanghwang." 24 August 2011. Available online: http://www.goscon.co.kr/news/articleView.html?idxno=27974 (accessed on 9 October 2015).

45. Hoe-Gwŏn Kim (professor, Sungsil University), in conversation with Ch'ong Pak. "Pogŭm kwa Sanghwang." 27 January 2012. http://www.goscon.co.kr/news/quickViewArticleView.html?idxno=28114 (accessed on 11 October 2015).

46. Chik-Han Ko (executive director, Young 2080), in discussion with the author, 16 August 2010.

47. Chong-Ch'ŏl Yi. "80-yŏndae kidok haksaeng undongsa (IV) (Christian student movement in the 1980s, IV)." *Pogŭm kwa Sanghwang* 9 (1992): 128–35.

48. Han'guk Pogŭmjuŭi Hyŏbŭihoe. "Hyŏn siguk e taehan pogŭmjuŭijadŭl ŭi cheŏn (A suggestion of evangelicals concerning the current state of affairs)." In *Han'guk Pogŭmjuŭi Hyŏbŭihoe Sŏngmyŏngsŏ Moŭmjip (Anthology of Public Statements of Korean Evangelical Fellowship)*. Edited by Myŏng-Hyŏk Kim. Seoul: Kidokkyo Munsŏ Sŏn'gyohoe, 1998, pp. 10–13.

49. Donald N. Clark, ed. *The Kwangju Uprising: Shadows over the Regime in South Korea*. Boulder: Westview Press, 1988.

50. Linda Sue Lewis. *Laying Claim to the Memory of May: A Look Back at the 1980 Kwangju Uprising*. Honolulu: University of Hawaii Press, 2002.

51. Hwang Pyŏng-Jun's public testimony, delivered at the Turanno Kyŏngbae wa Ch'anyang in Seoul National University on 29 October 1989. The transcribed text of this testimony was sent to the author via personal email communication by his cousin and colleague, Hwang Pyŏng-Gu, on 20 July 2011.

52. Kyo-Hyŏng Ku (pastor, Ch'annŭni Kwangmyŏng Church), in discussion with the author, 25 August 2010.

53. Yŏng-Gyu Pak. *Han'guk Kyohoe Rŭl Kkaeun Pogŭmjuŭi Undong (The Evangelical Movement that Waked up the Korean Church)*. Seoul: Turanno, 1998.

54. Chŏl-Ha Han. "Sŏng'gyŏng i Karŭch'inŭn Hyŏnsil Ch'amyŏ (What the Bible Teaches about Christian Socio-Political Involvement)." *Sŏnggyŏng kwa Sinhak* 1 (1983): 7–28.

55. Pong-Ho Son. "Haebang sinhak [Liberation theology]." *Sŏnggyŏng kwa Sinhak* 1 (1983): 246–54.

56. Myŏng-Hyŏk Kim. "Minjung sinhak pip'an 1: Sinhak undong anin sahoe undong (Criticism of Minjung theology 1: Not a theology, but a social theory)." *Sŏnggyŏng kwa Sinhak* 1 (1983): 257–63.

57. Yŏng-Hwan Kim. "Minjung sinhak pip'an 3: Minjung sinhak e taehan sŏngsŏjok kaehyŏk sinhakchok ch'aksang (An examination of Minjung theology from the biblical, reformed perspective)." *Sŏnggyŏng kwa Sinhak* 1 (1983): 273–79.

58. Citizens' Coalition for Economic Justice. "Inaugural Declaration." 1989. http://www.ccej.or.kr/index.php?mid=page_org_7&type=aoa (accessed on 11 October 2015).

59. Kyŏng-Sok Sŏ. "Minjung sinhak ŭi wigi (Crisis of Minjung theology)." *Kidokkyo Sasang* 417 (1993): 187–204.

religions

MDPI

Article

Globalization and Orthodox Christianity: A Glocal Perspective

Marco Guglielmi

Human Rights Centre, University of Padua, Via Martiri della Libertà, 2, 35137 Padova, Italy;
marco.guglielmi.3@phd.unipd.it

Received: 14 June 2018; Accepted: 10 July 2018; Published: 12 July 2018

Abstract: This article analyses the topic of Globalization and Orthodox Christianity. Starting with Victor Roudometof's work (2014b) dedicated to this subject, the author's views are compared with some of the main research of social scientists on the subject of sociological theory and Eastern Orthodoxy. The article essentially has a twofold aim. Our intention will be to explore this new area of research and to examine its value in the study of this religion and, secondly, to further investigate the theory of religious glocalization and to advocate the fertility of Roudometof's model of four glocalizations in current social scientific debate on Orthodox Christianity.

Keywords: Orthodox Christianity; Globalization; Glocal Religions; Eastern Orthodoxy and Modernity

---

Starting in the second half of the nineteen-nineties, the principal social scientific studies that have investigated the relationship between Orthodox Christianity and democracy have adopted the well-known paradigm of the 'clash of civilizations' (Huntington 1996). Other sociological research projects concerning religion, on the other hand, have focused on changes occurring in this religious tradition in modernity, mainly adopting the paradigm of secularization (in this regard see Fokas 2012). Finally, another path of research, which has attempted to develop a non-Eurocentric vision, has used the paradigm of multiple modernities (Eisenstadt 2000). In his work *Globalization and Orthodox Christianity* (2014b), Victor Roudometof moves away from these perspectives. He prefers to adopt the concept of globalization as a theoretical framework to investigate the historical trajectories of Christian Orthodoxy and its recent transformations. In this article, our aim is to sociologically develop this paradigm, following a path that analyses the main points of the aforementioned work (Roudometof 2014b) and connecting them to various sociological theories and major research regarding this religion.

This paradigm of globalization arises from the theories which the sociologist Roland Robertson began to develop in the nineteen-eighties. Robertson defines globalization as "the compression of the world and the intensification of consciousness of the world as a whole" (Robertson 1992, p. 8). With the term 'compression', he refers to the accelerated pace of contact among cultures, peoples, and civilisations or conveys the sense that the world is a single place. The confrontation of different world views means that globalization involves the "comparative interaction of different forms of life" (Robertson 1992, p. 27). As a process that both connects and stimulates the awareness of connection, globalization dissolves the autonomy of actors and practices in contemporary world order. In this process, all units engaged in globalization are constrained to assume a position and define an identity relative to this interdependence (Robertson 1992, p. 29). Moreover, global interdependence and consciousness of the world as a whole precede the advent of capitalist modernity through a process continuing over various centuries.

According to Roudometof (2014b, chp. 1, pp. 1–17) this theoretical frame appears to be an appropriate choice for the purpose of investigating Eastern Orthodoxy: it retains perspectives less focused on the West and presents multiple definitions. It interprets globalization not as a consequence of Western-European modernity or as the result of a 'second' modernity that developed after the

Second World War. On the contrary, it places modernity in Western Europe and North America within the historical panorama of globalization. As mentioned above, this vision manages to free the study of Orthodox Christianity from the narrative of Western modernity and the conventions of the debate on secularization. Following this vision, Peter Beyer (2006) argues that the idea of 'religion' itself, as it is commonly construed, is the product of a long-term process of intercultural interaction subject to debate within the context of globalization. Beyer claims that the social scientific study of religion must be founded within a perspective of 'global society': "far from remaining more or less constant during these transformations and thereby suffering or at least being challenged to reassert itself, religion has actually been a critical carrier and example of the entire process. Religion, like capitalism, the nation-state or modern science, has been a carrier of modernization and globalization, not a barrier or a victim" (2006, p. 300).

Roudometof thus investigates with a historical and sociological approach the public role of Orthodoxy and the forms it has assumed in different contexts within the historical framework of globalization. This view seems unprecedented with respect to the main narrative in sociological literature on Orthodoxy and globalization (in this regard see, for example, Payne 2003). It does not interpret globalization as a phenomenon of the modern world which may be seen as an 'external' dimension with respect to the Orthodox world, and a 'modern enemy' of a religion which places great importance on traditions and the past. On the contrary, it proposes a long-term view of globalization which will analyse its interaction with this religion, starting from its constitution. It moreover identifies in the processes of negotiation and in the adaptation of Orthodox Christianity or, in other words, its many *transformations*, its religious responses to the evolution and socio-cultural changes occurring in the world.

Analysing Eastern Orthodoxy from both the historical and sociological points of view, Roudometof hypothesized a model of four distinct types of glocalization (Roudometof 2013; 2014a; 2014b). These glocalizations offer concrete examples that involve a fusion between religious universalism and local particularism: *vernacularization, indigenization, nationalization*, and *transnationalization*. Each of the above presents a specific form of 'blending' with respect to universal religion and particular human settings (e.g., empire, ethnicity, nation-states, and transnational migration). These forms are not distinct merely on account of their historical specificity; they are distinct because each form offers a discrete analytical concept to analyse the combination of global and local dimensions. In our opinion, these four forms of religious glocalization are the main theoretical legacy of Roudometof in the study of glocal religions. However, Roudometof's model fits better for some case studies about religions than others, and it does not fit for an analysis of all churches of the Orthodox world. For instance, it holds some limits for a study of the Russian case, i.e., the largest Orthodox jurisdiction. Starting from this awareness, in this article, we will stress the fertility of each form of religious glocalization in the current social scientific debate on Orthodoxy[1].

The first part of the work (Roudometof 2014b, chp. 2, 3 and 4, pp. 18–79) analyses the initial development of Orthodoxy, and investigates the historical period from the ninth century to the final siege of Constantinople (1453). This historical perspective offers an interpretation of the *crystallization* of Orthodoxy in a religious tradition, focusing on the pre-modern era of globalization and the ways in which it accentuates the differences between Eastern Orthodoxy and Western Christianity. In this long historical period, it is possible to outline the foundations of glocalization's beginning of this religious tradition. This article has mainly sociological aims, and for this reason, we do not focus on the historical trajectories of this period. We would solely like to stress that in this stage, there are several glocal processes and cultural encounters both among religious elites (for instance in the 'Third Rome' idea rise in Russia from 1510) and among the lower classes within the aforementioned diversification

---

[1]   These forms of glocalization are used to analyse the historical phases and the socio-religious and political processes of Orthodox Christianity through the entire research. In our article, we focus on one of these paths of hybridisation in each chapter (or theoretical section) of the work.

processes. In particular, these last processes are shown through two key processes or forms of religious glocalization: the *vernacularization* of Christianity (the fusion of religious universalism with specific languages) and the *indigenization* of Orthodoxy (the fusion of religious universalism with a particular ethnicity). These socio-cultural processes facilitate the polarization of these two traditions of Christianity and especially in their interaction, ranging from the first crusade to the second fall of Constantinople. Moreover, these two forms of glocalization allow for an investigation of the different historical trajectories that distinguish the Russian Empire and the Ottoman Empire in their transition towards modernity. The divergences identified in the historical experiences of these two territories are relevant, in particular in the constitution of the Church-state relations and, as mentioned, in the creation of a link between faith and ethnic roots, religion, and language in the life of a community and in liturgy.

This perspective appears to provide an adequate approach to address the debate on the question of the 'unsolved' relationship of Orthodox Christianity with modernity. This religion has a strong link with tradition and with the past. For example, we may reflect on the importance attached to the first ecumenical councils or the teachings of the Fathers of the Church. It has succeeded in developing processes of modernization and in facilitating important historical changes, while maintaining nonetheless a set of reservations with respect to some typical demands (or basic elements) of the contemporary world. A multidisciplinary perspective focusing on the historical trajectories of this religion is therefore suitable in an analysis of the current tensions of this religion with respect to some modern phenomena (for example, we may think of the contribution of religious studies (Makrides 2012a, 2012b; Agadjanian 2003)). This vision 'from the past' sheds light on the current patterns of settlement, on the models of action of this religion, and on its attitude towards some contemporary challenges. As stated by Makrides (2012b), the solid reference towards the past of this religion favored the establishment of an Orthodox traditionalism that influences Orthodoxy's interactions with the socio-cultural reality and contemporary challenges:

> The purpose of this continuous quoting was to justify traditionalist policies and orientations and to condemn various attempted changes or innovations. Characteristically enough, we are not talking here about religious and theological contexts alone. The same holds true for secular contexts as well, which were equally influenced by this kind of Orthodox traditionalism. The question is whether there is an intrinsic connection between the Orthodox and the social traditionalism or if these are simply parallel and coincidental phenomena. The Orthodox usually try to find pertinent answers or solutions with reference to a normative and binding past, which is somehow regarded as a panacea beyond time and space. It appears, however, that there was indeed a strong interplay between Orthodox and social traditionalism in certain historical periods, although always in relation to the overall conditions of the time and numerous other factors (2012b, p. 21).

Regarding the current socio-cultural trajectories of this Orthodox traditionalism, in a recent study, Djankov and Nikolova (2018) show how deep-rooted theological differences between Orthodoxy, Catholicism, and Protestantism, affect life satisfaction and other attitudes of those with a Christian faith in Europe. Comparing these three different Christian traditions, they find that those that are faithful belonging to Eastern Orthodoxy have less social capital and prefer old ideas and safe jobs. In addition, those that are Orthodox faithful approve of left-leaning political preferences and stronger support for government involvement in the economy. Firstly, this study suggests how the study of religion relates to a comprehensive analysis of the socio-cultural reality, even of its components that do not belong to the religious sphere. In fact, if on one hand communist elites attempted to eradicate Orthodox churches in Eastern Europe, on the other hand, it seems that communists maintained many points of Orthodox theology which were suitable for the progress of the government's doctrine. Secondly, this study indicates the reach and temporal continuity of religious beliefs in contemporary societies, even in those that are largely secularized. These results seem to suggest overcoming the views of conflict/severance among religion and globalization, and religious sphere and modern phenomena. They attempt, instead, to define cultural hybrids regarding attitudes and values raised within the social environment.

Moreover, the analysis of the history and doctrine of the Orthodox Church, and also the culture of the society in which it developed and evolved, allows for a greater understanding of the actual conflicts and changes, and avoids a 'limited' social-scientific approach which focuses solely on rational choice theory (for an assessment with this view, see Hamilton 2011). This is especially pertinent in a controversial issue such as Orthodoxy and democracy, in which the constituent elements—for example, the phenomenon of nationalism—are incomprehensible when detached from their historical and theological trajectories. The approach of religious glocalization points out both that religion involves active agency and that religious traditions at the local/global level may contain socio-cultural elements that do not follow a perspective of religious provision and consumption (also in their interaction within a condition of transnational religion).

Moving within this ambivalence of Eastern Orthodoxy, which alternates an open attitude and closure with respect to socio-cultural reality, Roudometof addresses the *nationalization* of this religion (the fusion of religious universalism with a particular nation). This author argues that the joining of a faith and a nation is a sort of *modern synthesis* that has characterised the relationship between church and nation in the Orthodox states to the present day (Roudometof 2014b, chp. 5, pp. 79–101). The principal difference between *nationalization* and the previous forms discussed is that the nation serves as a foundation for the religious institutions' claim to legitimacy. It operates through the use of religion as a potential source for the formation of nations or the intertwining of religious and national markers. Typically, *nationalization* operates through the construction and reproduction of a close relationship between confessional membership and modern national identities.

In fact, Roudometof claims that this form of religious glocalization is a recent historical process and identifies it in the historical developments of Orthodox Christianity during the advent of modern nationalism from the nineteenth century onwards. The Orthodox churches had to adopt elements of the past indigenization in the processes of formation of modern states. These political and religious dynamics define this *synthesis*, and "for the majority of these newfound Orthodox national churches, the continuing cultivation of the church-nation link remains either an incomplete or a recently completed process" (Roudometof 2014b, pp. 166–67). This vision allows for an investigation of the conflicts of the Orthodox churches in the processes of European integration in the countries of Eastern Europe. Moreover, it clarifies the genesis of the Church-state relations model of countries with an Orthodox majority founded on the concept of *symphony* or the symphonic model deriving from the Byzantine tradition. This means that church and state collaborate in a harmonious manner in a sort of alliance to pursue the common good of the people and to promote their spiritual and political interests, assigning a key national role to the church. In the current debate, social scientists and theologians raise questions concerning what political forms and expressions this model may assume within the European framework and in liberal democracies (Hovorun 2017a).

Also in social-scientific and theological literature on nationalism in Orthodoxy, the relationship of this religion with modernity appears to be a key issue, and its ambivalence and ambiguities with respect to phenomena and events of the modern world are emphasized (Demacopoulos and Papanikolaou 2016; Leustean 2014). For example, Daniel Payne (2007) suggests that it is the actual concept of a 'local church', which originally disavowed nationalism and affirmed the legitimate presence of a single church in a territory, that assumed another meaning from the nineteenth century onwards. On the one hand, the Orthodox churches accepted its new nationalist nuances, using them in a strategic way in the definition of the identity and role of the (local) church within the nation-state relationship; on the other hand, they insisted on the legitimacy of its original meaning, using it, as we shall see later, in conflicts for the defence of canonical territories against other churches. Moreover, according to some social scientists, once again considering the present-day situation, it is precisely in this synthesis and in this model of Church-state relations that the "burden of Eastern

Orthodoxy" resides (Radu 1998). From the historical point of view, they would have tended to favour the phenomenon of nationalism and compromised the civil and democratic development of countries with an Orthodox majority (Pollis 1993), and they make it difficult for Orthodoxy to incorporate modern phenomena such as human rights (Giordan and Guglielmi 2017; Agadjanian 2010). Regarding this latest issue, the concept of religious glocalization is an interesting choice for an examination of the position of religions towards human rights. When deemed to be useful, it is possible to adopt a perspective that may be defined as 'religious glocalization and human rights' which addresses this issue in a glocal key[2]. As mentioned briefly before, these analyses concerning human rights should not be interpreted as a set of processes disconnected from the settlement of churches in their societies, nor from their relationship with certain modernity issues. These are issues relating to the topic (a classic one in the field of sociology of religion) of the (glocal) relationship between religion and modernity.

The third form of religious glocalization is that of the *transnationalization* of Orthodoxy, because the global construction of nation-states has necessarily created the 'transnational' category. In this sense, *transnationalization* represents the other aspect of global nationalization and is seen as a form of hybridisation. In the context of migration, transnational people reconstitute their ties to both host and home countries, and they engage in a creative process of blending elements from both points of reference. As shown in many studies (Levitt 2001; Katzenstein and Byrnes 2006), transnational religiosity is a means of describing solutions to newfound situations that people face as a result of migration, and it presents as two quite distinct blends of religious universalism and local particularism.

In his work, Roudometof analyses the situation of the Orthodox diaspora in the United States. He analyses the de-ethnicisation or Americanisation of the Russian diaspora, the Orthodox Church in America (OCA), recognised as autocephalous since 1970, and focuses on the conflicts occurring within the Greek Orthodox Archdiocese of America (Roudometof 2014b, chp. 7, pp. 119–36). We will not dwell on a description of these case studies; however, an analysis of the same reveals some important indications that describe the tensions arising between the opposing positions of a church in diaspora and a local church. These elements make it possible to comprehend these two conditions and the relative processes of institutionalisation: use of the language of the host country as the liturgical language; the request for greater autonomy or autocephaly with respect to the church of origin; the presence of a collective identity that reproduces the national and ethnic identity of immigrants, or of a hybridized (also comprising various identities) or indigenized identity in the host country; and acceptance on the part of the diaspora religion of the cultural norms of the host country, such as its religious pluralism and religious economy[3].

This form of glocalization allows us to focus on two recent topics in the debate on Orthodoxy. The first concerns the now consolidated extension of the global trajectories of this religion. As stated by Roudometof (2015, pp. 223–24), it seems that Orthodox Christianity has assumed the traits of a transnational religion, and that through the migratory flows and its transnational ties, some of its paths may deviate from the historical experiences of Orthodoxy. In this scenario, in the main Orthodox jurisdictions, it is possible to identify institutional forms of transnationalism among the parishes of the diaspora and the church in the motherland, and forms of transnational religious practices among the followers of the Orthodox faith that relate to their religious sphere (Levitt 2007). The second topic, however, concerns the establishment of an authentic Orthodox dimension in Western Europe. It has been formed in the global spread of Orthodox Christianity over the last thirty years, and now has its own role and interests in international Orthodox affairs. Roudometof could have probably further

---

[2] In this case, we do not intend to define a theory, but to apply a specific investigative perspective to a subject of research.
[3] With regard to this last point, an in-depth analysis would have been interesting. Perhaps defining the sociological concepts of cultural norms and religious pluralism used in the theoretical frame, and indicating some forms or paths of their acceptance by Orthodox diasporas in a host country. There seems to be an increasing focus on this point in sociological research concerning Orthodoxy in the West, also with a path of qualitative studies on conversions to the Orthodox faith on the part of believers in Western countries (in the USA: Slagle 2011; Herbel 2014; Winchester 2015, Kravchenko 2018; in Europe: Giordan 2009; Kapaló 2014; Thorbjørnsrud 2015).

investigated this point. It is a social-scientific path which identifies in some Orthodox diasporas in this European region important forms of adaptation in the host context (Hämmerli and Mayer 2014; Giordan and Guglielmi 2018). In these diaspora religions, processes of hybridization with the new socio-cultural reality appear to be identifiable, in addition to a change in the Orthodox tradition whereby certain specific elements of the European context are acquired[4].

In this regard, the question of ethnophyletism deserves our attention as currently, it relates not only to the phenomenon of nationalism in Orthodoxy—mentioned earlier, but also to Orthodox diaspora's issue (Hämmerli 2010). This idea means the principle of nationalities applied in the ecclesiastical field, i.e., the idea that a local autocephalous Church should be based not on a local ecclesial criterion, but on a national one. It was condemned as a modern ecclesial heresy, such as religious nationalism, by the Pan-Orthodox Synod in Constantinople on 10 September 1872. This concept is often used in the conflict between Orthodox jurisdictions to denounce the condition of Orthodox diasporas (in Western Europe and North America) and parallel jurisdictions in some Orthodox countries (such as Moldova and Estonia). With respect to its original theological meaning, this concept is often exploited in political and religious conflict. As suggested by Hovorun (2017b), a clarification of this concept in its theological declinations can favor an understanding of some dynamics of international Orthodox affairs and of the religious positions and orientations of the Orthodox churches in the current socio-religious contentions (such as the next mentioned ones occurring within *deterritorialization/reterritorialization* processes).

Indeed, another perspective examined in Roudometof's work and which allows us to comprehend the historical developments of Orthodoxy is that of the dialectic occurring between *deterritorialization* and *reterritorialization* (Roudometof 2014b, chp. 8, pp. 137–54). Globalization functions through this dialectic: on the one hand, it increases cross-cultural contact, and on the other, it facilitates the possibility of reconstructing or creating 'locality', by modifying the religious panorama. During the 19th century and the first half of the 20th century, this dialectic was expressed through the gradual fragmentation of the Ottoman Empire and the reterritorialization of authority within the South-eastern European nation-states. It undergoes further change in the *global* condition of the current historical period, in which there is a simultaneous and/or synchronous experience of events and relationships on the part of people which generates hybridization. This dialectic is more evident in the recent attempts of Orthodox jurisdictions to become established outside their national borders and to assume a role in the fragmented international scenario. Orthodox ecclesiastic institutions must therefore devise forms of religious response to address these changes that favour migratory flows and cultural and religious pluralism. In this regard, Roudometof focuses on defining the international activity of the Ecumenical Patriarchate. It operates both as a *transnational* institution that maintains ties with the Greek communities in the diaspora and as a *global* institution focused on its traditional status as *primus inter pares*, which intervenes in the processes of *deterritorialization* and as an impartial referee in the 'affairs' of the Orthodox world.

This last vision appears to shed new light on the role of the Orthodox churches as stakeholders in the international arena and in Western countries marked by an increasing religious differentiation, as well as in the exercise of 'soft power' in the geopolitical interests of their countries. If in the case of the Russian Orthodox Church the so-called *Russkii Mir*—the religious policy pursued by the Russian Patriarchate in spreading the 'Orthodox World' outside the national borders—has been examined by social scientists (in this regard see Sidorov 2006; Suslov 2014; Payne 2010), little attention seems to

---

4   In this regard, Chapter 6 (Roudometof 2014b, pp. 102–18) focuses on the case of Cyprus, and 'enters into conflict' with the more general view adopted in the research. This examination of the encounter between colonialism, the 'dark side' of Western modernity, and the history of the Orthodox Church of Cyprus, allows us to tackle an important issue in the study of the Orthodox diaspora. The study analyses the cultural hybrid that develops in an Eastern socio-cultural context 'entangled' in Western and European trajectories and patterns. In a somewhat different light, but still relating this religion to colonialism and the Western world, Demacopoulos (2017) reinterprets and clarifies 'traditional Orthodoxy' as a post-colonial movement: a "more loosely organized but similarly aimed subgroup within the Orthodox Church whose animating spirit is resistance to the perceived threats of a Western and/or modern contamination of Orthodox teaching and practice" (2017, p. 476).

have been paid to international policies involving the other churches of the Orthodox Communion. However, events related to the Pan-Orthodox Council held in Crete in June 2016, which, following considerable tension and controversy, was attended by 10 of the 14 Orthodox jurisdictions, recently revealed to the entire world the geopolitical significance of this religion. The Council appears to have drawn attention to the role exercised by the individual jurisdictions in the diplomatic world and in international relations and to the complex geopolitical framework created around this particular event, and to the extent that it is possible to identify an analytical category in geopolitics, permitting a more in-depth examination of this religion (Giordan 2016; Ladouceur 2016; Leustean 2018).

The foregoing elements and topics are eventually summed up in the description of the concept of glocalization (Roudometof 2014b, chp. 9, pp. 155–72; or Roudometof 2016a). This concept provides a theoretical framework suitable for the study of the relationship of this religion with globalization, and a fertile point of view in the study of religion. As we have tried to show in the analysis of the work, the glocal stance expresses the dual nature of globalization, focusing on both the global and local levels. Within the processes of the four forms of glocalization (*vernacularization, indigenization, nationalization,* and *transnationalization*), the glocal view studies the formation of cultural hybrids that merge religious universalism with the forms of local particularism. This perspective of *multiple glocalizations* allows us to examine the religion beyond the dimension of the 'Western imagination'; indeed, as a religious tradition marked by a rich and varied cultural and historical past, a *religious panorama* composed of societies, identities, and cultures on which globalization has an effect.

Since the late 1980s and the early 1990s, the concept of *glocalization* has been referred to in various fields[5]. The concept of *glocal religion* in fact abandons the narrative of secularization and focuses on a meeting of cultures and a valorization of the interaction occurring between local and global dimensions (Beyer 2007). Rather than considering cultural units as fixed elements or as exclusive units, it is possible to concentrate on the various processes referred to as *hybridization* or *glocalization* (Beyer 2007). Instead of underestimating the scope and influence of traditional local cultures, structures, and settings, it assumes that global processes interact with them. Robertson's goal in introducing this concept is to make the duality of global processes visible. They do not oppose or occur outside local forces; on the contrary, both global and local processes are established on a reciprocal basis. This concept shows how the global world cannot be conceived as existing in opposition to or as isolated from local reality, and that both form part of contemporary society.

As Robertson suggests, glocalizations offer a means to interpret and acquire a more profound comprehension of the *hybridity* and *fragmentation* of the cultural context within the framework of global-local relations. Within this framework, in their localization, religions form new *cultural hybrids* that blend religious universalism with forms of local particularism. The processes of globalization in fact promote multiple glocalizations (Beyer 2007), i.e., universal religion, thematized alongside local particularity. These multiple glocalizations should not be seen as mechanically linked to specific historical periods, but as synchronously interacting in the various historical periods and influenced by the political and cultural conditions of each age. Such a perspective allows us to comprehend the historical discontinuities or continuities and changes in the religious phenomenon, focusing on the hybrid nature generated by local and global processes in the geographical regions considered. For example, the model of "multiple glocalizations of Christianity in Europe suggests that this model offers a conceptual map that accounts for religious change and fragmentations both in Western and Eastern Europe" (Roudometof 2014c, p. 76).

To conclude, this research perspective may be appropriate for researchers of all disciplines involved in the study of Orthodox Christianity thanks to its unprecedented vision with respect to historical and sociological changes in this religious tradition. Furthermore, it examines the relationship

---

[5] For an in-depth examination of the concept of glocalization with respect to its various interpretations, its tense relations with other fields of interest, and its influence in various areas, see (Roudometof 2016b).

of Orthodoxy with global processes through a framework that is not merely conflictual, depicting a theoretical turn not only in the literature on this religion, but in the entire theme of the relationship between religion and globalization. In fact, for scholars engaged in this field, it may provide some suggestions by elaborating in a meaningful way the conceptual framework of this relationship and by proposing an original application of the concept of glocalization in the study of a religious tradition.

Conflicts of Interest: The author declares no conflicts of interest.

References

Agadjanian, Alexander. 2003. Breakthrough to Modernity, Apologia for Traditionalism: the Russian Orthodox View of Society and Culture in Comparative Perspective. *Religion, State and Society* 31: 327–46. [CrossRef]

Agadjanian, Alexander. 2010. Liberal Individual and Christian Culture: Russian Orthodox Teaching on Human Rights in Social Theory Perspective. *Religion, State and Society* 38: 97–113. [CrossRef]

Beyer, Peter. 2006. *Religions in Global Society*. London and New York: Routledge.

Beyer, Peter. 2007. Globalization and Glocalization. In *The SAGE Handbook of the Sociology of Religion*. Edited by James A. Beckford and N. J. Demerath III. Los Angeles: Sage, pp. 98–117.

Demacopoulos, George E. 2017. "Traditional Orthodoxy" as a Postcolonial Movement. *The Journal of Religion* 97: 475–99. [CrossRef]

Demacopoulos, George E., and Aristotle Papanikolaou, eds. 2016. *Christianity, Democracy, and the Shadow of Constantine*. New York: Fordham University Press.

Djankov, Simeon, and Elena Nikolova. 2018. Communism as the Unhappy Coming. Policy Research Working Paper 8399, World Bank Group: Development Economics Office of the Chief Economist, Washington, DC, USA. Available online: http://documents.worldbank.org/curated/en/303241522775925061/pdf/WPS8399.pdf (accessed on 7 July 2018).

Eisenstadt, Shmuel Noah, ed. 2000. *Multiple Modernities*. New Brunswick: Transaction Publishers.

Fokas, Effie. 2012. 'Eastern' Orthodoxy and 'Western' Secularisation in Contemporary Europe (with Special Reference to the Case of Greece). *Religion, State and Society* 40: 395–414. [CrossRef]

Giordan, Giuseppe. 2009. Conversion as Opposition. In *Conversion in the Age of Pluralism*. Edited by Giuseppe Giordan. Leiden: Brill, pp. 243–62.

Giordan, Giuseppe. 2016. Grande e Santo, salvo imprevisti: Il Sinodo Panortodosso tra Geopolitica e Religione. *Religioni e Società* 85: 61–70.

Giordan, Giuseppe, and Marco Guglielmi. 2017. Ortodossia Cristiana, Modernità e la Questione dei Diritti Umani: Prospettive Teoriche. *Religioni e Società* 87: 41–49. [CrossRef]

Giordan, Giuseppe, and Marco Guglielmi. 2018. Be Fruitful and Multiply . . . Fast! The Spread of Orthodox Churches in Italy. In *Congregations in Europe*. Edited by Jörg Stolz and Christophe Monnot. Cham: Springer, pp. 53–69.

Hamilton, Malcolm. 2011. Rational Choice Theory: A Critique. In *The Oxford Handbook of the Sociology of Religion*. Edited by Peter B. Clarke. Oxford: Oxford University Press, pp. 116–33.

Hämmerli, Maria. 2010. Orthodox Diaspora? A Sociological and Theological Problematisation of a Stock Phrase. *International Journal for the Study of the Christian Church* 10: 97–115. [CrossRef]

Hämmerli, Maria, and Jean-François Mayer, eds. 2014. *Orthodox Identities in Western Europe: Migration, Settlement and Innovation*. Farnham: Ashgate.

Herbel, Oliver D. 2014. *Turning to Tradition: Converts and the Making of an American Orthodox Church*. Oxford and New York: Oxford University Press.

Hovorun, Cyril. 2017a. Is the Byzantine 'Symphony' Possible in Our Days? *Journal of Church and State* 59: 280–96. [CrossRef]

Hovorun, Cyril. 2017b. Ethnophyletism, Phyletism, and the Pan-orthodox Council. *The Wheel*. Available online: https://www.wheeljournal.com/blog/2017/9/14/cyril-hovorun-ethnophyletism-phyletism-and-the-pan-orthodox-council (accessed on 7 July 2018).

Huntington, Samuel P. 1996. *The Clash of Civilizations and the Remaking of World Order*. New York: Simon & Schuster.

Kapalò, James A. 2014. Mediating Orthodoxy: Convert Agency and Discursive Autochtonism in Ireland. In *Orthodox Identities in Western Europe: Migration, Settlement and Innovation*. Edited by Maria Hämmerli and Jean-François Mayer. Farnham: Ashgate, pp. 229–50.

Katzenstein, Peter J., and Timothy A. Byrnes. 2006. Transnational Religion in an Expanding Europe. *Perspectives on Politics* 4: 679–94. [CrossRef]

Kravchenko, Elena. 2018. Becoming Eastern Orthodox in Diaspora: Materializing Orthodox Russia and Holy Rus'. *Religion* 48: 37–63. [CrossRef]

Ladouceur, Paul. 2016. The Holy and Great Council of the Orthodox Church. *Oecuménisme/Ecumenism* 51: 18–39.

Leustean, Lucian N., ed. 2014. *Orthodox Christianity and Nationalism in Nineteenth-Century South-eastern Europe*. New York: Fordham University Press.

Leustean, Lucian N. 2018. Eastern Orthodoxy, Geopolitics and the 2016 'Holy and Great Synod of the Orthodox Church'. *Geopolitics* 23: 201–16. [CrossRef]

Levitt, Peggy. 2007. *God Needs No Passport: Immigrants and the Changing American Religious Landscape*. New York: The New Press.

Levitt, Peggy. 2001. *The Transnational Villagers*. Oakland: University of California Press.

Makrides, Vasilios N. 2012a. Orthodox Christianity, Modernity and Postmodernity: Overview, Analysis and Assessment. *Religion, State and Society* 40: 248–85. [CrossRef]

Makrides, Vasilios N. 2012b. Orthodox Christianity, Change, Innovation: Contradictions in Terms? In *Innovation in the Orthodox Christian Tradition? The Question of Change in Greek Orthodox Thought and Practice*. Edited by Trine Stauning Willert and Lina Molokotos-Liederman. London and New York: Routledge, pp. 19–50.

Payne, Daniel P. 2003. The Challenge of Western Globalization to Orthodox Christianity. In *Orthodox Christianity and Contemporary Europe*. Edited by Jonathan van den Sutton and Wil Bercken. Leuven: Peeters Publishers, pp. 133–44.

Payne, Daniel P. 2007. Nationalism and the Local Church: The Source of Ecclesiastical Conflict in the Orthodox Commonwealth. *Nationalities Papers* 35: 831–52. [CrossRef]

Payne, Daniel P. 2010. Spiritual Security, the Russian Orthodox Church, and the Russian Foreign Ministry: Collaboration or Cooptation? *Journal of Church and State* 52: 712–27. [CrossRef]

Pollis, Adamantia. 1993. Eastern Orthodoxy and Human Rights. *Human Rights Quarterly* 15: 339–56. [CrossRef]

Radu, Michel. 1998. The Burden of Eastern Orthodoxy. *Orbis* 42: 283–300. [CrossRef]

Robertson, Roland. 1992. *Globalization: Social Theory and Global Culture*. London: Sage.

Roudometof, Victor. 2013. The Glocalizations of Eastern Orthodox Christianity. *European Journal of Social Theory* 16: 226–45. [CrossRef]

Roudometof, Victor. 2014a. Forms of Religious Glocalization: Orthodox Christianity in the Longue Durée. *Religions* 5: 1017–36. [CrossRef]

Roudometof, Victor. 2014b. *Globalization and Orthodox Christianity: The Transformations of a Religious Tradition*. London and New York: Routledge.

Roudometof, Victor. 2014c. The Glocalizations of Christianity in Europe: A Global-Historical Perspective. In *European Glocalization in Global Context*. Edited by Roland Robertson. London and New York: Palgrave McMillan, pp. 62–81.

Roudometof, Victor. 2015. Orthodox Christianity as a Transnational Religion: Theoretical, Historical and Comparative Considerations. *Religion, State and Society* 43: 211–27. [CrossRef]

Roudometof, Victor. 2016a. Globalization. In *Handbook of Religion and Society*. Edited by David Yamane. New York: Springer, pp. 505–24.

Roudometof, Victor. 2016b. *Glocalization: An Introduction*. London and New York: Routledge.

Slagle, Amy. 2011. *The Eastern Church in the Spiritual Marketplace: American Conversions to Orthodox Christianity*. DeKalb: Northern Illinois University Press.

Sidorov, Dmitrii. 2006. Post-Imperial Third Romes: Resurrections of a Russian Orthodox Geopolitical Metaphor. *Geopolitics* 11: 317–47. [CrossRef]

Suslov, Mikhail D. 2014. "Holy Rus": The Geopolitical Imagination in the Contemporary Russian Orthodox Church. *Russian Politics & Law* 52: 67–86.

Thorbjørnsrud, Berit Synøve. 2015. Who is a convert? New members of the Orthodox Church in Norway. *Temenos* 51: 71–93.

Winchester, Daniel. 2015. Converting to Continuity: Temporality and Self in Eastern Orthodox Conversion Narratives. *Journal for the Scientific Study of Religion* 54: 439–60. [CrossRef]

MDPI

St. Alban-Anlage 66

4052 Basel

Switzerland

Tel. +41 61 683 77 34

Fax +41 61 302 89 18

www.mdpi.com

Religions Editorial Office

E-mail: religions@mdpi.com

www.mdpi.com/journal/religions

www.ingramcontent.com/pod-product-compliance
Lightning Source LLC
Chambersburg PA
CBHW051315020426
42333CB00028B/3351